Abortion:

Ethical Issues and Options

Abortion:

Ethical Issues and Options

Edited by

David R. Larson

Loma Linda University
Center for Christian Bioethics
Loma Linda, California

Center for Christian Bioethics
Loma Linda University
Loma Linda, CA 92350

Cover Art: Cheryl Lessard
Typesetting and Page Design: Richard Weismeyer
Editorial Assistance: Gary Chartier, Duane Covrig, Gayle Foster,
    Gwendolyn Utt, Richard Utt, Nancy Yuen

Printed in the United States of America

Library of Congress Cataloging-in-Publication Data

    Abortion : ethical issues and options / edited by David R. Larson.
        p. cm.
        Includes bibliographical references and index.
        ISBN 1-881127-00-1 (alk. paper) :
            1. Abortion—Religious aspects—Seventh-day Adventists
        2. Abortion—Moral and ethical aspects. 3. Abortion—United States.
    I. Larson, David R. (David Ralph), 1946-
    HQ766.25.A26   1992
    363.4'6—dc20   92-28584

To:

Erik, Krister and Rakel

Contents

Contributors ix

Preface: Let All Be Persuaded in Their Own Minds xi

Part One
Medicine and Morality

1. Observations on Abortion: One Perinatologist's Viewpoint 3
   Elmar P. Sakala

Part Two
Scripture and Tradition

2. Adventists, Abortion, and the Bible 27
   John C. Brunt

3. A Biblical Perspective on Abortion 43
   Niels-Erik Andreasen

4. Abortion: Some Questionable Arguments 55
   Tim Crosby

5. The View of John Harvey Kellogg on Abortion 71
   Dalton Baldwin

Part Three
Theology and Ethics

6. Immortality of the Soul and the Abortion of the Body 89
   Sydney Allen

7. Abortion and Adventist Interpretation: Significant Theological Themes . .99
   Ginger Hanks-Harwood

8. Reverence for Life and the Abortion Issue 113
   Jack W. Provonsha

9. A Compassionate and Christian "Quality of Life" Ethic 125
   Richard Fredericks

10. Control of the Body—Control of the Mind: Autobiographical and
    Sociological Determinants of a Personal Abortion Ethic in
    Seventh-day Adventism 143
    Michael Pearson

11. The "Hard Cases" of Abortion 155
    Teresa Beem

Part Four
Church and Society

12. Adventist Guidelines on Abortion 173
    James W. Walters

13. Abortion and the "Corporate Conscience" of the Church 187
    Diane Forsyth

14. Communicating Grace: The Church's Role in the
    Abortion Controversy 205
    Sara Kärkkäinen Terian

15. Abortion and Public Policy 221
    Michael Angelo Saucedo

16. Abortion Policies in Adventist Hospitals 237
    Gerald R. Winslow

Appendix: Seventh-day Adventist Abortion Guidelines 251

Index of Scriptural References 265

Index of Proper Names 268

Index of Subjects 271

Contributors

Sydney E. Allen, Jr., Ph.D.
Associate Professor of Philosophy
San Bernardino Valley College

Niels-Erik Andreasen, Ph.D.
President
Walla Walla College

Dalton Baldwin, Ph.D.
Professor of Christian Theology
Loma Linda University

Teresa Beem
President, Adventists for Life
Keene, Texas

John C. Brunt, Ph.D.
Vice President for Academic Administration
Walla Walla College

Timothy Crosby, M.Div.
Producer, Voice of Prophecy
Newbury Park, California

Diane Dunlap Forsyth, M.A.
Chaplain
Glendale Adventist Medical Center

Richard Fredericks, Ph.D.
Associate Professor of Religion
Columbia Union College

Ginger Hanks-Harwood, Ph.D.
Assistant Professor of Religion
Pacific Union College

Michael D. Pearson, D.Phil.
Senior Lecturer in Ethics and
  Philosophy
Newbold College

Jack W. Provonsha, M.D., Ph.D.
Emeritus Professor of Philosophy of
  Religion and Christian Ethics
Loma Linda University

Elmar P. Sakala, M.D., M.P.H.
Associate Professor of Obstetrics
  and Gynecology
Loma Linda University

Michael Angelo Saucedo, J.D.
Legal Analyst for the State of
  California
Sacramento, California

Sara Kärkkäinen Terian, Ph.D.
Vice President for Academic Administration
Columbia Union College

James W. Walters, Ph.D.
Professor of Christian Ethics
Loma Linda University

Gerald R. Winslow, Ph.D.
Professor of Ethics
Chair, Department of Religion
Pacific Union College

Preface

Let All Be Persuaded in Their Own Minds

The sixteen essays in this volume are selected from thirty-six presentations made at a conference entitled "Abortion: Ethical Issues and Options" held November 14-16, 1988 at Loma Linda University, under the auspices of the Center for Christian Bioethics. Loma Linda University is a health sciences campus in Southern California administered by the Seventh-day Adventist denomination. No attempt was made at the conference to reach a consensus regarding the morality or immorality of abortion. Neither did the conference try to formulate recommendations to Seventh-day Adventism's leadership about the matter. The purpose of the conference was to enable qualified Seventh-day Adventists from around the world to voice differing views concerning the morality of abortion in an atmosphere of open dialogue and Christian candor and cordiality.

The theological assumption that guided conference organizers was the belief that controversial matters are more clearly understood by a Christian community when its members honestly share their convictions and eagerly listen to the views of others. This fosters not only a sensitivity for each other but also for the presence of the One in whom all live and move and find being. Only this approach will ensure that pronouncements from religious administrators will appeal and persuade the general membership. When such exchanges occur, they often succeed in fostering the needed consensus that pure administrative actions alone can not engender.

The 1988 Loma Linda conference on abortion was a success in at least three ways. First, a tenor of Christian collaboration permeated the proceedings from beginning to end. This was possible despite the variety of ethical and professional perspectives from which the presenters and auditors spoke and listened. This was also possible despite the cultural diversity of the participants, representing countries as far away as Argentina, Australia, Brazil, Denmark, England, Germany, Jamaica, New Zealand and Yugoslavia. One Adventist administrator voiced the general feeling of most when he said that rarely had he experienced a series of meetings in which people with such different views collaborated so effectively.

The conference also indirectly influenced Adventist guidelines about abortion by stimulating the establishment of the Christian View of Human Life Committee led by Dr. Bruce Whiting of the Health Department of the General Conference of Seventh-day Adventists in Silver Spring, Maryland. Subsequently, this committee has done much work to update and improve the 1970s guidelines about abortion. The reader will note the differences in the Appendix where the 1970s guidelines and the recently proposed guidelines are printed in their entirety. The participation of Dr. Whiting and his committee in the 1988 Loma Linda abortion conference was extremely helpful. It fostered a cooperative relationship that has continued during subsequent years between the Center for Christian Bioethics and the Christian View of Human Life Committee.

Lastly, the conference resulted in this book which, I believe, will enable Seventh-day Adventists, as well as those who belong to other communities of faith, to understand the range of views regarding abortion that exist within this community. Such a survey will be of historical interest to many who are curious about how those who belong to a small denomination that makes large investments in health care view the matter of abortion. But it will also be of ethical interest to those who wish to formulate their own views about the morality or immorality of abortion with awareness of a variety of thoughtful alternatives. "Let every man be fully persuaded in his own mind," wrote the Apostle Paul to the first Christians in Rome about a very different matter that was threatening to divide them. This is sound advice for Christians and others today about issues like abortion. But it is easier to follow this counsel wisely if one knows what the options are.

Regretfully, we are unable to publish all thirty-six papers from the conference. Such a volume would have been so large that it would have discouraged even the most eager. These sixteen essays were selected to exemplify the range of alternatives represented at the conference without unduly challenging the reader.

Discerning students of this book will note that the technical possibility of aborting human fetuses poses not one but at least three different kinds of ethical questions. At the personal level, women must ask themselves about the circumstances, if any, in which it would be ethically appropriate for them to seek abortions and for men to support them in doing so. At a more professional and institutional level, the question focuses upon the cases in which it would be ethically appropriate for physicians to perform abortions or for institutions to offer them. At the societal level, the question concentrates upon what the laws of a state or nation should allow regarding abortion. There is a tendency among some to assume that an answer to any one of these questions must be the same as the answer to the others. This is not necessarily the case. As the essays in this volume demonstrate, it is possible to focus upon one of these three questions to the virtual exclusion of the others or to advance different answers to each of them.

Some may wonder why this volume includes no extensive study of the views of Ellen White. One answer is that she wrote little or nothing on the topic of abortion. Another is that Michael Pearson examines this issue in *Millennial Dreams and Moral Dilemmas: Seventh-day Adventism and Contemporary Ethics* (Cambridge: Cambridge University Press, 1990). Readers of this book are invited to consult Pearson's discussion for further information about Ellen White's views.

I am grateful to all who made the conference and this resulting volume possible. My colleagues at the Center at that time, James Walters and Gerald Winslow, were most supportive. Mrs. Gwendolyn Utt, the Center's Office Supervisor, was a model of efficiency that was so effective as to appear effortless, as always. Elders Neal Wilson and George Reid of the General Conference of Seventh-day Adventists were helpful behind the scenes. Several presidents of Divisions of the General Conference sent delegates to the conference from their parts of the world. Many members of the Loma Linda community devoted three days of their lives to responding to the presentations. And those who established the Center for Christian Bioethics with their financial contributions made this and other conferences possible. Most importantly, there would have been no conference if thirty-six Seventh-day Adventists from around the world had not responded to the Center's call for papers on the controversial topic of abortion.

A number of persons participated in the preparation of this volume. These include Richard and Gwendolyn Utt, Gary Chartier, Katherine Ching, Duane Covrig, Gayle Foster, Cheryl Lessard, Richard Weismeyer, and Nancy Yuen. Without them, this book would not have been published. I am grateful to each of them.

I dedicate this book to my three children: Erik Provonsha Larson, Krister Provonsha Larson and Rakel Provonsha Larson. Each was wanted. Each was planned. And, most importantly, each is loved.

This book is not published as the last word on the ethics of abortion. We hope it is a responsible contribution to many continuing conversations about abortion among Seventh-day Adventists and others. We also hope that those who read these essays will do so with an eager but patient desire to listen and respond to the divine Word that threads its way through human words, frail and faulty though they are.

David R. Larson, D.Min., Ph.D.
Associate Professor of Christian Ethics
Co-Director, Center for Christian Bioethics
Loma Linda University

Part I

Medicine and Morality

1 Observations on Abortion: One Perinatologist's Viewpoint

Elmar P. Sakala

I. Introduction

By profession I am a physician, with specialty training in obstetrics and gynecology and with subspecialty training in maternal-fetal medicine. As a perinatologist my practice is limited to high-risk and problem pregnancies. My goal is to realize an optimum outcome for both mother and fetus. In the majority of cases this goal is achieved. It is impossible to describe adequately the heartfelt thanks from couples who previously were unable to have a successful pregnancy but who now hold in their arms the newborn baby they have longed for.

With current technology we can peer into the womb with ultrasound technology and examine in detail both the anatomy and physiology of the fetus to a degree previously impossible. In advanced pregnancies it is feasible to assess the state of fetal well-being through high resolution ultrasound, chorionic villous sampling, fetoscopy, percutaneous umbilical blood sampling, a wide range of amniotic fluid analyses, and maternal serum alpha-fetoprotein assessments. Physiological evaluations of the fetus are now possible that were previously never imagined: cardiac contractility, urine production, breathing movements, gross body motion and extremity movements. There is also an increasing array of intrauterine therapies to treat the fetus *in utero*—transplacental and transamniotic medications and nutrition, modalities to enhance blood flow through the placenta, and, to a limited extent, fetal surgery. What then does a perinatologist who seeks to save fetuses have to do with abortion procedures?

My involvement with abortion[1] is largely in the setting of the "doomed" fetus. Most of these pregnancies are wanted and desired, yet the fetus has such major malformations or abnormalities that it cannot survive outside the uterus. It is from this context that I approach the issue of abortion. I realize this is in stark

3

contrast to the vast majority of elective abortions performed in this country and around the world: pregnancies that although unplanned, unwanted, and undesired, yet have normal developing fetuses.

Since one of the key figures in an abortion is the fetus, it is appropriate to examine who or what is being aborted. The term "products of conception" or "POC" is a generic medical phrase often used when abortion is being discussed. Use of the term POC serves a useful purpose, when dealing with spontaneous abortions, to collectively designate the residual uterine contents, including placental fragments, chorionic and amnionic membranes, and remnants of fetal tissue.

This same phrase, "products of conception," however, is now also used in dealing with elective induced abortions of intact fetuses. Employment of this euphemism avoids reference to the fetus and provides a surgical context for the abortion. The expression, however, tends to downplay and obscure the striking and exquisite development of even a first trimester fetus. Even early abortion procedures do not involve formless blobs of protoplasm but delicate, finely orchestrated embryological processes following a sequence meticulously devised by the Creator Himself.

In dealing with the appropriateness and morality of abortion I have had to come to grips with the significance of human prenatal life and existence. My objectives in this essay will be to initially present an overview of the reproductive process from ovulation to fertilization, implantation and subsequent development of the fetus. In the appendix I will summarize legal abortion methods in use, the pregnancy stage in which they are utilized, and their risks. Lastly I will outline my thoughts in dealing with abortion of the normal fetus, the "doomed" fetus and the abnormal fetus.

II. Egg Transport

Human development begins when the sex cell from a female, an ovum, is fertilized by the sex cell from a male, a sperm. Each sex cell or gamete contains 23 chromosomes, half the number needed to constitute a full human chromosome number of 46.

An ovum measures 1/175th of an inch in diameter and weighs 1/20 of a millionth of an ounce. Although the ovum is one of the largest cells in the human body, all the ova required to create the entire population of the world could be put into a single cookie jar. A sperm, including the tail or flagellum, measures 1/500th of an inch in length but weighs only 1/90,000th the weight of an ovum. All the sperm required to create the entire population of the world could be put into a thimble.

4

At ejaculation an average of 250 million sperm are deposited in the vagina, yet less than 200 sperm are successful in achieving proximity to the egg. Fertilization of the ovum occurs in the ampullae or distal part of the oviduct or fallopian tube. The transit time for spermatozoa to reach the ampulla from the vagina through the cervix and uterus can be as short as five minutes, although a more usual time is four to six hours.

The motion of the sperm tail or flagellum alone cannot account for such rapid travel of the sperm through the female reproductive tract. There must be other mechanisms that provide for the accelerated sperm transport. The sperm probably burrow, by chemical and mechanical means, through the mucus that fills the cervical canal.

The leaders among the sperm very likely break down or depolymerize the cervical mucus by releasing enzymes called proteases that are contained in the acrosome or sperm head. The proteases render the mucus more easily penetrable by the sperm that follow. The uterine cavity itself may be nearly obliterated except for canals that extend the length of the uterus from the cervical internal os or opening to where each oviduct joins each cornu or horn of the uterus and the oviduct. By means of such canals, sperm are directed to the oviduct.

The ovulated egg is surrounded by a mass of thousands of much smaller follicular cells called a cumulus. The ovum with its corona of cells adheres to the surface of the ovary. Delicate fimbriae, finger-like projections of the terminal end of the fallopian tube, sweep over the ovary in order to pick up the egg.

Entry into the oviduct is facilitated by muscular movements that bring the fimbriae into contact with the ovary surface. Hair-like cilia on the surface of the fimbriae have adhesive sites which initially move the egg into the tubal opening. Then the unidirectional beating of the cilia in the oviduct move the egg in the direction of the uterus. Muscular contractions of the oviduct, with a to-and-fro movement, result in a three-day transport time through the tube to the uterus. It takes 30 hours for the egg to reach the ampullary-isthmic junction. It remains at this point another 30 hours until it begins its rapid transport through the isthmus of the tube.

III. Fertilization

The fertilizable life span of human gametes is uncertain. The best estimate is that ova can be fertilized for up to 24 hours after ovulation and sperm can be fertilized for up to 24 to 28 hours after ejaculation. Contact of the sperm with the egg appears to be random; no current evidence suggests that the egg lures the sperm onto its surface.

The covering membrane of the ovum, the zona pellucida, contains species-specific sperm receptors. Only sperm of the same species as the ovum can normally attach to the zona. Once the zona is penetrated by the fertilizing sperm it becomes impervious to other sperm. The egg membrane engulfs the sperm head, and there is fusion of egg and sperm membranes.

Gamete pronuclei from the male and female will merge to form the nucleus of the new zygote. The limiting membrane of each pronucleus breaks down and the 23 pairs of chromosomes combine, forming a complement of 46 chromosomes, the diploid number. The complete genotype is now present which will be a characteristic of each cell of the developing organism.

The 46 chromosomes arrange themselves in pairs on a spindle forming the stage for the first cell division. Failure to divide the chromosomes equally between the two daughter cells at this point may result in a host of chromosomal abnormalities. If unequal cell divisions result in either excessive or deficient numbers of critical chromosomal material, the outcome is predictably lethal.

Of clinically detectable pregnancies that have implanted, at least 15 percent are spontaneously aborted. Over half of these losses are chromosomally abnormal. Use of sensitive pregnancy tests suggests that up to 50 percent of conceptions may be lost before they are clinically perceived.

IV. Implantation

Implantation is the process whereby an embryo attaches to the uterine wall and penetrates the epithelium and then the woman's circulatory system. The morula stage prepares the way for implantation. By the time the dividing zygote has entered the uterus it will have undergone four cell divisions, becoming a mass of 16 cells resembling a mulberry, hence the name "morula." This dividing of cells continues in a systematic sequence.

By day 6 the morula has grown into a blastocyst, a hollow-shaped structure of 60 to 200 cells. At this point the cells have already begun to differentiate. Only a small percentage of the blastocyst cells, however, will actually form the embryo.

Ten percent of the total cells gather at one side of the spherical blastocyst, forming the "inner cell mass" or embryoblast from which the embryo will develop. Various sites on the cells of the inner cell mass can already be identified as being destined to form organ systems such as the brain and spinal cord, heart, stomach and liver. Ninety percent of the cells take different positions, forming the "outer cell mass" or trophoblast, preparing to provide protective cover and support systems. From these cells the placenta will form.

Synchronous events must occur for successful implantation to result. The uterine fluid must be hospitable to the embryo, the embryo must be at an appropriate maturational stage and the epithelial lining of both blastocyst and uterus must be prepared for implantation. A number of events bring about this preparedness.

Delicate hair-like projections known as microvilli are present on the surface of the blastocyst and the uterine lining cells. Surface glycoprotein molecules on the blastocyst microvilli undergo a transition increasing their stickiness to the uterine epithelium. The blastocyst epithelial cells themselves increase their negative charge.

It is probable that the embryo signals the inner cells lining the uterus, thus bringing about a favorable site of implantation. Release of carbon dioxide by the embryo raises the pH of the embryo surface in turn, also increasing its stickiness. The conceptus also produces a hormone known as HCG (human chorionic gonadotropin) at about the time of implantation on day 6 of the pregnancy. HCG increases production of progesterone, a steroid hormone that enhances the receptiveness of the uterine lining to implantation.

The blastocyst secretes enzymes which can digest the intercellular matrix that holds the uterine epithelial cells together. This allows the trophoblast to penetrate through the basement layer on its way to the maternal blood vessels.

The blastocyst attaches to the endometrium with the inner-cell mass adjacent to the uterine cells. The trophoblastic cells proliferate rapidly, penetrating between the endometrial epithelium and anchoring the blastocyst securely. The blastocyst appears to sink entirely into the endometrium by a combination of collapse of the blastocyst cavity along with endometrial proliferation at the edges. The trophoblast between the inner cell mass and the endometrium is destined to become the placenta. This point in development is approximately day 7 following ovulation/fertilization. There is still a week to go before the woman misses her menstrual period.

The focus of the second post-conception week is the formation of a two-layer or bilaminar germ disk. By day 8 the blastocyst is partially embedded in the endometrial stroma of the uterine lining. The embryoblast forms into two layers, thinner hypoblast and thicker epiblast. The amniotic cavity appears as a small cleft. There are scattered endometrial blood vessels. The surface defect where implantation occurred is still open.

Birth-control.[2] Methods that may prevent implantation include: the "morning-after pill," intrauterine contraceptive device and RU486 (see Appendix).

V. Embryological Development

By day 9 the bilaminar germ disc has increased in size. The yolk sac is forming, as is an early amniotic cavity. The endometrial blood vessels also have increased in size. The original surface defect has now been closed by a layer of fibrin.

By day 12 the blastocyst is completely implanted. The trophoblastic cells or early placental tissue are in open connection with the maternal blood vessels or sinusoids establishing the uteroplacental circulation. The yolk sac is enlarging.

By the end of the second week after conception, around the time of the expected menstrual period which will not come, the germ disk is well established. At one end a thickening, the prochordal plate, is developing. This marks the location of the future head. The placenta is also well established with the development of primary stem villi. The future umbilical cord location can be seen as the connecting stalk.

Abortion Method. Menstrual Extraction or Menstrual Regulation (see Appendix).

The focus of the third post-conception week is the formation of the third germ layer, the mesoderm, leading to a trilaminar germ disc. This activity centers around the "primitive streak," a narrow groove with slightly bulging regions on either side which develops on the end of the germ disk opposite the prochordal plate. The epiblast cells migrate inward in the direction of the primitive streak. On arrival at the region of the streak they detach from the epiblast, slip underneath it and form an intermediate layer called the mesoderm, sandwiched between the upper ectoderm and lower endoderm. The formation of this third germ layer is known as gastrulation.

During the fourth to eighth week of development, the embryonic period, each of the three germ layers gives rise to specific tissues and organs.

From the ectodermal germ layer those organs and structures that maintain contact with the outside world are formed: central and peripheral nervous systems, and skin including hair and nails. On the embryonic disc opposite to the primitive streak forms the neural groove from which will form the brain and spinal cord. Failure of closure will result in either anencephaly, a lethal malformation, or spina bifida.

The mesodermal germ layer gives rise to the supporting structures of the body: muscles, bones, cartilage, ligaments, and tendons. It also forms the heart, blood vessels, and urogenital system. Failure of formation of the kidneys results in renal agenesis, a lethal malformation.

The endodermal germ layer gives rise to the lining of the gastrointestinal tract, respiratory tract and urinary bladder. Failure of the formation of the lungs results in pulmonary hypoplasia, also lethal.

At the end of the fourth week from conception one can identify the primordia of the eye, the ear, the limbs and the heart. The embryo is half an inch long and is developing fore-and hindlimbs as paddle-shaped buds. At this stage the embryo can be visualized with high resolution ultrasound imaging and cardiac motion can be identified.

With further growth the terminal portions of the limb buds flatten and become separated from the proximal, more cylindrically shaped segment. The four radial grooves separating five slightly thicker areas appear on the distal portion of the buds, foreshadowing the formation of the digits. The prominent eye and enormous size of the head stand out in comparison to the remainder of the body. The head constitutes approximately one-half the embryo's crown-rump length.

In week eight, while the fingers and toes are being formed, a second constriction, to become the elbow or knee, divides the proximal portion of the buds into two segments. The three parts characteristic of the adult extremities can now be recognized.

During the third month the face becomes more human in appearance. The eyes, initially placed on the lateral side of the head, become located on the front and the ears take their place on the side of the head. The lengths of the limbs in relation to the body begin to assume a more mature proportion. Gender differences are becoming evident in the external genitalia. The intestinal loops—up to this point herniated into the enlarged mumbilical cord—begin withdrawing into the abdominal cavity.

At 9 weeks post-conception the placental villi appear fine and delicate. Biopsy of these chorionic villi allows early identification of the embryo's chromosomes with the first trimester.

Abortion Methods — First Trimester. Ninety percent of abortions are performed in the first 10 weeks from fertilization. Procedures include vacuum dilatation and curettage (D&C) and sharp D&C (see Appendix).

VI. Fetal Development

The fetal period begins from the third month and continues to delivery. No new organs form, but there is growth and maturation of the existing organs. No malformations arise from this period, but growth disorders can occur. Rapid growth follows.

Initially the intestinal loops cause a large swelling in the umbilical cord, but by the end of the 11th week they withdraw into the abdominal cavity. By week 12, post-fertilization the external genitalia are developed adequately that the sex of the fetus can be determined by external examination. At this stage of the pregnancy, using high-resolution ultrasound, one can see both gross body movements of the fetus and extremity motion. These, however, are not perceived yet by the mother.

Now the 18-week fetus is connected to the placenta by its umbilical cord. During the fourth and fifth months the fetus lengthens rapidly. At 20 weeks its crown-rump length is half the total length of the term newborn, though it only weighs about 500 grams. The skin of the fetus is thin, lacking subcutaneous tissue. The fetus is covered with fine hair called lanugo hair. Eyebrows and head hair are also visible. About this time the mother begins to feel fetus movements.

During the last half of the pregnancy the weight of the fetus increases almost tenfold. A fetus born prior to the 24 weeks gestation has great difficulty surviving due to gross immaturity of many organ systems. The greatest problems arise from primarily from pulmonary immaturity. This stage in fetal development appears to mark an anatomic survival threshold. Advances in neonatal intensive care may well increase survival rates after 24 weeks in years to come but it is doubtful significant improvements in mortality statistics will occur when birth occurs earlier in gestation.

In the last eight weeks prior to term, the fetus doubles its weight. The rounded contours of a mature fetus develop as a result of deposition of subcutaneous fat. The fat is important for the fetus to maintain normal body temperature after birth. At term the fetal skin is covered by vernix caseosa, a whitish, fatty substance produced by the sebaceous glands of the maturing fetal skin.

Abortion Methods — Second Trimester. Only 10 percent of abortion procedures are performed after 12 weeks' gestation. Procedures include dilatation and evacuation (D&E); intraamniotic infusion; intravaginal suppositories; and hysterotomy (see Appendix).

VII. Human Tissue Or Person?

A key ethical question is "When in reproductive development does a new 'person' exist?" Over the millennia many "moments" of metamorphosis have been suggested: *fertilization*—with formation of a new unique genotype; *implantation*— with direct vascular contact with the mother; *fetogenesis*—when the embryo becomes a fetus; *cerebrogenesis*—with onset of brain-wave activity; *quickening*—with perception by the mother of fetal movement; *delivery*—with physical severance of the newborn from its mother; *respiration*—with breath of life entering the newborn.

The evidence is clear that reproductive development does not occur in neatly partitioned stages but on a continuum. Portrayal of development in stages is artificial and unnatural, and performed for ease of discussion only. I perceive no clearly demarcated moment or milestone in prenatal development when human cells become a human person. It thus is presumptuous, in my judgment, to attribute major ethical or moral significance to any specific developmental event.

The Human Zygote. The uniting of the DNA contributed by both ovum and sperm result in the formation of a unique gene sequence within the nucleus of a conceptus that over time will develop into a functioning human being. But is the zygote human *tissue* or a human *person*?

It is tempting to bypass the question of transition to personhood and attribute personhood to the zygote at the moment of fertilization. In such a view, this earliest developmental stage of a new and unique human genotype, the conceptus, has the same rights of existence and claims to protection as a term fetus, newborn or even adult human. Since the conceptus is a product of God's creation, since it is of human origin and since it is alive, its life is sacred and should not be violated. Some who believe in a human soul contend this is the point in development where the soul enters this new human life. Disruption of even a conceptus is the moral equivalent of murder, in this view, for a human soul has been destroyed. If the earliest stages of human development are not protected, what is there to a prevent a slide down the "slippery slope" to destruction of any other human organism deemed "unworthy" of life?

Such an argument has many appeals. Consistency is easier when there are no gradations of value, significance or meaning to stages of human development. The "hard questions" disappear when one no longer seeks the "moment of metamorphosis." From my perspective the so-called sanctity-of-life view leaves too many unexplained problems and unanswered questions.

While the zygote does represent the first step in the cascade of development that will lead to a new person, in my judgment, the zygote is not yet either a potential person or a new person. There are at least three reasons why I come to that conclusion.

First, only part of the zygote contributes to the development of the fetus. While each daughter cell that develops from the zygote receives an identical nucleus, this is not true of the cytoplasm. The bulk of the zygote's cytoplasm does not go to the inner cell mass, from which the fetus will develop, but rather forms the outer layer of the blastula, the anlage of the placenta and membranes. While recognizing the biologic elegance of the conceptus, I have difficulty conferring on it the corresponding significance and meaning as a viable, mature-term fetus, let alone a normal newborn infant.

Second, the high rate of early spontaneous pregnancy losses, most of which occur before the pregnancy is even recognized by the woman, makes me hesitate to attribute significant moral worth to a conceptus or zygote. Most conceptions that fail undergo developmental arrest due to major chromosomal or structural defects incompatible with life. Attributing eternal significance to zygotes, a majority of which will never develop to the embryo stage, seems meaningless to me. I cannot believe the hereafter will be largely populated by "persons" who never developed even to the embryo stage.

The third problem I have with calling the zygote a new person arises from formation of multiple identical fetuses. The division of a single zygote into identical twins or triplets occurs within the first 12 days post-fertilization. If at fertilization the zygote becomes a new person, what happens when that one new "person" divides into two or more "persons"? Does a second or third soul enter the additional blastocysts when the division takes place, often many days after the initial fertilization?

The Human Embryo. The one-celled zygote undergoes a series of eight cell divisions before becoming a 350-cell embryo at four weeks' gestation. Direct vascular contact has been established between the embryo and the mother. The vast majority of zygotes with lethal chromosomal malformations have undergone developmental arrest and have either been reabsorbed or spontaneously aborted. The embryos that remain have a 98 percent probability of developing to viability. At this stage we can state with reasonable certainty that the implanted embryo has a reasonable potential of becoming a person, a rational and functional human being.

I therefore view implantation as marking the beginning of potential personhood and therefore the point beyond which disruption of the reproductive process would be considered an abortion. Any disruption of the reproductive process prior to implantation I consider as contraception, not abortion.

VIII. Abortion of the Normal Fetus

With advancing development there is an increasing moral meaning and value to the embryo/fetus as a potential person. The significance of a fetal loss, whether it occurs spontaneously or by induced abortion, is greater as each week and month of the pregnancy passes. Although abortion should never be undertaken thoughtlessly regardless of the stage of pregnancy, the further in gestation the pregnancy has progressed, the weightier the reasons for abortion should be.

In pregnancies of early gestational age, the limited potential personhood of the fetus demands less weighty indications for abortion than a more advanced gestation. An abortion at eight weeks' gestation requires significantly less compelling evidence than an eighteen-week one. Similarly an eighteen-week abortion requires less pressing rationale than a twenty-eight-week delivery. Notwithstanding this gestational age-contingent criterion, no abortion or premature delivery is trivial. While an embryo is not a human person, it is more than mere human tissue. Abortion of even an early embryo is never the moral equivalent of removing an unwanted skin tag or wart.

The grounds for aborting a pregnancy need to be increasingly grave the further along the developmental continuum the fetus has progressed. However, delivery of even an immature or premature fetus in the third trimester of pregnancy would be justified if extreme maternal risks are present. Late abortion, in the presence of a fetus with increasing potential personhood, is justified when the mother's life is in jeopardy (e.g., severe pregnancy-induced hypertension, disseminated intravascular coagulopathy).

It is important in the decision-making, prior to any abortion, for all parties to ensure that there are increasingly weighty indications for abortion corresponding to the gestational age. There is a moral imperative for significant responsibility and personal honesty on the part of the woman, her partner and her physician.

This is not to say the embryo or fetus is without value, but rather that the strength of the grounds to abort the pregnancy exceed the claims of the embryo or fetus to continue the pregnancy. Since the fetus is inextricably linked to the mother for its existence, when a pregnancy is terminated early, the separation of the fetus from its mother will lead to death for the fetus. In most cases the fetus is developing normally and over time would mature into a term newborn. Yet the abortion or premature delivery comes about from no fault of the fetus. The fact that a pregnancy is being intentionally terminated should not change the care and concern given to the newborn.

When a premature delivery is required for reasons of maternal jeopardy, it is only proper to render fitting care to the immature or premature newborn as would enhance its developmental progression toward personhood. The premature, yet intentionally, delivered newborn should be handled in the neonatal period just as any other similar gestational-age newborn who was born early but unintentionally. If the neonate can be saved *ex utero*, enabling it to proceed on the developmental continuum to personhood, it should be given that opportunity.

If the biological mother is unable to care for the newborn or if she chooses not to accept responsibility for the newborn's care, many adoptive parents are ready to do so. With a fetus of survivable gestational age, the method of abortion should be chosen so as to deliver the fetus with the least trauma and in the best possible condition for pediatric care and resuscitation.

My hope for every abortion would be that every normal fetus and placenta could be removed intact and without damage from the biological mother and placed either in a hormonally prepared adoptive mother or artificial uterus. There it could be nourished and sustained, allowing it to continue growth and development until term. This proposal, although philosophically and ethically appealing to me, currently is medically and scientifically impossible at the gestational age of most abortions. The current state of neonatal intensive care and our present understanding of developmental limits suggest a lower boundary of survivability at 24 menstrual weeks of gestation. Abortion or immature delivery prior to 24 completed weeks of gestation will almost certainly preclude neonatal survival.

IX. Psychosocial Indications For Abortion

The most vexing dilemmas in considering the issue of abortion surround the legitimacy of psychosocial indications for abortion. Most abortions in the United States as well as worldwide are performed for psychosocial rather than medical indications. One point of view expressed frequently today equates psychosocial indications for abortion with trivial, elective and convenient abortions. From such a perspective, only medical reasons for abortion are considered legitimate. This position seems too restrictive and narrow to me.

Even the most vigorous opponents of abortion generally agree that morally acceptable reasons for abortion include: (1) rape, (2) incest, and (3) jeopardy to the woman's life. Each of these conditions poses serious threats to the pregnant woman. More significantly, they reflect the notion that justifiable grounds for abortion include not only a threat to the woman's physical life and health but also her psychosocial well-being.

I believe that mankind was created by God as a multidimensional being in whom balance and harmony in all dimensions, psychosocial as well as physical, are necessary for an abundant life. It appears artificial to accept only physical threats to a woman's life and health as legitimate indications for abortion but not recognize psychosocial threats.

Psychosocial indications may seem "soft" and lack credibility for any of the following reasons: (1) they are often perplexing to validate objectively, (2) it is

14

difficult to assess reliably their severity, and (3) they are subject to feigning and fabrication. Yet it seems naive to deny that certain psychosocial hazards of an unwanted pregnancy may be just as real and menacing to the pregnant woman involved as physical or medical perils. Violent rape and incest represent two indications for abortion at one end of the psychosocial spectrum. However, many psychosocial situations of lesser degree could be cited that could cause extreme and prolonged distress to a pregnant woman.

The previous discussion on abortion has developed the following ethical principles: (1) birth control by contraception is morally preferable to abortion; (2) an embryo/fetus has moral worth above ordinary human tissue due to its potential for personhood; (3) the moral claims of an embryo/fetus increase with advancing gestational age; (4) an abortion is morally justified at a given gestational age only when the threat to the mother exceeds the moral claim of the embryo/fetus.

Consideration of these ethical principles gives rise to three crucial questions that are appropriately considered by every woman/party involved in decision-making regarding a possible abortion: (1) How much moral claim does an embryo/fetus have at a given week of gestational age? (2) What degree of psychosocial stress/threat is the mother experiencing? (3) Does that degree of psychosocial stress/threat exceed the moral claims of the embryo/fetus at a given gestational age?

When applied to specific situations the answers to these questions will depend heavily on the woman's previous experience, her belief system and her value structure. Consider the two following cases: Nancy is an unmarried 14-year-old inner-city adolescent who was pressured by her boyfriend into unprotected intercourse one time, which resulted in pregnancy. Mary is a married 35-year-old mother of two teenagers planning to return to college. She was scheduled for a tubal ligation but finds herself pregnant from a diaphragm failure. Both Nancy and Mary find themselves pregnant under conditions of psychosocial stress. How will these women answer the three crucial questions regarding abortion? Clearly responses cannot be assumed the same for both women.

The private and personal nature of psychosocial stresses/threats makes their objective verification perplexing and assessment of their severity difficult. Yet in spite of the lack of assessment precision, an unverified assertion of psychosocial stress may not be adequate justification for every requested abortion. The key issue is gestational age. If at the time of prospective abortion gestational age has progressed to where the moral claims of the fetus are substantial, attempts to verify the presence and degree of psychosocial stress may be justified. At still more advanced gestational ages, with even further development of fetal moral claims, no degree of psychosocial stress can justify an abortion.

15

Verification unnecessary. In a free and pluralistic society the personal autonomy of its citizens is valued highly. In early pregnancies the moral claims of the embryo/fetus are the least, and maternal physical risks are negligible. Together with the imprecision of psychosocial stress assessment, these considerations suggest that in the first trimester the woman should be able to request an abortion without third-party verification of her stated psychosocial threat. This is not to say that all first trimester abortions performed for psychosocial indications are morally justified. Rather, this position ensures that the freedom and autonomy of a pregnant woman will not be trivially dismissed.

Verification needed. As the pregnancy progresses into the second trimester, the moral claims of the fetus increase to where they may outweigh trivial maternal psychosocial stresses. At this stage of potential personhood, the fetal claims to continue the pregnancy may exceed the autonomy of the woman. Society may need to prevent abortion of potential persons of substantial development for trivial reasons. It may be reasonable to require, between 12 and 20 weeks' gestation, objective third-party verification of the presence and degree of the stated psychosocial stress/threat. This will not ensure that all abortions performed in this gestational-age window would be morally justified, but it may prevent indiscriminate destruction of many normal fetuses well on their developmental journey.

Verification superfluous. At 20 weeks' gestation the fetus is almost at the halfway point of intrauterine development, equidistant between fertilization and term delivery. In just a few more weeks the fetus will be able to survive outside the uterus. Any abortion procedure now carries considerable risks to the woman. The moral claims of the fetus are substantial at this advanced stage of development. Abortion of a normal fetus at the midpoint of pregnancy requires evidence of a major threat to the woman's life. In my judgment no psychosocial threat of any degree would outweigh the moral claims of a fetus past 20 weeks of pregnancy. Other therapeutic remedies than abortion, such as psychotherapy and medication, are available to support the woman until delivery. After 20 weeks' gestation, objective verification of the nature and degree of psychosocial threat is not only unnecessary but superfluous.

X. Abortion of the "Doomed" Fetus

The technological advances discussed earlier in this essay have enabled the identification of a wide range of fetal abnormalities that previously went unrecognized until birth. Some fetal abnormalities are relatively minor and have little clinical or functional significance. Others are so major as to preclude survival outside of the uterus: major chromosomal anomalies, severe heart defects, failure of kidney development, failure of lung development, many kinds of conjoined twins. Previously such "doomed" pregnancies would have continued to term only to have the newborn die from untreatable, uncorrectable abnormalities. These lethal anomalies can now be diagnosed early in pregnancy, often in the first or early second trimester.

Inevitable questions arise such as the following: If the fetus will die before or at birth is, there any point in carrying on with the pregnancy? What values are there to either mother or fetus in continuing a pregnancy in which survival outside the uterus is impossible? Is abortion of such a pregnancy appropriate? These are decisions facing the mother and physician that seldom had to be faced before.

When the fetus has no possibility of realizing any degree of personhood, there appears to be nothing gained for either the fetus or the mother by pregnancy continuation. The question is not *"Will* premature death occur?" but *"When* will premature death occur?"

Although the fetus possesses sensory capabilities *in utero*, the pain and suffering of a dying fetus/neonate is not presently quantifiable. It is reasonable to assume that the more advanced the maturation of the fetal/neonatal peripheral and central nervous system, the greater the chance the fetus will experience pain and suffering. Fetus suffering may well be lessened by allowing inevitable death to occur earlier than later.

From the standpoint of the mother, her physical morbidity and mortality risks are increased directly as the gestational age increases. An early abortion would pose fewer risks to the mother than a delivery later in pregnancy. Once it is clear the fetus has no chance of extrauterine survival, I believe it is morally justified to offer a mother the option of aborting the "doomed" fetus regardless of gestational age.

On the other hand, a mother may feel she should not actively contribute to the premature death of her fetus, even if that death is ultimately unavoidable. She may wish to allow the natural course of events to occur, even at the greater risk to her physical health. I believe her decision to continue a "doomed" pregnancy should also be supported.

XI. Abortion of the "Abnormal" Fetus

Over two percent of all babies at term will have some identifiable birth defect. Fortunately, many of these defects are of a mild and relatively innocuous nature. Some, however, can be severe with major disability and/or profound mental retardation. With increasing use of the prenatal diagnostic modalities previously described, many of these fetal abnormalities that previously went unrecognized until birth are now being identified *in utero*, some early in pregnancy. What ethical principles can be applied to the management of the abnormal fetus? Under what conditions is abortion of an abnormal fetus justified? I will discuss this issue first from the perspective of the mother and then of the fetus.

The woman may experience variable psychosocial stress upon learning her fetus has an abnormality. Her response will vary depending on the nature of the abnormality. Research studies have documented the impact of major neonatal disability on the family: marital breakup, economic jeopardy, effect on siblings, etc. These considerations may lead the woman to request an abortion. As described, the basis for this request is the psychosocial impact on the woman and her family. Such abortion requests should be handled as previously discussed over psychosocial indications for abortion.

The second perspective is that of the fetus. A fundamental assumption is that for some fetuses abortion and non-survival is to be preferred over continuation of the pregnancy and probable survival. Are there fetal conditions in which nonexistence is preferable to existence? Prior to addressing this question, we need to deal with the inherent limitations in diagnostic accuracy, disability prediction and quality-of-life assignment.

Limitations of diagnostic accuracy and disability prediction. Many factors can diminish the accuracy of ultrasound diagnosis. These include: fetal factors (small fetal size, early gestational age, orientation in the uterus), maternal factors (low amniotic fluid, abdominal wall obesity), technical factors (resolution ability of the ultrasound equipment, inadequate technique and inexperience of the ultrasonographer). Each of these areas needs to be closely scrutinized prior to accepting a diagnosis of a fetal abnormality. A given degree of structural abnormality often has a wide range of functional disabilities. Even if an accurate structural diagnosis is made, it is often difficult to predict the degree of newborn or childhood disability. The impact on the newborn is not the structural abnormality but the functional disability. The impreciseness of predicting functional disability must be weighed when considering abortion of pregnancy for a prenatally diagnosed fetal abnormality.

Limitations of quality-of-life assignment. A more difficult question is the relationship between functional disability and quality of life. Even if the fetal diagnosis is correct and disability prediction is accurate, it is problematic in many cases to predict what effect that disability will have on the quality of life of the surviving infant. An abortion for fetal indications is performed because the predicted neonatal/childhood quality of life is no better/worse than nonexistence. The obstacles to making such a judgment *in utero* are evident.

Now that I have pointed out the limitations of prenatal diagnosis, disability prediction, and quality-of-life assignment, I must stress that there are severe fetal abnormalities, particularly those of the brain and central nervous system, in which accurate diagnosis and disability prediction is possible. Although these newborns may survive for prolonged periods of time, they will have such severe and profound mental retardation they lack even a sense of self-awareness. Examples include: porencephaly, holoprosencephaly, anencephaly. Although these conditions are not lethal (in the sense that extrauterine survival is impossible), their severity precludes achievement of personhood by the newborn/child just as surely as in the doomed fetus. I perceive no benefit to the fetus of continuing the pregnancy in these cases where self-awareness is lacking. I would manage such a pregnancy just as I would that of the doomed fetus.

After excluding fetuses with no chance of achieving personhood (the doomed and self-awareness absent fetuses), what principles apply to abortion of the remaining "abnormal" fetuses? This group has some hope of potential personhood, although the degree to which it will be realized will vary. Recognizing the limitations of prenatal assessment as well as the increasing potential personhood of the fetus with advancing gestational age, I would manage abortion requests according the previously discussed psychosocial indications for abortion.

XII. Summary

1. From its earliest stages reproductive development involves a finely orchestrated sequence of exquisite processes devised by the Creator.

2. Any intentional disruption of the reproductive process *prior* to implantation I consider as contraception, whereas *after* implantation it would be an abortion. Contraception is to be morally preferred to abortion.

3. The implanted normal embryo has moral worth as a potential person, since it represents the first step in reproductive development toward a rational, functional human being.

4. The moral claims of a normal embryo/fetus increase with advancing gestational age.

5. An abortion is morally justified at a given gestational age only when the threat to the mother exceeds the moral claim of the normal embryo/fetus.

6. Psychosocial threats of pregnancy represent a valid justification for abortion of the normal fetus. Third party verification of the nature and degree of

psychosocial threat is inappropriate up to 12 weeks' gestation, but reasonable between 12 and 20 weeks' gestation. No degree of psychosocial threat can justify an abortion past 20 weeks' gestation.

7. Abortion of the "doomed" fetus (with no chance of extrauterine survival) or the severely impaired fetus (without capability of self-awareness) is a morally acceptable option any time in the pregnancy.

8. Abortion of the fetus with lesser degrees of abnormality should be managed as the normal fetus.

Endnotes

[1] The words "abort" and "abortion" are often employed in their restricted sense referring only to pre-viable gestational ages. In this essay I will use these words in their broadest sense to refer to intentionally ending a pregnancy prematurely regardless of the gestational age.

[2] Birth control includes both contraception and abortion. I will define 'contraception' as any intervention to prevent pregnancy prior to implantation and 'abortion' as disruption of an established pregnancy after implantation has taken place. Subsequent discussion will develop the basis for the assertion that an implanted normal embryo has moral value beyond that of an ovum, sperm or even a fertilized zygote. Accordingly, I believe that birth control by contraception is to be morally preferred over abortion.

APPENDIX

I. Contraceptive Methods to Prevent Implantation

The Morning-after "Pill." This is really not a pill but a series of hormone pills taken on a number of successive days. The mechanism of action is to hormonally render the lining of the uterus, the endometrium, hostile to successful implantation, should an ovum have been fertilized.

The Intrauterine Contraceptive Device. The intrauterine contraceptive device or IUD has a variety of possible mechanisms of action. The IUD does induce a local foreign body inflammatory response, resulting in injury to the cell wall of the blastocyst and sperm. It can thus prevent implantation. However, the IUD also may operate by other mechanisms to prevent fertilization. These include increased motility of the ovum in the fallopian tube and immobilization of sperm as they pass through the uterine cavity. IUDs placed in the uterus after implantation may also cause a mechanical disruption of the implanted blastocyst from the endometrium.

RU-486. This is an experimental anti-progesterone drug developed in France. It can function as a contraceptive by rendering the uterine lining hostile to implantation. It has also been used to cause expulsion of a normally implanted embryo, resulting in a chemically induced abortion.

II. Methods of Abortion: First Trimester

Menstrual Extraction or Regulation. This procedure removes the uterine contents from a woman who is at risk of being pregnant before she can be declared "obviously pregnant" by clinical examination and other diagnostic measures. It is performed between the 5th and 14th days following day 1 of the expected but missed period. Pregnancy testing is not considered mandatory.

Dilatation of the cervix may not be needed, and anesthesia is often unnecessary. A sterile 5 to 6 mm. plastic cannula is inserted through the cervix into the uterine cavity until the top of the fundus is reached. Suction is then applied to withdraw the endometrial contents. The cannula is rotated until tissue flow ceases and air bubbles appear, indicating the extraction is complete.

After the procedure all tissue is examined grossly for confirmation of pregnancy tissue. If none is found, the patient should have a follow-up pregnancy test 10 days after to rule out a failed procedure or possible tubal pregnancy. The risks of menstrual extraction are negligible.

Vacuum Dilation and Curettage (D&C). Ninety percent of all abortion procedures are performed within the first 12 weeks of pregnancy and involve either menstrual extraction or a D&C. The D&C removes the uterine contents from a woman who has been diagnosed as being pregnant between the 6th and 12th week of pregnancy. Dilatation of the cervix is necessary, and anesthesia is needed. A paracervical anesthetic block is usually employed for pain relief. Tapered metal dilators are forced through the cervical opening in serial fashion. The dilators open the cervix in 1 mm. increments until adequate dilatation is reached. A sterile 8 to 10 mm. plastic cannula is then inserted through the open cervix into the uterine cavity. The fetus, placenta, amniotic fluid and membranes are vacuum- aspirated through the cannula, which is rotated or moved in a forward-backward motion. When tissue flow ceases and air bubbles appear the procedure is complete.

The D&C procedure used to be performed using only a sharp curette without the vacuum. Blood loss and uterine perforation risks are greater than those for the vacuum D&C. The sharp D&C is seldom used today.

As with the previously described menstrual extraction procedure, all tissue is examined grossly for confirmation of pregnancy tissue. Failure to identify fetal parts or placental tissue suggests a failed procedure or possible tubal pregnancy.

Legal abortion procedures at 12 weeks' gestation or earlier are relatively safe. The mortality risk to a woman of an induced abortion procedure prior to 12 weeks is 1.3 per 100,000 abortions, 11 times lower than her risk of dying from pregnancy and childbirth.

Morbidity risks of early vacuum curettage abortions include: hemorrhage (4 per 1,000), pelvic infection (7 per 1,000), cervical injury (10 per 1,000) and uterine perforation (2 per 1,000). The most consistent factor associated with abortion complications is advancing pregnancy duration. Each additional week of gestational age increases D&C morbidity risks by 25 percent and D&C mortality risk by 50 percent.

III. Methods of Abortion: Second Trimester

Dilation and Evacuation (D&E). The D&E and D&C are similar in that both are surgical procedures and local anesthetic block is necessary. However, with the pregnancy further advanced (14-20 weeks' gestation), the uterus is bigger and the fetus larger. No longer can the fetus be easily aspirated through cannula as with the D&C. In order to remove the fetal parts completely, the cervix needs to be dilated to a greater degree. The fetus must be crushed with embryotomy forceps and removed in fragments. Even more than with the D&C, the fetal skeletal anatomy must be reconstructed to ensure complete removal of bony parts, especially of the skull, pelvis and long bones of the extremities.

In general, the complications associated with D&E are similar to those of earlier curettage procedures, but are increased in frequency and severity. Morbidity risks of D&E abortions include: hemorrhage (38 per 1,000), pelvic infection (38 per 1,000), cervical injury (10 per 1,000) and uterine perforation (7 per 1,000).

Maternal mortality from D&E procedures overall is 9.9 per 100,000 abortions, seven times higher than with a D&C procedure. The most consistent factor associated with abortion complications is advancing pregnancy duration.

Intraamniotic Infusion (IAI). IAI is not used until after 16 weeks' gestation because of a high failure rate when used in pregnancies of lesser duration. An 8 cm. long 18 gauge needle is placed under local anesthesia through the woman's abdominal wall into the amniotic sac surrounding the fetus. A variety of agents may be infused through the needle into the amniotic fluid in order to initiate uterine contractions. These agents lead to labor with progressive cervical dilation and, ultimately, expulsion of the fetus. The average infusion to expulsion time is about 15 hours. Narcotic pain medication is usually required.

All agents have maternal complications or side effects. Hypertonic saline ('salting out') has been associated with hypernatremia, water intoxication and coagulopathy. Hypertonic urea has been associated with failed or incomplete expulsion. Prostaglandin F2-alpha is associated with high incidence of nausea, vomiting and diarrhea. Fetal death almost always occurs with hypertonic saline and urea. Use of prostaglandins results in frequent live-born fetuses.

Morbidity risks of IAI abortions include: hemorrhage (38 per 1,000), pelvic infection (38 per 1,000), cervical injury (10 per 1,000) and uterine perforation (7 per 1,000). Maternal mortality from IAI procedures overall is approximately 17 per 100,000 abortions, twice as high as with a D&E procedure, and 13 times higher than with a D&C. Hypertonic saline infusion has somewhat higher risks than other agents. The most consistent factor associated with abortion complications is advancing pregnancy duration.

Intravaginal Suppository. A variety of chemical agents can be absorbed through the vaginal lining resulting in the induction of uterine contractions. As with IAI, these contractions lead to labor with progressive cervical dilation and expulsion of the fetus.

These agents are contained in a vaginal suppository which melts when exposed to body heat within the vagina. Prostaglandin E_2 vaginal suppositories are commercially available in the United States. The gestational age and maternal risks are similar to the IAI procedure in which prostaglandin agents are used.

Hysterotomy/Hysterectomy. A hysterotomy is basically a mini-cesarean procedure used to remove a fetus that is either dead or prior to viability. The fetus is removed from the uterus through an abdominal incision. The vertical uterine incision is susceptible to rupture with contractions and so renders subsequent labor dangerous. This destines the woman with a previous hysterotomy to a cesarean without labor for any ensuing delivery. It is the rarest of all abortion procedures and is used almost exclusively when a D&E or IAI abortion fails.

A hysterectomy is a major surgical procedure to remove a uterus. It is not a true abortion procedure and is used almost exclusively when there is a medical indication for removing the uterus in which there is a coincidental pregnancy. The pregnant uterus with intact fetus is removed by either abdominal or vaginal route, depending on the gestational age and uterine size.

Since both hysterotomy and hysterectomy are major surgical procedures, they require either regional or general anesthesia. Maternal mortality risks are higher than with any other abortion procedure: 45 deaths per 100,000 abortions.

Bibliography

Berger, G. S., W. E. Brenner, and L. G. Keith, eds. *Second-Trimester Abortion: Perspectives After a Decade of Experience.* Boston: John Wright-PSG Inc., 1981.

Creasy, R. K., and R. Resnick, eds. *Maternal-Fetal Medicine: Principles and Practice.* 2nd ed. Philadelphia: W. B. Saunders Company, 1989.

Goodwin, J. W., J. O. Godden, and G. W. Chance, eds. *Perinatal Medicine: The Basic Science Underlying Clinical Practice.* Baltimore: The Williams & Wilkins Company, 1976.

Nilsson, L. *Behold Man: A Photographic Journey of Discovery Inside the Body.* Boston: Little, Brown & Company, 1973.

Pritchard, J. A., P. C. MacDonald, and N. F. Gant. *Williams Obstetrics.* 17th ed. Norwalk, CT: Appleton-Century-Crofts, 1985.

Sadler, T. W. *Langman's Medical Embryology.* 5th ed. Baltimore: The Williams & Wilkins Company, 1985.

Sakala, E. P. "Ethical Issues in the Management of the 'Doomed' Pregnancy." In *Clinical Decisions in Obstetrics and Gynecology,* ed. R. C. Cephalo. Rockville, MD: Aspen Publishers, 1990.

Shettles, L. B. and D. M. Rorvik. *Rites of Life.* Grand Rapids, MI: The Zondervan Publishing House, 1983.

Williams, N. B., ed. *Contraceptive Technology, 1986-1987.* 13th ed. New York: Irvington Publishers, 1986.

Zatuchni, G. I., J. J. Sciarra, and J. J. Speidel, eds. *Pregnancy Termination: Procedures, Safety and New Development.* Hagerstown, MD: Harper & Row, 1979.

Part II

Scripture and Tradition

2 Adventists, Abortion, and the Bible

John C. Brunt

For almost two decades Adventist periodicals (especially *Ministry* and *Spectrum*) have, with moderate frequency, included discussions and debates on the problem of abortion. It is hardly surprising, given the Adventist commitment to the authority of Scripture, to find that the Bible plays a prominent role in these discussions. This study seeks first to survey, analyze and evaluate the way the Bible has been used in the discussion of abortion in American Adventism, and then to offer some concluding suggestions about how the Bible should and should not be used in this and similar discussions of the moral life. The purpose of the study is not to offer a position on the question of abortion itself. It is rather to lay some hermeneutical foundation on which future discussions may build.

The survey and analysis is divided into five sections. Four of them enumerate ways that Scripture is used in discussion of abortion: as a source of specific rules, as an arbiter of specific facts, as a source of moral principles, and as a source of analogies relevant to abortion. Before considering these different ways Scripture has been used, however, we begin by looking at reactions to the fact that the Bible gives no explicit advice on abortion.

Reactions to the Bible's Silence

Arguments from silence can produce an interesting variety of conclusions, and the use that Adventist authors have made of the Bible's silence is no exception. On the one hand, as early as 1971 Harold Ziprick, a physician, used the Bible's silence to argue against hard and fast prohibitions of all "therapeutic" abortions. Although he warns against hasty decisions, he would allow abortion when it makes "troubled life tolerable," as he concludes in his article:

The decision to take the life of a fetus should not be taken hurriedly. The decision to sacrifice an unborn life should be made only when it is the best way to make a troubled life tolerable. Since the problem of abortion is not delineated in the Bible, we should show by our actions that we have reverence and regard for the life God has created, and that we are trying to do his will. . . . Perhaps because we have been given freedom to make decisions about this difficult problem, we will become more responsible and mature Christians.[1]

At the other extreme Richard Müller, who strongly opposes abortion, interprets the Bible's silence by saying: "The thought of abortion is so foreign to Judeo-Christian thought that it is not even mentioned in Scripture."[2] James Londis is on safer ground when he uses the silence of the Bible to argue for tolerance and warns against those on either side of the issue becoming dogmatic and judgmental.[3]

In rare cases it is even possible for Adventists to discuss the topic of abortion with little or no reference to Scripture. This is the case with physician, theologian, and pioneering ethicist Jack Provonsha[4] and one of the church's premier Bible scholars, Sakae Kubo.[5]

One of the most interesting reactions to the Bible's silence is denial that the Bible really is silent. Since some have used this silence to argue for abortion, certain opponents have been anxious to deny that the Bible is silent. The argument has taken the form of an implicit syllogism: The Bible speaks to all important topics; abortion is an important topic; therefore the Bible speaks to abortion. Thus Richard Fredericks responds to Adventists who hold that Scripture has nothing to say about abortion: "This, to me, is a view that discredits Scripture and God Himself. Would God be silent on a matter of such great moral import, leaving everyone to do what is right in his own eyes?"[6] Müller expresses the same sentiments by saying: "The Bible can never be neutral on such vital questions of life and death."[7]

John and Millie Youngberg express a similar view when they speak specifically to the question of when life begins:

The argument has been put forth that we do not know enough about Biblical anthropology to define the subtleties of when life begins. . . . To say this is ultimately to malign God Himself, for how could He leave us in such darkness that we are unable to make intelligent choices that involve life and death?[8]

This latter reaction to Scripture's failure explicitly to address the issue of abortion reflects a strong impetus in Adventism to ground moral decision-making in the Bible. Although this stance is commendable, it can be a serious temptation to misuse Scripture. The desire to find answers in the Bible can be so strong that biblical statements and stories are twisted to fit the issue of abortion with little regard for the real issues at stake in their original historical and literary context. On the other hand, there can be a positive result from a refusal simply to set Scripture aside on the question of abortion, for it can lead to a legitimate search for deeper Scriptural guidance in relationship to this issue. This, for instance, is what Fredericks claims to do when he, subsequent to the previous quotation, attempts to set forth biblical principles that speak to the issue.

At the same time, Londis' caution is important. Any discussion of abortion that makes use of the Bible must remember that there is a silence, at least at the level of explicit teaching. Thus warnings against dogmatism are appropriate.

The next four sections of this study provide the opportunity to evaluate how successful Adventist authors have been in their attempt to use Scripture to seek guidance on this topic while avoiding the temptations of dogmatism and the misuse of Scripture.

The Bible as a Source of Specific Rules

Few Adventists have attempted to make Scripture yield specific rules governing abortion, but some of the strongest opponents of abortion have come very close in their use of the sixth commandment in Exodus 20:13, "Thou shalt not kill." Ardyce Sweem, for example, uses Exodus 20:13 and Genesis 9:6 to show that the Bible forbids violence and killing and then concludes: "The techniques of abortion are violent acts of killing."[9]

Müller reaches the same conclusion through a series of rhetorical questions. After quoting the commandment he asks:

> Is this commandment not straightforward, clear in itself?... Some might argue that the commandment in its original setting speaks about murdering, not about accidental killing, but is not murdering exactly what we find in cases of abortion?... Is this not one of the most brutal forms of murder?[10]

Fredericks is slightly less emphatic when he sets forth his first in a series of four Old Testament principles as the principle that God is against abortion. Again he uses the sixth commandment and argues that even though this commandment may allow for some forms of capital punishment or self-defense, it never allows for the taking of innocent life by violent means.[11]

In all three cases the sixth commandment becomes a specific rule against abortion, because abortion is defined as murder. If the Bible says "Thou shalt not murder" and abortion is murder, the Bible does give an explicit rule against abortion. But is this simple equation of abortion with murder justified? Does it produce an explicit biblical rule against abortion?

It is not within the scope of this study to answer the question of whether abortion is murder. But from a hermeneutical standpoint it is important to notice that none of the authors who find a specific rule against abortion in the sixth commandment makes a *biblical* case for why abortion should be considered murder. That endeavor would appear necessary in order to nail down a clear biblical rule against abortion. Otherwise, these authors are open to the challenge that the biblical concept of murder does not include abortion. The equation of abortion and murder is overly simplistic in its attempt to make Scripture provide a specific rule against abortion. The biblical data are simply not sufficient to establish this case.

The Bible as Arbiter of Facts

Adventist authors have also looked to Scripture in order to settle certain factual matters. They have done this either by bringing specific questions, such as when life begins, to the text or by looking at texts that appear to have some relevance for abortion and asking about their significance.

Some of the strongest Adventist opponents of abortion have used Scripture to show that human life begins at conception. Müller takes the close relationship between conception and birth in Genesis 4:1 (Adam knew his wife, and she conceived and bore a son) and Luke 1:31 (she conceived a son) as evidence that "the beginning of personhood starts with conception."[12] In addition, texts such as Job 31:15, Psalms 71:6, Isaiah 44:24, Psalms 139:16, Jeremiah 1:5, and Galations 1:15 reveal that the making of a human is not a biological development but a creative act of God forming a person in the womb.[13]

Fredericks uses Jeremiah 1:5 and Psalms 139:13-16 as support for what he calls the "principle" of the value of life. But his conclusion is not so much a principle as a statement that life begins before birth. He says:

> He [God] views the unborn not as potential life but as persons, individuals with identity and worth for whom He already has a destiny.[14]

Sweem also uses Scripture to argue that life begins before birth. She points out that passages such as Genesis 16:11; 19:36; and Matthew 24:19 refer to pregnant women as being "with child" and that texts such as Jeremiah 1:5, Luke 1:13-17, and Galations 1:15 show God's involvement with persons before birth. She concludes: "God looks at fetuses as having personhood prior to their birth."[15]

Walter R. Beach acknowledges that some use Genesis 2:7 to suggest that life begins with the first breath, but he then goes on to point to Ecclesiastes 11:5, which says that the spirit (or breath) comes into the womb.[16]

Maureen Maxwell and Clarice Woodward use Genesis 2:7 to posit that it is the breath of life that leads to a living being. After pointing out that the fetus is not viable until 20 weeks' gestation, without giving specific endorsement, they conclude: "According to the Genesis approach, the infant would become a human being when it has taken its first breath and is able to live apart from the mother."[17]

Kevin Paulson objects to arguments such as those of Muller, Sweem and Fredericks in a letter to the editor of *Ministry*. He says: "Adventist doctrine and practice should be based on a plain 'Thus saith the Lord.' And nowhere does Inspiration declare that personhood begins at conception."[18]

Does the Bible solve the problem of when life begins? Certainly no biblical writer addresses that question in a specific way. All of the texts cited by the above authors have quite a different purpose in their original historical and literary contexts. This is not to say that the texts have no significance for the question of abortion, but they will give no generally accepted answer to the question of the moment when human life or personhood really begins.

In fact, Gerald Winslow correctly shows that there is no specific moment when life or personhood begins. He says that, since creation, human life never begins but is passed on as a gift from one life to another, and each of the times that has been proposed as the beginning of life is significant. There is no time before which this emerging life can be considered unimportant, and each "time" reminds us that "the unique form of human life initiated at conception is on its way to becoming *personal*."[19] This calls into question the whole endeavor of ascertaining the exact moment that life or personhood begins. But even if it were possible to find this moment on other grounds, we can hardly make Scripture yield this information.

Another factual question faced by authors on abortion has been the interpretation of Exodus 21:22-25 and its significance for the abortion question. The passage reads:

> When men strive together, and hurt a woman with child, so that there is a miscarriage, and yet no harm follows, the one who hurt her shall be fined, according as the woman's husband shall lay upon him; and he shall

pay as the judges determine. If any harm follows, then you shall give life
for life, eye for eye, tooth for tooth, hand for hand, foot for foot, burn
for burn, wound for wound, stripe for stripe (RSV).

The major difficulties with this verse are the meanings of the words translated
"miscarriage" and "harm." Is the contrast being made in the passage between
a premature birth where the fetus lives and one where it dies, or is it between
a miscarriage that does no injury to the mother and one that injures her? If the
latter is in view, the passage places less value on the fetus than the life of the
mother. If the former, the fetus is valued as a life.

Some authors use the text in one way or the other without any
acknowledgment that it could have a different interpretation. Thus John Duge,
in the course of stating a position that would allow for certain abortions and that
would protect individual choice rather than have a church-wide decision, says
that the passage shows that violently induced miscarriage, although a serious
matter, is still not murder.[20] And Ralph Waddell, in an effort to give scriptural
justification for the three acceptable reasons for "therapeutic" abortion that were
proposed in the guidelines set forth by the General Conference in 1971, used
this passage to show that higher priority is placed on the mother's life than on
the unborn embryo in Scripture. This gave sanction to abortion when the mother's
life was in danger.[21]

On the other hand Muller takes "harm" to refer to the accidentally aborted
fetus and concludes that if the child survives, there is only a fine; but if the child
dies, the one causing the miscarriage must die.[22]

Other authors recognize that interpretation is problematic and use the text
with more caution. Londis says that a number of scholars see a clear distinction
between the life of the fetus and the mother, making the mother a person in
a sense that the fetus is not in this passage, but he goes on to admit that universal
agreement is "unfortunately" lacking.[23] Charles Wittschiebe recognizes the different
possibilities and opts for a still-different view that comes from rabbinic
interpretation. It holds that according to Leviticus 24:18 "life for life" can refer
to mere monetary compensation, thus in no case is the "harm," whatever it is,
punished by death.[24]

As is frequently the case, Winslow, who has written extensively on the topic,
gives the most complete survey of the options and their implications.[25] He
concludes that whichever interpretation is valid, one must remember that no
interpretation leads to the conclusion that the fetus is without value and that
the text is not about intentional abortion.[26]

The use of this text reveals several interesting things. First, it shows that the Bible can be used in quite different, indeed almost opposite, ways, depending on the perspective one brings to the text. Second, it reveals how little attention is given to the process of exegesis by most of those who use the text. It is more often a justification than part of a serious attempt to understand Scripture. Third, one would hope for a more forthcoming posture from some that would at least recognize the difficulties.

In actual fact the text is probably not very helpful to the ongoing debate on abortion, since its interpretation is so problematic. A review of any good commentary will show the complexities of the text and the numerous attempts at its interpretation.[27]

Therefore both of these examples of attempts to find factual data in the Bible to speak to abortion lead to conclusions that are less than satisfying. Not only does Scripture fail to give any specific and clear commands about abortion, it does not appear to provide direct factual data about when life begins or about abortion as such.

The Bible as a Source of Principles

By far the majority of appeals to Scripture in Adventist discussions of abortion are at the level of principle rather than that of specific rule or fact. In other words, most appeals do not attempt to see the Bible addressing the issue directly, but see the Bible revealing broader values and themes that then have implications for the abortion question. Since there is so much material that falls into this category, a complete survey is impossible. Thus this section will only briefly survey the major principles and concerns to which Adventist authors appeal.

By far the most popular and frequently utilized principle is that of the *value of life*, especially as it is seen in God's personal valuing of human life. It is often pointed out that this value that God places on life includes fetal life. The most frequently used text to support this principle is Psalms 139:13-16, which reads:

> For you created my inmost being;
> > you knit me together in my mother's womb.
> I praise you because I am fearfully and wonderfully made;
> > your works are wonderful, I know that full well.
> My frame was not hidden from you
> > when I was made in the secret place.
> When I was woven together in the depths of the earth,
> > your eyes saw my unformed body.

> All the days ordained for me were written in your book
> before one of them came to be (NIV).[28]

Frequent use is also made of passages which speak of God's purpose for specific individuals while they were still in the womb. These include Jeremiah (Jer. 1:5), John the Baptist (Luke 1), and Paul (Gal. 1:15).[29] Numerous other biblical appeals to God's value for life include Genesis 2:7,[30] the "lost" parables of Luke 15,[31] John 3:16,[32] Jesus' warning against despising "little ones" in Matthew 18:10,[33] and the Bible's pervasive regard for life in general.[34]

A second biblical principle or theme that receives frequent attention is that of *justice*, or *God's impartiality and even special concern for the vulnerable.* In at least three different articles Winslow calls this the principle of justice and uses Deuteronomy 10:17-18 and Matthew 5:43-48 for support.[35] Fredericks appeals to Psalm 82:3-4 to show God's special regard for the vulnerable and goes on to argue, on the basis of texts such as Romans 5:6, Ephesians 2:3-6, and 1 Timothy 1:15, that God's unconditional acceptance of human beings apart from their achievements precludes any kind of quality-of-life ethic.[36]

Waddell refers to a principle he calls the *person-image concept* which he takes from the creation story in Genesis 1. This is part of his attempt to give biblical support for the specific reasons for "therapeutic" abortion given in the 1971 General Conference guidelines. Since God intended for humans to be born in His image within the context of family, this "concept" supports the legitimacy of abortion in cases of deformed fetuses who cannot be "normal" and in cases of rape and incest.[37]

A principle which is used in different ways by different authors is the principle of freedom. Winslow calls this the principle of "choice"[38] or "respect for personal automony."[39] For Winslow this principle means that even though he personally opposes abortion when carried out merely for convenience and would see only a limited number of "exceptional" cases as legitimate, he nevertheless opposes efforts to remove the choice from the pregnant woman.[40] Others specifically argue that reverence for life has primacy over freedom of choice. The Youngbergs use Deuteronomy 30:19 to support this,[41] and both they and Fredericks appeal to 1 Corinthians 6:19-20 to show that since the body belongs to God a woman does not have the right to choose what she will do with her own body.[42]

In a letter to the editor of *Ministry*, Fredericks specifically attacks Winslow's use of this principle as totally unbiblical.[43] He holds that the Bible calls individuals to repentance, which means turning from personal autonomy to obedience to God's will. But in a sense Fredericks is talking past Winslow here. Winslow is not using the concept of freedom to conclude that humans are autonomous and may do anything they wish to do vis-a-vis God. He uses it to argue that Christians should show respect for each other's freedom, a principle that certainly is biblically valid. (See Paul's advice concerning food offered to idols, for instance, in 1 Cor. 8-10.)

Another principle that is used by a couple of authors is that of *forgiveness*. Winslow appeals to Colossians 1:13-14,[44] and Duge to the *pericopae adulterae* of John 8 (some manuscripts).[45] Winslow stresses the need for forgiveness to be mediated to all concerned in the tragedy of abortion, and Duge stresses that the result of the anti-abortion argument is often a punishment of the victim, which is not in keeping with the spirit of Christ.

A final principle to be mentioned (although this list is by no means exhaustive) is Fredericks' appeal to the principle of the *love of money and danger of wealth*. He shows the danger of the love of money and greed from texts such as 1 Timothy 6:5-11, Colossians 3:5, and Ephesians 5:5, and then goes on to add that James (4:2; 5:5-6) even shows a link between greed and violence against the innocent. For Fredericks this rules out economic factors as a reason for abortion.[46]

With the exception of the "person-image concept," which seems quite problematic, the principles and themes in this list all appear to be valid biblical emphases which do indeed have at least some relevance for the question of abortion. This method of using principles from Scripture appears to be the most fruitful of the various uses we have surveyed so far. Yet there are problems with the manner in which the Bible is utilized here as well.

Most of the authors line up biblical principles to buttress a certain position without any acknowledgment that a given principle might be applied in a different way and without any recognition that different biblical principles might at times come into legitimate conflict. For example, almost everyone would agree that the principle of God's concern for the vulnerable and oppressed has significance for the question of abortion. But when a fifteen-year-old girl is raped and becomes pregnant, who is the "vulnerable one" who should be in focus? A given principle might be very clear in the abstraction, but it might also become quite problematic when we realize that there are legitimate claims and interests that can be brought on behalf of different subjects, i.e., the fetus and the pregnant woman.

It is also possible for different values and principles to come into conflict. Personal autonomy and freedom can conflict with our desire to preserve life, for example. In other words, the line from biblical principle or theme to specific decision on a topic such as abortion is not as straight and uncluttered with complexity as many of our authors assume. The one person who gives explicit recognition to this potential conflict between principles is Winslow. He sees such conflicts as an opportunity for moral maturity:

> Tough dilemmas, such as abortion, may also lead us toward moral maturity. The fact that an issue is called a moral dilemma generally reveals that two or more of our firmly held values are in conflict. If we do not rush to resolve the conflict in facile, one-dimensional ways, if we pause long enough to explore in some depth our colliding values, we may become clearer about why the problem troubles us so. And, as a result, we may be able to state with greater clarity and force those principles which we must balance if we are to remain true to our Christian convictions and honest about the complexity of the moral dilemma confronting us.[47]

Too much of the use of major biblical principles in the literature surveyed here is facile and one-dimensional in its failure to explore the complexity of the interaction between these principles and the real world of conflicting interests and claims, as well as its failure to acknowledge legitimate conflicts between principles.

The Bible a Source of Analogies

The final use of the Bible to be explored overlaps with the previous one, but there is a distinction between them. Here the focus is not on broad biblical themes and principles, but on individual stories and incidents that are used as analogies to speak to some aspect of the abortion issue. In each case the author sees some analogous features between the biblical incident and the current problem of abortion. We will look at but three examples.

The Youngbergs use God's reaction to humans when they sinned as a model for the woman faced with an unwanted pregnancy. They argue that when humans sinned God could have had a cosmic abortion, but instead he chose cosmic sacrifice.[48] In a subsequent letter to the editor a reader challenges them, however, and retorts that God did do a cosmic abortion—the flood.[49]

Muller points to God's anger at the nations around Israel for their disregard for unborn life as an analogy pointing to God's disapproval of abortion. He mentions incidents such as those recorded in Isaiah 13:18; Hosea 13:16; and 2 Kings 8:12; 15:16-18, where enemies slash open the wombs of pregnant women, killing both mother and unborn child, and then concludes:

> These acts are presented in Scripture as acts of sinful cruelty because they reveal a total disrespect for unborn life.[50]

The reader is left to wonder if perhaps a small part of God's anger might have been caused by what was done to the women.

Winslow offers the most self-conscious use of biblical analogy. He explicitly states that even though the Bible offers no specific instruction on how prenatal life should be treated, the Bible nevertheless informs our decision-making in more than direct commands. It also enlivens our moral imagination. As an example he presents the analogy of the birth story of John the Baptist recorded in Luke 1. He points out that John's conception was a miraculous fulfillment of a divine mandate, that his mission was designated prior to his conception, that his prenatal movements were given symbolic significance, and that his name was chosen prior to his birth. Thus we see that the fetus is one whom God calls by name. This analogy helps us see the value of fetal life.[51]

Such analogies cannot be expected to give unambiguous answers to modern dilemmas. The chief difficulty is the question of control of the analogous features. How does one decide what really counts as a valid analogy when there are always elements that are not analogous? For example, Müller's analogy may say something about the value of the unborn, but the differences between the violent murder of a pregnant woman and abortion are quite marked. Even for one who strongly opposes both, we all know that whatever the similarities might be, Charles Manson's murder of Sharon Tate is something different from abortion.

And even in Winslow's analogy there are factors that could lead one to argue in a very different way. For example, Winslow shows that John's mission is designated *prior* to his conception. Why could not this analogy be used to speak for the value of potential life before conception and thus lead one to oppose birth control?

These objections certainly do not rule out the use of analogies to "enliven our moral imagination." In fact, these stories do much to shape our characters at a level deeper than that of specific decision-making. Biblical analogies are important to moral discourse, but seldom do they produce unambiguous conclusions to specific dilemmas. Rather they lend support to broader biblical themes and principles.

Concluding Observations

The preceding survey and evaluation of various uses of the Bible in Adventist literature on abortion lead to several concluding observations about how Scripture should be used in discussions of abortion and other contemporary moral issues. What follows is by no means a complete or systematic hermeneutic, but it is hoped that these general principles will aid in the continuing discussion of abortion by sharpening the use made of the Bible in the discussion. Those who use the Bible in this discussion should exhibit:

1. *Respect for the Bible's Own Agenda.* This means that every passage must be considered in the light of its own literary and historical context to determine the author's own agenda and concerns. Our use of Scripture must be consistent with that original intent.

Respect for the Bible's agenda would result in the following specific guidelines for our agenda as we move from Scripture to the issue of abortion.

a. There must be less lining up of texts to support a position and more interpretive analysis of texts to determine whether they actually speak to the question of abortion. If they do, further analysis must determine how they speak to it and with what limitations. Interpreters must be sensitive to the kind of literature they are interpreting and must show how stories they utilize are analogous to the abortion issue.

At the same time, the skills needed to bring the Bible to bear on contemporary moral issues are more than those of technical exegesis. One must be sensitive to the basic directions Scripture is moving and the true issues that are at stake in biblical materials of moral significance. Those issues must then be translated into our own circumstances so we may discover where they intersect with our life and culture. This may necessitate challenging important values and customs in our world.

b. Respect for the Bible's agenda includes respect for its silence. We must allow it to be silent when it is silent. The Bible simply does not give a clear, unambiguous answer to the problem of abortion, and we must let that silence stand. This does not mean the Bible is irrelevant for the question. But the Bible should not be pressed to speak directly to issues on which it is silent merely because we believe it should address such an important issue.

c. Respect for the Bible's agenda means honestly balancing biblical evidence with other relevant data. The Bible is not our only source of evidence, even if it is the central controlling norm. Obviously our experience and empirical data will condition our views, and this must be admitted.

For example, if one believes, as does Sweem, that abortion always causes severe emotional damage to the woman,[52] his or her application of the principles of both compassion and justice might be quite different than for one who believes, as does Ziprick, that "few psychiatric disturbances occur in the aborted patient, since her feeling is mainly that of outstanding relief."[53] The answer to such a question is and should be important to our discussion, but empirical data, not the Bible, must solve it. We must acknowledge what the Bible can and cannot do and balance biblical and non-biblical data.

2. *Recognition of the Nature of Principles.* Appeals to biblical principles to speak to the abortion issue must show awareness of both the importance and limitations of principles. On the one hand, this is the most fruitful area for biblical exploration on issues such as abortion, but on the other, principles do not stand alone. They must be weighed along with other principles. We do face situations in a sinful world where various biblical principles can point in different directions and where the legitimate interests of different parties can be in conflict. This means that exceptions may be possible even when general biblical mandates are quite clear.

A biblical example of this may be seen in Paul's discussion of divorce in 1 Corinthians 7. Although he makes it clear that the principle of the permanence of marriage is important even in cases where a believer is married to an unbeliever, and admonishes believers to preserve their marriages to unbelievers, he also allows for divorce when the unbelieving spouse wishes to leave on the basis that "God has called us to peace" (1 Cor. 7:15). In this case the principles of peace and allowing freedom to others cause Paul to override the strong principle of the permanence of marriage.

If we fail to acknowledge the possibility of conflicting principles, we may well hear only a part of the biblical witness and miss the wide spectrum of its notes and tones.

Therefore, an adequate understanding of the nature of biblical principles will lead us to:

a. Weigh various principles and show on what basis one should take precedence over another in conflict dilemmas. This includes showing the kind of burden of proof that is necessary to override values and principles.

b. Weigh the conflicting claims of various beneficiaries of the principles set forth in Scripture. In other words, in abortion all the principal subjects, including both mother and fetus, must be taken into consideration.

3. *Commitment to Community-wide Reflection.* When confronted with difficult dilemmas, we need each other. Our different backgrounds, perspectives and ways of thinking all contribute to making us the body of Christ with its many members. Moral reflection is most effective in an atmosphere of give-and-take and mutual respect. The Bible is not the private possession of any one of us. It is the community's instrument for listening to God's voice, and that voice is heard best when the whole body, with its diverse parts, participates together.

This commitment will also have a direct influence on the way we go about utilizing Scripture in discussions of abortion.

    a. It will motivate us to listen carefully to each other with respect and a spirit that fosters rather than shuns discussion.

    b. It will give us a spirit of restraint and humility.

Once we have set these ground rules for the discussion of abortion as it relates to biblical evidence, is there any hope that our study of Scripture will yield positive results? Will it be possible for the Bible to bring us to any kind of consensus, or must we remain in a sea of confusion?

Given the nature of the biblical evidence, we must admit that it will never resolve all of our differences. Even though the Bible will lead those committed to its teaching to value life, it will never give unambiguous and undisputed answers to difficult cases where conflicting values are present. We will have to rely on Spirit-guided, reasoned reflection to evaluate these specific dilemmas. To reject such reflection in favor of an all-or-nothing position on abortion is in itself unbiblical.

However, the degree of positive consensus already demonstrated in the literature surveyed in this study should not be overlooked or underestimated.

All of our authors appear to be shaped by a commitment to God and to Scripture, and there is an impressive degree of consensus. All agree the Bible teaches that God values life highly and that we should respond to this gracious God by valuing it as well. All agree that this important biblical principle has serious implications for the question of abortion. No one sanctions the kind of wholesale abortion of convenience that has become commonplace in our society. Differences center on the kinds of principles that must be weighed along with this basic commitment to the value of life and the kinds of considerations that would make abortion the lesser of evils in certain situations. My hope is that we will celebrate this consensus, let our continuing conversation on our areas of differences build up our moral commitment and our sense of community, and demonstrate our commitment to Scripture by listening to its voice with both intensity and care.

Endnotes

[1]Harold F. Ziprick, "Abortion in Our Changing World," *Spectrum* 3 (Spring 1971):11.
[2]Richard Müller, "Abortion: A Moral Issue?" *Ministry* 58 (January 1985):19.
[3]James J. Londis, "Abortion: What Shall Christians Do?" *Insight* (March 19, 1974):17.
[4]Jack W. Provonsha, "An Appraisal of Therapeutic Abortion: The View of Christian Ethics," *Spectrum* 3 (Spring 1971):29-36.

[5]Sakae Kubo, *The Theology and Ethics of Sex* (Washington, DC: Review and Herald Publishing Association, 1980), 93-98.

[6]Richard Fredericks, "Less Than Human?" *Ministry* 61 (March 1988):13.

[7]Müller, 31.

[8]John and Millie Youngberg, "The Reborn and the Unborn," *Ministry* 58 (November 1985):12.

[9]Ardyce Sweem, "Three Perspectives on Abortion: Perspective 1," *Adventist Review* (September 25, 1986):11.

[10]Müller, 20.

[11]Fredericks, 13.

[12]Müller, 18.

[13]*Ibid.*, 19.

[14]Fredericks, 14.

[15]Sweem, 10.

[16]W. R. Beach, "Abortion?" *Ministry* 44 (March 1971):6.

[17]Maureen Maxwell and Clarice J. Woodward, "The Nurse and Abortion," *Spectrum* 3 (Spring 1971):21.

[18]Kevin Paulson, letter to the editor, *Ministry* 59 (January 1986):2.

[19]Gerald Winslow, "Adventists and Abortion: A Principled Approach," *Spectrum* 12:2 (December 1981):12.

[20]John Duge, "The Abortion Issue: Must the Church Decide?" *Lake Union Herald* (May 21, 1985):13.

[21]Ralph F. Waddell, "Abortion Is Not the Answer," *Ministry* 44 (March 1971):7.

[22]Müller, 19.

[23]Londis, 15.

[24]Charles E. Wittschiebe, *God Invented Sex* (Nashville: Southern Publishing Association, 1974), 130.

[25]He adds the LXX reading that makes the punishment dependent on whether the fetus is fully formed.

[26]Gerald Winslow, "Abortion and Christian Principles," *Ministry* 61 (May 1988):13-14.

[27]See, for example, Brevard S. Childs, "Old Testament Library," chap. in *The Book of Exodus: A Critical, Theological Commentary* (Philadelphia: Westminster Press, 1974), 469-470.

[28]Authors using this text include Daniel Augsburger, "Abortion: Don't Believe All You Hear!" *Ministry* 49 (September 1976):25; W. G. Dick, "A Look at Abortion," *Review and Herald* (May 13, 1971):11; Ardyce Sweem, "Abortion's Effects," *Ministry* 61 (July 1988):14-16; and *Adventist Review*, 9-10; and Gerald Winslow, "Three Perspectives on Abortion: Perspective Three," *Adventist Review* (September 25, 1986):10, 13; and *Ministry*, 13-14.

[29]Augsburger, 25; Dick, 11; Sweem, *Ministry*, 16; Winslow, *Adventist Review*, 10-11; and *Ministry*, 13-14.

[30]Winslow, *Spectrum*, 10.

[31]Frank B. Holbrook, "The Christian and Abortion," *These Times* (April 1975):21; Müller, 21.

[32]Holbrook, 21.

[33]Miriam Wood, "The Right to Live," *Adventist Review* (September 7, 1978).

[34]Leonard McMillan, "To Abort or Not to Abort: That Is the Question," *Ministry* 51 (March 1978):13.

[35]Winslow, *Adventist Review*, 12-13; *Ministry*, 15; and *Spectrum*, 13-15.
[36]Fredericks, 14.
[37]Waddell, 7-9.
[38]Winslow, *Adventist Review*, 11-12.
[39]Winslow, *Ministry*, 14-15; and *Spectrum*, 12-13.
[40]Winslow, *Ministry*, 15.
[41]Youngberg, 13.
[42]*Ibid.*, and Fredericks, 15.
[43]Fredericks, letter to the editor, *Ministry* 61 (September 1988):26.
[44]Winslow, *Adventist Review*, 9-10; and *Ministry*, 13.
[45]Duge, 13.
[46]Fredericks, 15.
[47]Winslow, *Spectrum*, 6-7.
[48]Youngberg, 12.
[49]David Hampton, letter to the editor, *Ministry* 59 (May 1986):30.
[50]Müller, 19.
[51]Winslow, *Spectrum*, 10-11.
[52]Sweem, *Ministry*.
[53]Ziprick, 10.

3 A Biblical Perspective on Abortion

Niels-Erik Andreasen

> The sleeping, and the dead, are but as pictures...
> Yet who would have thought the old man to have had so much blood in him?
> Shakespeare, *Macbeth* (II.2:V.1)

These two lines, separated in the play by murder, reveal common attitudes associated with the contemplation and execution of a plan to terminate life. The first minimizes life, especially life of the sleeping, the still, the inactive, on the borders of existence, as but a picture of which one can dispose with little or no harm and pain. The second recoils in horror at the realization of how much life (blood) actually circulates in an apparently still life on the borders of human existence. These two attitudes also represent two common responses to the question of abortion. One holds that the unborn fetus is but a still life, a picture of what may become a person. The second measures the immense amount of life spilt in the death of such a fetus.

In contemplating these two responses to the question of abortion, everyone influenced by the Judeo-Christian ethic in general, and confessing Christians in particular, should consider the biblical perspective on the matter. The Bible does not address the issue of abortion explicitly, but it demonstrates a unique understanding of the early life process from conception to birth, and it expresses particular perspectives upon a variety of potential disruptions to that process.

I
The Early Life Process from Conception to Birth

(a) *Conception.* According to the Bible, human life began with the creation of a man and a woman who together expressed the image and likeness of the creator (Gen. 1:26f.; 2:7). That beginning also provided for the continuation

43

of human life through procreation, already within the creation story (Gen. 1:28). Nevertheless the details of procreation, though hinted at in Genesis 2:24, first emerge explicitly in Genesis 4:1, where again it begins with complete unity between the two persons, man and woman. As the Bible puts it, the man "knew" his wife.

Of course, that complete unity of man and woman is anticipated in Genesis 2:24 where the marriage relationship is described without specific reference to conception of new life. Consequently, the marriage relationship takes priority over procreation in the story of creation. That priority is confirmed later in the story of Hannah and Elkanah (1 Sam. 1:5), underscoring the biblical principle that marriage was established first for the benefit of the two partners, and only secondly for procreation. In short, the unity of the two does not exist primarily for the sake of procreation, but points to the single source of human life, God himself, whose image comes to expression in the creation of the two of them, man and woman, in relationship with each other and with their creator (Gen. 1:26). Procreation, meanwhile, is moved discretely outside the garden (Gen. 4:1), thereby establishing the fact that conception is always preceded by something else, namely a fundamental and harmonious human relationship reflecting the image and character of God.

Thus in order for conception to occur, the man must first "know" his wife. The word know (*yadah*) has been examined in this context and shown to mean "experience," "form a relationship," "meet." It describes the total harmony and love for which man and woman were destined, and brings about the oneness with which they are capable of expressing the image of God according to which they were created. This suggests, according to the Bible, that conception imitates creation itself. Indeed the very expression "know" describes God's relationship with the life not yet conceived (Jer. 1:5; Gal. 1:15). As man and wife "know" each other in the process of conceiving, so God "knows" that which he will create in the womb. According to the Bible, the unborn life, therefore, is fashioned by God, and not "poured out like milk" (perhaps a reference to spilt semen), but rather curdled like cheese, before being clothed with skin and flesh and knitted together (Job 10:8-11). The womb in which this creation takes place is characterized as a sacred place, deep in the earth, where, beginning with an unformed substance, God initiated this creation-inspired conception (Ps. 139:13-16).

The resulting close relationship between creation and conception in the Bible explains the deep satisfaction and joy attending both. By contrast, ancient Near Eastern creation stories generally focused on violent activity, namely division, separation, warfare, or at best construction and growth. Only a very few introduce creation as a single moment of design or joyous planning. Thus the Egyptian theology of Memphis (2700 B.C.) reads: "Indeed, all the divine order really came into being through what the heart thought and the tongue commanded" (J. B. Pritchard, ed. *Ancient Near Eastern Texts Relating to the Old Testament*, 5). The Babylonian story of creation, *Enuma Elish*, makes at least one such brief reference to the creative plan for mankind: "Opening his mouth, he (Marduk) addressed Ea to impart the plan he had conceived in his heart. . . . Verily, savage-man I will create" (*ANET*, 68). However, these are rare occurrences, overshadowed by pictures of creation through conflict or struggle. The Bible, on the other hand, portrays the initiation and execution of creation in a way not found elsewhere, namely through the creative word (Gen. 1:3; Ps. 33:6,9; John 1:1). Indeed the biblical story of creation distinguishes itself from most other ancient stories of creation precisely by pointing out that creation began in the mind of God, when he brought the world into existence using only his word.

The Hebrew term for word (*dabar*) means not simply a sound, but a thought, a matter, a concern, a plan. According to the Bible, creation began at this point, and so does conception, when a man "knows" his wife. To be sure, the laws and narratives in the Old Testament indicate that after the fall into sin, conception could and did occur in accidental or "ill-conceived" ways, something these many laws and customs attempted to regulate for the protection of the innocent. But whenever the Bible focuses on the meaning of procreation, it speaks of what follows a thought, a matter, a concern, a plan—of what is conceived in the mind before being conceived in the body (Gen. 16:4; 21:2; 25:21; Ex. 2:2; Isa. 8:3). It is a deliberate thought, desire or plan to initiate life anew. The union of man and woman for the purpose of conceiving, according to the Bible, represents an imitation of creation, a plan rather than an accident, a purpose rather than a chance, a desire rather than a fright, and is attended by joy.

(b) *Gestation.* Ancient people must have been puzzled by the period of gestation, from the moment at which two unseen cells united until nine months later a child was born. However, although the process of a developing fetus was not understood scientifically then, the stages of fetal growth were probably known through observation of various types of mishaps or violence interrupting the gestation period (Num. 12:12; Ezek. 16:6; Amos 1:13).

The most common pictures employed in the ancient world to describe the making of human life portray mixing, shaping, growing, building or weaving. Thus the Atrahasis epic reports the creation of mankind as a mixing of clay and the blood of a sacrificed god (Lamberton and Millard, *Atrahasis*, I, 208-260). The Sumerian hymn to the mattock describes the first humans as plants which grew out of the ground split open by the mattock (W. Beyerlin, *Near Eastern Religious Texts Relating to the Old Testament*, 75f.). The Genesis account of creation tells of God making mankind from the dust, shaping it the way a potter shapes clay (Gen. 2:7; cf. Job 10:8). Both Job and Psalms portray human formation as a weaving of threads of knitting (Ps. 139:13; Job 10:11).

These pictures are of uneven religious and spiritual quality. For example, the mixing of clay with the blood of a sacrificed god does serious injury to the biblical concept of creation, which draws a sharp distinction between Creator and creation, between divinity and humanity. Nevertheless, these pictures of the gestation period do connect that process of human formation before birth conceptually with the process of forming and shaping in the work of creation. Thus, according to the Psalmist, it was precisely God's creative and universal powers that enabled him to know human life from conception through gestation when its parts were "knit together" in a secret place, deep in the earth (Ps. 139:13-18). The unborn life was fashioned by God in the same way God had shaped the first man from clay, except that the gestation process is much slower, compared to milk curdling into cheese, to skin, bone and flesh being joined, and to a naked body being clothed (Job 10:8-11). The entire description is reminiscent of Genesis 2:21f. in which the woman was formed bone of bone and flesh of flesh.

Thus, although the scientific aspects of the gestation period were little understood in the time of the Bible, with the possible exception of its duration (Job 39:1-4), the biblical description of it does convey an interesting fact regarding this early development of human life: It cannot be slowed or advanced by its parents, once the conception has occurred, for its course is determined by an external force, God, and depends entirely upon God for success. Moreover, the emerging life was considered human throughout the process. Thus a pregnant woman is said to be with child (Amos 1:13), that is, bearing a human being within her. According to one passage, such an unborn person (in sharp distinction to a dead person) can respond to God. Thus Luke's gospel reports about Elizabeth, the mother of the unborn John the Baptist, that he (the babe) "leaped in her womb" (Luke 1:41) in response to excitement at the news of Mary's pregnancy. While this expression may merely express extraordinary excitement, it is worth noting that the word "babe" (*brephos*) describes both the unborn fetus (Sir. 19:11) and the infant (1 Macc. 1:61), implying that no sharp distinction was made between life after and before birth. In short, the period of gestation, like conception, is presented in the Bible as an aspect of creation, namely that divine activity in which the creator shaped human life and breathed life into it.

(c) **Birth**. The Bible describes childbirth as painful joy (Gen. 3:16)—painful because of the difficulties, or death, attending the birth process (cf. Gen. 35:17-19), even for the hardy Hebrew women (Ex. 1:19). Indeed we may assume that death to mother or child probably occurred with considerable frequency (Gen. 35:17; 2 Sam. 12:18). But even under the best of circumstances childbirth could be painful, and its imagery served the prophets to portray coming troubles in Israel and in the world (Isa. 13:8; 26:17; Jer. 4:31; 22:23). Therefore, expectant mothers were assisted by midwives (Gen. 35:17; 38:28, Ex. 1:15).

But childbirth was also a joyful experience, for children represented a gift and blessing from God (Gen. 12:2f; 28:14; 24:60; Ps. 127:3; 128:113). The occasionally expressed preference for male offspring (Jer. 20:15; 1 Sam. 4:20; Gen. 30:2) suggests that children were considered to be economic assets, providing a sense of security to the parents. But more importantly, having children enabled parents to make sons and daughters after their own image, the way God made people after his own image (Gen. 5:1-3). The gift of conception, gestation and birth thus invites parents to share in the work of creation in an unprecedented way, in the sense that they can produce many things using existing materials; but in giving birth to children, parents can make brand-new people in their own image, without using any materials at all. Only love between man and woman is needed to bring a new life into existence. This, perhaps, is as close as any created beings can ever come to participate in the work of creation. In sum, according to the biblical perspective, conception, gestation and birth represent an imitation of creation within human experience.

II
Disruptions to the Early Life Process

(a) *Inability to conceive.* Barrenness, the inability of a woman to conceive, was considered a tragedy by the people of the Bible (Gen. 16:1f.; 25:21; 30:1f.) that only divine intervention could overcome (Gen. 30:2; Isa. 54:1; Luke 1:7,13). Thus Proverbs compared barrenness to the grave and the parched land deprived of life-giving water (Prov. 30:16), and individuals unable to have children apparently were called barren in a pejorative sense (Deut. 7:14; Luke 1:36).

Curiously some of the ancestors in Israel suffered this problem, including Abraham's wife Sarai (Gen. 11:30), Rebekah (Gen. 25:21), and Rachel (Gen. 29:31). Apparently this condition was thought to be caused by God and thus could be rectified only by him (Gen. 29:2). Consequently, any correction of barrenness became a cause celebre, as in the case of Sarai who at God's instigation became pregnant at the age of 90 and had her name changed to Sarah in honor of her motherhood (Gen. 18:15-21). Similarly, Samson and Samuel were born of women presumed barren, following divine intervention (Judg. 13:2f.; 1 Sam. 1:19,20). But God's intervention could also produce barrenness. Thus Michal, David's wife, was unable to bear children after her outspoken criticism of the king during the triumphant entrance of the ark into Jerusalem, perhaps because David put her away, or because in offending the king she had also offended God. According to Hosea, God's punishment of Israel would include imposing the inability to conceive (Hos. 9:11), and in a moment of despair over his troubles Job wished to eliminate from the calendar the night in which he was conceived (Job 3:3-6).

Throughout the Bible, the barren womb, like the world before creation, was considered a tragedy, comparable to death, a desert, or a dry land that had not yet benefited from God's creative and life-giving power (Gen. 2:4-5). Conversely, the ability to conceive life was seen as a fulfillment of the promises of God for a better future (Ex. 23:26; Deut. 7:14; Cant. 4:2; 6:6; Isa. 54:1). However, even when the ability to have children failed, whether in men or women, they were no less human, and were not deprived of the opportunity to find fulfillment in life, as noted earlier (cf. 1 Sam. 1:8; Isa. 56:4f.).

(b) *Inability to bring a pregnancy to term.* The verb describing the birth process, "come out" (*ys*), generally portrays a normal, successful birth (Gen. 25:25f.; 38:27-30; Ex. 21:22; Job 1:21; 3:11; Jer. 1:5). An exception is Numbers 12:12 where it may describe a malformed infant or a stillbirth (cf. Job 3:11). A second verb, "bereaved" (*skl*), exhibits two main usages in the Old Testament. Generally it speaks of the bereavement caused by the loss of children (Gen. 27:45; 42:36; 43:33; Lev. 26:22; Deut. 32:25; Jer. 15:7; Ezek. 5:17), but in a few instances it refers to miscarriage caused (or even prevented) by one factor or another (Gen. 31:38; Job 21:10; Ex. 23:26; 2 Kings 2:19-21; Hos. 9:14). Evidently the Old Testament viewed the loss of children to death in the same way it viewed the inability to bear a fetus to term. Both represented either a tragedy or a divine punishment (Hos. 9:14), and both robbed the parents of their most profound participation in God's creative work and, of course, of their desired offspring.

The New Testament term *ektroma* (1 Cor. 15:8) describes a premature birth or a miscarriage. In this text the apostle Paul employed the term to denote his own late call to apostleship, depriving him of a proper acquaintance with Jesus, or possibly to note his abrupt, premature, call to apostleship on the road to Damascus, robbing him of a proper "gestation" period for faith development. Beyond this metaphorical reference to the deplorable experience of untimely spiritual birth, indicating either deprivation or missing formation, the New Testament is silent on the matter.

(c) *Disruption of the pregnancy.* One law in the so-called Book of the Covenant (Ex. 21-23) deals with miscarriage or early delivery (lit. her children go out) of an expectant mother who suffered blows in a fight among men (Ex. 21:22-25). Any adverse consequences for the mother or infant required penalty according to their level of severity. Thus "if no harm follows" (presumably mother and newborn were both well in spite of the ordeal of a premature birth), an appropriate fine would be levied upon the offending party. But "if any harm follows" (either mother or child or both did not survive) the talion principle would be invoked, i.e., a life for a life. Understood this way, the law does not differentiate between harm to the mother and to the fetus and thus does not permit a distinction between the relative value of life before and after birth. At any rate, the law does not deal with voluntary abortion. However, it does address the general regard and protection a pregnant mother and an unborn child were to enjoy in society. See Keil and Delitzsch, *Exodus*, 134f.; Cassuto, *Exodus*, 123.

An alternate interpretation of this difficult biblical law holds that the differentiation between "no harm" and "any harm" applies only to the mother and not to the fetus. In that case a fine would be levied at fighting men causing a miscarriage or a stillbirth, whereas the talion principle would only be invoked if the mother was harmed. This interpretation, accepted by the majority of recent Bible translations and commentators, and finding some support in certain ancient Near Eastern laws dealing with similar cases, distinguishes between the value of life before and after birth. Thus the lost life of the unborn, unlike the mother's life, could be compensated with a fine. Best known among the ancient Near Eastern parallels are the following:

The code of Hammurabi, approx. 17th cent. B.C. (par. 209-214; *ANET*, 175) stipulates a fine for a fetus lost to a woman struck by blows. The size of the fine (10,5,2 shekels of silver) depended upon the relative social status of the woman. If the woman herself died as a consequence of the blow, the laws required a much larger fine (one-half to one-third mina of silver) for a commoner and a slave respectively. But in the case of a gentleman's daughter (a member of the nobility) the talion principle was invoked.

The Middle Assyrian laws, approx, 15th-12 cent B.C., complicate matters a little (par. 21;50-53, *ANET*, 181,184f.). Someone causing the daughter of another to miscarry would be fined, flogged and made to perform public service. However, someone causing another man's wife to miscarry must pay for the lost fetus with a life and for the eventual death of the mother with his own life—unless the pregnant mother "does not rear her children," in which case the fetus was compensated with a fine. Finally, a miscarriage (abortion) induced by the mother herself carried the death penalty.

What weight do these parallels have on the interpretation of the biblical law (Ex. 21:22-25)? First of all, the text itself does not speak of a miscarriage, but of a birth, as noted above, possibly a premature birth, but a birth without harm. For causing this a fine is levied. The harm (*swn*) to which the next verse refers generally means deadly mishap (Gen. 42:4; 44:29) and is punishable with retribution and therefore must involve loss of life, but whose life? The life of the mother, implying a depreciation in the value ascribed to the life of the unborn; or the life of the unborn, implying an appreciation of the value of its life, equal to that of the mother?

In general the Old Testament laws differ from the ancient Near Eastern parallels by not distinguishing between the relative status in life of injured parties. Thus the biblical law does not inform us if the pregnant Hebrew woman belonged to the leading families, the common people, the slave class, the *gerim* (resident aliens) or if she was married. Evidently the value placed upon the loss of life would not be affected thereby. Perhaps the Old Testament laws differ from their counterparts precisely at this point; they consistently place the highest value on life, regardless of the relative social value ascribed to it. This equalizing perspective presumably also extended to the life of the unborn. As the life of king and pauper, rich and poor, noble and common was thought to possess equal inherent value, so the life of young and old, indeed of the very young and very old, even the life of the one whose existence was just conceived in a creative design, must also possess equal inherent value in the Bible's scheme of things.

The Bible nowhere speaks of voluntary or induced abortion, even though it was well known in the ancient world, both in the east, among the Egyptians, and among the Greeks and Romans in the west. The New Testament refers to *Pharmakia* (and derivates), meaning sorcery, magic, poison, always in a condemnatory way (Gal. 5:20; Rev. 9:21; 18:23; 21:8). But it offers no indication that drug-induced abortions lie behind this condemnation. However, such practices are known in the Graeco-Roman world.

(d) *Stillbirth, infant mortality and infanticide.* The books of Job and Jeremiah speak vividly and bitterly about stillbirth as a desired solution to deeply felt sufferings in life. "Why did I not die at birth, come forth from the womb and expire?" (Job 3:11). ". . . because he did not kill me in the womb; so my mother would have been my grave, and her womb forever great" (Jer. 20:17). However, this does not represent a standard biblical position on birth. On the contrary, grief and bitter weeping express the common response to lost offspring during or after birth (Gen. 37:33-35; 2 Sam. 12:15-18; 18:33; 1 Kings 17:17f.; Jer. 31:15). For that reason infanticide, in the form of exposure and child sacrifice was met with horror and pity (Ex. 1:16,22; 1 Kings 16:34; 2 Kings 16:3, 17:16f.; Jer. 7:30f.; Ezek. 16:1-5; Matt. 2:16-18). Nevertheless, the Bible does seem to recognize that under certain circumstances life in this world can be so distorted that not only death but non-existence seems preferable (cf. Matt. 24:19).

We can only guess at the frequency with which children were lost to death at birth or in infancy, but most families likely experienced such loss of life, for ancient tombs reveal a significant proportion of infant burials. And while infanticide found no place in the Bible, awareness of this practice among the people in Mesopotamia, Anatolia and Carthage must be supposed. (See L. E. Stager and S. R. Wolff, "Child Sacrifice at Carthage," *Biblical Archaeology Review* 10/1, 31-51). That the Bible largely ignored these tragedies and practices only confirms our conclusion that both are incomprehensible to biblical thought for at least two reasons: first, due to its strong emphasis on the equal value of all life, including life at the borders of human existence, and second, due to its understanding of the very beginning of life (conception), gestation and birth, as a "creation-like" work.

III
Summary and Conclusion

We can now summarize our findings regarding the biblical understanding of the process of procreation and its potential disruptions. In so doing we note that the Bible differentiated between the stages of conception, gestation and birth in this process and identified potential disruptions at each stage within it.

(a) Conception is a harmonious expression of love whereby two individuals, a man and a woman, imitate creation by becoming life givers.

(b) Gestation is a process beyond the control of parents, whereby the new life becomes formed, as once man and woman were formed by God when in creation he shaped them into his image.

(c) Birth is an intense, laborious, yet joyful experience, whereby the seriousness and satisfactory completion of the creative act are expressed.

(d) The new life, conceived, formed, and brought forth, creation-like, is of equal value to that of its parents, for it represents an image of their very being.

(e) The process of procreation from conception to birth can be interrupted at various points, and in that respect it differs from God's creation, which became distorted only after its completion. Such interruptions may occur at the point of conception, during the period of gestation or even at birth. In our time contraception, abortion, inability to conceive and stillbirth would illustrate such interruptions. The Bible shows familiarity with only the latter two interruptions to the process and generally views both as inexplicable tragedies that only God can rectify. However, the desperate contemplations of Job and Jeremiah, that conception should not have occurred, that gestation should not have run its course or that birth should have failed to produce life, and the warning to women with child during the time of trouble, give biblical expression to the idea of interrupting the process of procreation. The reason given for such a wish appears to be that under certain narrowly defined circumstances, actual life had (or will) become so distorted that an interruption in the process of procreation, as opposed to death, is desirable, i.e., that non-existence seemed preferable to existence.

This brings us to some concluding assessments of the biblical perspective on abortion. Does life ever become distorted to such a degree that not only its termination by death may seem better than life (Cf, 1 Sam. 31:3f.; 1 Kings 19:4; Jonah 4:3), but that non-existence is preferred to existence (Job 3:3-19; Jer. 20:14-18)? The answer to this question must not be sought merely in the degree of suffering, indignity, depression or failure to which a person may fall, leading to the contemplation of capital punishment, suicide or euthanasia. Instead we must consider the potential distortions in the procreation process itself to discover if they reach such magnitude that an interruption in that process can be justified. For unlike God's creation, the creation-like process of procreation can go desperately wrong before reaching its fulfillment, due to sin. Again the Bible differentiates between the stages of conception, gestation and birth within that complex process, and any consideration of abortion must take account of each of these stages.

(a) At the point of conception a distortion may occur, for example, in the case of rape, incest or intercourse between totally incompetent individuals. In such cases the experience of conception is characterized by struggle, division, separation (typical of the ancient Near Eastern creation stories), rather than by harmony, unity and becoming one (typical of the biblical concept of creation). This may well warrant interruption of the pregnancy for the sake of the unborn life and its parents. However, abortion may not always be necessary, since the power of God's love is both creative and recreative, and may with time be able to overcome the distortion and violence of such a conception.

(b) During the gestation period the formation of the new life may go astray so as to produce death rather than life, for example, in AIDS-infected parents. Since the process of formation lies beyond the control of the parents (or nearly

52

so), with the result that they cannot repair what is going wrong, a new life so distorted as to produce destruction rather than creation may warrant an abortive interruption during the gestation period.

(c) At the moment of birth, complications may threaten the life of mother or child or both, so that one life must be abandoned in order to save another. Whereas the people of the Bible probably had little choice in the matter, thanks to technology we are frequently in a position to choose the life of the mother.

(d) Finally, since the entire process of a new life, according to the biblical perspective, corresponds to the fulfillment of creation, it is in harmony with biblical principles to prevent that birth process from commencing, if it is certain to produce destruction and death rather than life, fulfillment and perfection. This recommends the use of contraception to protect families from becoming too large or from having children too soon for the available resources needed for their health and support, as well as to prevent the conception of life doomed from the beginning.

However, resorting to an interruption of a pregnancy (abortion) merely as a convenient means of contraception is contrary to the Bible's perspective, for it diminishes the Bible's respect for life and for the extraordinary creative process God has entrusted to humans. Human beings need not procreate in order to be fulfilled, but if they begin the process of procreation, respect for the creative powers God has placed within them requires that the process not be interrupted except when that process was so ill-intended or has failed so badly as to produce death rather than life. While some ancient peoples attempted to procure such interruptions in the pregnancy by various means, probably frequently for the wrong motives, the Bible only expresses the thought that in certain instances it would have been better if conception, gestation or birth never had occurred. Thus, from a biblical perspective, abortion must always be seen as a way to hinder death and destruction, not as a means to terminate life already conceived. Christian practitioners of medicine and Christian ethicists are responsible for making this distinction in deciding on abortion cases.

This cautious biblical attitude towards even the idea of interrupting a pregnancy urges that whenever a decision must be reached in an abortion case, no matter how clear the evidence appears to be, great care must be exercised and much thought given to the matter. The biblical perspective (and indeed human history) offers two reasons for such a cautious and careful approach. The first is the great value of life to which the Bible bears unmitigated and untiring testimony. The second is the realization that when the value of life is depreciated near the borders of human existence, as Shakespeare pointed out, no life is really safe anywhere, even well within those borders.

4 Abortion: Some Questionable Arguments

Tim Crosby

It would be wonderful if Scripture provided answers to all social, ethical, and philosophical questions, but how should the church make ethical decisions in areas where the Bible gives no explicit counsel? Is everything that is not explicitly condemned in Scripture a matter of private choice, or does the church have the right to forbid certain things which are not forbidden in Scripture? This paper will focus on the issue of abortion.

Neither the Bible nor Ellen G. White[1] address the issue of abortion. This is puzzling, for the practice was widespread and the question was widely discussed in biblical times. In spite of the fact that the Greeks "advised and even demanded abortion in some cases,"[2] it is forbidden in the Oath of Hippocrates (460-357 B.C.):

> I swear by Apollo Physician, by Asclepius, by Health, by Panacea, and by all the gods and goddesses, making them my witnesses, that. . .I will use treatment to help the sick according to my ability and judgment, but never with a view to injury and wrong-doing. Neither will I administer a poison to anybody when asked to do so, nor will I suggest such a course. Similarly, I will not give to a woman a pessary to cause abortion.

Among the Jews, abortion was generally condemned, as illustrated in Pseudo-Phocylides 184-5, Sibylline Oracles 2:339-42, and in Josephus:

> The law orders all the offspring to be brought up, and forbids women either to cause abortion or to make away with the fetus; a woman convicted of this is regarded as an infanticide, because she destroys a soul and diminishes the race.[3]

55

The earliest non-canonical Christian documents take a firm stand against abortion. Didache 2:2 forbids abortion along with murder, adultery, pederasty, fornication, theft, magic, and witchcraft. It is also forbidden in the epistle of Barnabas, Clement of Alexandria, Athenagoras, and Tertullian.

It could be hazardous to speculate why the Bible is silent on an issue that occupied other religious writers of the times.[4] Whatever the reason, this silence has not deterred proponents on both sides of the debate from finding support for their positions in Scripture.

Modern debates about abortion often center around the question of exactly when human life begins. Appeal is made to scriptural texts that indicate that God forms the fetus in the womb as proof that life begins at conception and that termination of the conceptus for any reason thereafter is murder. An examination of some of the most frequently cited passages suggests the hazards of using a passage to prove a point that was not under consideration in the mind of the original writer.

Texts such as Job 10:8-12; 31:1-5; Psalm 139:13-17; and Isaiah 49:5 describe God as forming the fetus in the womb, but they do not allow us to pinpoint the moment of personhood. Psalm 139 is particularly interesting. This text seems to teach a rigid predestination; it says that the days of our lives are planned in advance, and written down in some heavenly book before we are ever born. Is this literal truth, or is it a poetic way of saying that God knows all about us and cares for us? The passage also asserts that we were formed "in the depths of the earth." Is this literal or metaphorical?

Now there is a valid use of proof texts—indeed, there is no other way to do systematic theology—but only when the texts, taken in context, speak to the point at issue. It is dangerous to take scriptural assertions—particularly when they occur in biblical poetry—and use them to prove a point that is different from the point the writer was trying to make. For example, when Job wrote "Did not He who made me in the womb make them [Job's slaves]? Did not the same One form us both within our mothers?" (31:15). His point was that all men are brothers, equal before God. He was not addressing the modern question of exactly when life begins. Similarly, Psalm 51:5, "Surely I have been a sinner from birth; sinful from the time my mother conceived me" teaches the sinfulness of humans, not their exact moments of origin.

The problem with such texts is that they prove too much, for there are passages that seem to indicate that personhood exists *before* conception. For example, Job 10:10 says, "Did you not pour me out like milk and curdle me like cheese?" This is probably an allusion to the seminal fluid. The fact that it is called "me" might seem to imply life before conception. An even clearer passage is Hebrews 7:9-10, which states that Levi paid tithes to Melchizedek long before Levi was conceived, because he was in the body of Abraham when Abraham paid tithes. Jeremiah 1:5 says, "Before [not "when"] I formed you in the womb I knew you, before you were born I set you apart; I appointed you as a prophet to the nations;" and God outlined the career of Cyrus (Isa. 44:24 - 45:5) long before he was conceived. These passages could be taken to imply that personhood exists before conception—a ridiculous concept.

None of these passages is helpful in deciding when life begins; they are probably examples of biblical prolepsis, a principle stated in Romans 4:17: "God calls things that are not [yet] as though they were."

But what about texts such as Isaiah 49:1, "The Lord called me from the womb, from the body of my mother he named me" (cf. "from birth" Gal. 1:15, Luke 1:15)? If God lays plans for a person before he is born, then isn't abortion frustrating the will of God? But in the Bible it is only living people who are said to have been foreknown by God. God is not foolish; He would not have pre-ordained Isaiah or Jeremiah to be prophets if He had known they were not going to survive.

One text that explicitly mentions conception is Matthew 1:20, "that which has been conceived in her [Mary] is of the Holy Spirit." But this says nothing about the status of the conceptus except to reveal who the "father" was. Even if it did, Christ might be considered a special case.

Other passages indicate that life begins at birth. Genesis 2:7 says that "man became a living being" at the moment he began to breathe. Other texts such as Job 27:3; 33:4; Ezekiel 37:5; and Psalm 104:29-30 explicitly equate life with breath; these passages weaken the objection that Adam is a special case, and might be understood as paradigmatic for all human life.

Yet the concept that the "soul" or "life" is in the blood (Deut. 12:23; Lev. 17:10-14) might imply that personhood begins as soon as there is heartbeat and circulation.

Although many of these passages confirm the worth of the fetus, they cannot be used to pinpoint the beginning of personhood. Using these texts to resolve the abortion debate is like using Psalm 93:1 or 96:10, "The world is firmly established, it cannot be moved," to resolve the fifteenth-century debate over whether the earth goes around the sun or not. The pro-life proof texts simply do not speak to the modern issue of exactly when life begins.

The most discussed text is Exodus 21:22-24. Since capital punishment is imposed only in the case of the death of the adult, not the fetus, it is alleged that this implies that the fetus has a lesser status. The majority of the rabbis so taught and held, as in Roman law, that the fetus is a part of the mother;[5] though some said that if the fetus is unformed (under 40 days) only a fine is called for, but if formed (and hence fully human) life for life is demanded.[6] Josephus gives the typical Jewish understanding of this verse:

> He that kicketh a woman with child, if the woman miscarry, shall be fined by the judges for having, by the destruction of the fruit of her womb, diminished the population, and a further sum shall be presented by him to the woman's husband. If she die of the blow, he also shall die, the law claiming as its due the sacrifice of life for life.[7]

Bruce Waltke[8] argues that the evidence for this interpretation is strengthened by a comparison of the biblical text with ancient Middle Eastern parallels. But others, such as Clifford E. Bajema[9] and Norman Geisler[10] dispute this because the attack on the fetus could be regarded as unintentional, and in cases of accidental death the penalty was not capital punishment but only a fine; or because the passage might refer not to miscarriage but to premature birth, with the penalty applying to the death of either the mother or the baby.

But all of this is beside the point, for Exodus 21:20-21, when compared with v. 12, clearly implies that the life of a slave is of lesser value than the life of a free man. Yet we would not accept this as normative for us today, would we? Therefore, even if Exodus 21:22f. provided unambiguous evidence that the life of the fetus was regarded as of less value than the life of an adult, it would not settle the question.

Finally, it is not helpful to cite the sixth commandment and charge abortionists with murder. First, the Bible does not precisely define the beginning of life; and second, the sixth commandment ("Thou shalt not murder") does not forbid the taking of life under all circumstances. This commandment does not use the general-purpose word for killing (Hebrew *mooth*), but the more precise Hebrew word *ratsch*, which generally means "murder"—i.e., killing which is malicious and unauthorized by higher authority. The sixth commandment was never understood in Bible times to condemn capital punishment or killing in war; i.e., it allows killing as long as the one who takes life is licensed to kill under civil authority. The question to be decided, then, is whether or not abortions fit into the category of murder. This is not something that can simply be assumed as a premise. Personally, I do not think it is possible to murder something that has no heart, no heartbeat, no brain, and no brainwaves—the state of the early embryo.

The Bible holds that it is morally justifiable to take human life under certain conditions—such as war—where those whose lives are taken may have no personal culpability. Neither in biblical nor secular philosophy is the preservation of life always an overriding ultimate value. The United States does not invade Cuba to free its political prisoners from Nazi-type concentration camps, or pay money to terrorists to save the lives of hostages.

Jesus sometimes ceased His work of healing to go aside and rest when there were doubtless still sick people waiting to be healed, some of whom probably died. Thus there were times when Jesus placed the value of relaxation above that of human life. It is critical to remember that, for the Christian, physical death is not the ultimate evil.

Some issues that arise in connection with abortion are simple to solve from a biblical standpoint. Pro-choice advocates maintain that a woman has the right to control her own body. This argument does not even stand up from a logical standpoint, much less a scriptural one. As far as Scripture is concerned, our bodies are not our own (1 Cor. 6:19-20). From a logical standpoint, the embryo is not a part of the mother's body. Paul Jewett comments:

> Of all the tissues in the body, it [the fetal tissue] alone has a fixed genetic make-up different from that of the body in which it is lodged. A woman cannot say of fetal tissue, this is mine, in the sense she can say of her kidney tissue, this is mine. She cannot keep it, any more than she can give it to someone else; she must surrender it at birth—or die.[11]

But what about the rights of the fetus? Since the fetus cannot choose, the argument goes, we have no right to deprive it of its right to life. But the argument can go either way. Who is qualified to define the rights of the fetus? Why must the fetus be forced to be born? Who will protect the right of the fetus not to be born? Bestowing the "right to life" upon the unborn may under certain circumstances be like forcing "life" upon a terminally ill patient who wishes to be allowed to die, or bestowing the great boon of salvation via forced conversion upon unwilling pagans. There may be times when, if the fetus were able to foresee its fate, it would choose not to be born. Job (3:1-26; 10:18-19) expressed regret that he had ever been born, and indicated that death is preferable to certain types of life. Jesus said of Judas that "it were better for that man if he had not been born" (Matt. 26:24, Mark 14:21). Thus the proper reply to the argument "What if the mother of Beethoven had had an abortion?" is "What if the mother of Hitler had had one?"

By now it should be clear that the matter of arriving at answers to questions that Scripture does not address is not as simple as it first seems. Where explicit biblical counsel is lacking, the proof-text method can lead us into a morass of confusion. We are trying to make Scripture say something it does not say. And if scriptural arguments against early abortion are somewhat weak, the logical arguments are not much stronger.

The pro-life position that life begins at conception is untenable. Clearly, life begins *before* conception. The unfertilized egg is alive, and has the capability to become a human being if it is fertilized by the sperm, just as the fertilized ovum has that capability if it is nurtured by the womb. An egg is a potential human being, and will become one given the right conditions. An unfertilized female egg is just as "human" as a fertilized egg—it certainly isn't reptilian. The unfertilized sperm even manifests goal-seeking behavior. I do not believe that human life begins at conception. It began in Eden.

It is true that only after fertilization does the cell have a complete complement of genes, giving it the potential to become an adult human being. The status of the embryo, then, boils down to its *potential;* that which it may become, given time. But, surely, potential things are less valuable than actual things. A potential election winner does not have the same rights as an actual election winner. A potential scholar does not enjoy the same respect as an actual scholar.

If it is true that having a full complement of genes constitutes personhood, then every cell in the adult human body is a "person." Even the requisite potential for differentiation may be present. If it should become possible to clone a human being from a single cell, then a cell from any part of the human body would be a potential human being (given the right conditions). In that case, should it be considered murder to destroy human cells by scratching oneself?

Since every living cell, fertilized or not, has life, the question is not "When does life begin?" but "When does personhood begin?"

This is, to some extent, a legal question. The state is forced to choose some point on the continuum of human growth as the point beyond which termination of life is immoral. The question is not unlike others where the state must create arbitrary moral boundaries on a continuum, such as the question of when a person becomes an adult, with the right to buy drinks and vote:

> Although we commonly believe that all adult human beings have basic political rights, just when an individual becomes an adult is, within limits, a legitimate matter for specific political decision. That is why different democratic communities can, without denying human rights, adopt slightly different ages of majority.[12]

An analogous problem is the speed limit. The 55-mph-limit does not correspond to any ontological discontinuity; it is an arbitrary legal decision. One might argue that, as speed is dangerous, and higher speeds are responsible for great loss of life every year in this country, the only logical and safe position is to avoid speed altogether; otherwise we might find ourselves on a slippery slope that leads to greater and greater speed and consequent loss of life. But this slippery-slope argument is hardly convincing. Even though the recent increase in the speed limit from 55 to 65 on interstate highways will probably result in the loss of thousands of additional lives—self-conscious, intelligent, adult lives—no one is accusing the legislature of legalizing murder.

I would argue that the very earliest the line of personhood could be drawn on the continuum of life would be late in the second month of pregnancy. Landrum Shettles, who argues that life begins at conception, writes:

> The so-called Harvard Criteria, established by a committee at the Harvard Medical School in 1968 to define death, would, if applied to the fetus, reveal a living human being. The Harvard Criteria, now widely used and accepted in medical schools and hospitals, state that death is determined by four things: lack of response to external stimuli, lack of deep reflex action, lack of spontaneous movement and respiratory effort, and lack of brain activity. . . . Movement of the fetus has been recorded on film as early as day 36, reflex mechanisms are definitely intact by day 42. The embryo responds to touch in the sixth week and sometimes earlier . . . . EEG tracings have been detected as early as the fifth week.[13]

Shettles' own data indicate that the embryo does not achieve "human life" until sometime in the second month of pregnancy. During the first month, although the organism is alive in the same sense as an amoeba or a tree, it is nevertheless "dead" according to the Harvard criteria. Surely an organism without breath or brain waves is not a living soul. We would not condemn a doctor for disconnecting a body with no brain from its life-support system; so we should not condemn a doctor for practicing menstrual extraction (the abortive procedure used up to the sixth week of pregnancy) for legitimate reasons, since, according to the Harvard criteria, the conceptus is no more alive than the vegetative, brain-dead body.

There are other indications that the early embryo is not a person. According to James J. Diamand,[14] in the light of biological evidence the conceptus cannot possibly be said to be a person before 14 to 22 days after conception, at which time a radical and categorical change in life form occurs. Before this point it is

61

undifferentiated (i.e., it is a collection of homogenous cells without specialization), there is a capacity for twinning, and the possibility of spontaneous abortion is greater than fifty percent. Henri Leridon finds that 56 percent of all embryos spontaneously abort,[15] while J. Biggers indicates this figure may be as high as two-thirds.[16]

The phenomenon of spontaneous abortion raises interesting questions. Are these spontaneously aborted embryos persons? Will they be resurrected? If so, they will vastly outnumber the righteous who were born and lived on earth.

Spontaneous abortion often indicates an abnormality in the embryo. This is, of course, a natural process, but nature often works imperfectly. This brings us back to the question of deformity. What if this natural process is not working correctly and allows grossly deformed children to be born? Should we help it along in the same way that we would facilitate the process of birth in case of a birthing emergency, or should we allow nature to take its faulty course in both cases (allowing the deformed fetus to be born and allowing one with the cord around its neck to die)?

If, as some argue, we have no right to play God, then we should not even perform abortions to save the life of the mother. What right do we have to decide that the mother should live if God/nature chooses to let the fetus live and the mother die? The false premise here is that things that are natural are right. But nature is fallen and sometimes needs our help. The "playing God" argument is an emotional red herring. Every surgeon who lifts the knife is "playing God." Legislators and judges "play God" every day.

If it is wrong to imitate nature and abort an embryo, then is it wrong to kill a mature deer who cares for her young and feels pain? The one difference between man and animals is that man is made in the image of God (Gen. 1:27). This cannot mean that man, in contrast to the animals, possesses an immortal soul, for in the creation account both men (Gen. 2:7) and animals (Gen. 1:24; 2:19) are called "souls" (Heb. *nephesh*, also translated "living creature"); and both are formed from the dust (Gen. 2:19). In fact, if the embryo did possess an immortal soul, that would weaken the pro-life case, for when we kill a deer we take all it has, but when we terminate a fetus we leave the essential part untouched (Matt. 10:28). To be consistent, pro-lifers should be vegetarians.

The statement that man is made in the image of God means, at the very least, that man is physically more like God than is any other animal on earth.[17] Ellen G. White defines the image of God as "the power to think and to do."[18] But regardless of how the image of God is defined, the embryo does not possess it. Even a normal (much less a deformed) embryo does not look human (it has a tail and apparent gills) and does not possess the power to think and to do. The image of God is something we grow into. We cannot leave the image of God undefined and argue that all fetuses possess it simply by virtue of being human. If that is so, then Hitler possessed just as much of the image of God as the greatest saint—an unacceptable conclusion.

Moreover, a deformed embryo has no hope of ever growing into that image. Anencephalic children, with little or no higher brain, die hours or days after birth. Children with Tay-Sachs disease develop normally at first but then go into prolonged deterioration leading to blindness, paralysis, and early death. There is no cure for these disorders. The argument that abortion is illegitimate in such cases because we do not kill adults who have similar maladies, such as cancer, is valid only on the questionable assumption that the fetus is on the same level as an adult.

Someone looking for a proof text that would settle the matter of deformed babies might seize upon Exodus 4:11, "Who has made man's mouth? Or who makes him dumb or deaf, or seeing or blind? Is it not I, the Lord?" This would seem to indicate that God causes deformity. But this text proves too much, for if deformity were truly God's will for a baby, then it would be wrong to frustrate His will by surgically correcting the deformity!

Can we, then, assume that if abortion is wrong, Scripture would condemn it? Should we conclude that anything not explicitly condemned in Scripture is allowed?

The church has not taken this position on other matters. Although slavery and polygamy are not explicitly condemned in Scripture, the church, along with society, has condemned these practices. Other practices, accepted by society, are proscribed by the church. Scripture is silent on the matter of attendance at the theatre (although the issue was discussed in biblical times),[19] yet the church has discouraged it. Another practice which is actually allowed in Scripture and is accepted by society, but which the church has chosen to take a stand against, is the drinking of alcoholic beverages.[20] But the fact that the Bible allows alcohol in moderation does not justify drinking today any more than the fact that it allows slavery or polygamy would justify those practices today. In the past God overlooked the times of ignorance (Acts 17:30) and allowed certain practices which should no longer be condoned in the light of advancing revelation (Matt. 19:4-8). Even in the Old Testament wine was forbidden to kings (Prov. 31:4), Nazarites (Num. 6:3), and priests (Lev. 10:9), indicating that, ideally, it was not fit to drink. Today there are good medical arguments that cast doubt on the premise that one can drink "to the glory of God."

Moreover, it could be argued that Matthew 16:19 gives the church a limited authority to forbid and permit within the guidelines of Scripture. In matters of practice, then, we must, as we have in the past, continue to move beyond the Bible, rather than attempting to maintain that anything allowed in Scripture is legitimate behavior for the Christian today.

Leaving behind the proof-text method, we now turn to a scriptural principle which, I feel, compels me to advocate a moderate pro-life position. It is the principle of Romans 14, which teaches that Christians should do nothing that would offend someone with a sensitive conscience. We should avoid the appearance of evil.

Although this principle is usually interpreted in an individualistic sense, it might also be applied to a church. This would imply that *the church should not practice something that is widely regarded as wrong in the Christian community.* Whenever any debatable practice brings shame on the church, as long as it is not enjoined in Scripture, it should be stopped. If society decides that sexual discrimination, racial discrimination, or polygamy is wrong, it is not a good idea for the church to continue to practice it, regardless of whether or not the Bible allows it. This is only common sense; to do otherwise is to cripple the church's witness.

Several caveats must be entered here. This does not mean, of course, that whenever a practice that is clearly condemned in Scripture comes to be perceived by contemporary society as excusable, that the church should abandon the scriptural stand against that practice. The church must condemn that which Scripture condemns regardless of the attitude of society.

Secondly, the church should not always play follow the leader to secular society; it should not always be the last to champion a good cause, such as racial equality. It should be at the forefront in advocating certain reforms, while others should be approached more cautiously.

Finally, it hardly needs to be stated that, where Scripture is silent, the church must obey the law. Only explicit scriptural commands can justify civil disobedience. It is true that the church practiced civil disobedience during the U.S. Civil War by flouting the fugitive slave law, but only because it had explicit scriptural support: Deuteronomy 23:15 forbids returning a runaway slave to his owner.

Although it is not currently illegal, abortion does fall into the category of a practice that is increasingly perceived as a social evil.[21] Hence the church must tighten up its guidelines, which seem far too loose at the present time, allowing abortion for virtually any reason. If the church wishes to maintain its integrity in the world, it must take a firm stand against elective abortion.

The abortion debate will never be resolved as long as we insist on applying all-or-nothing categories to what is obviously a gradualist situation. There are degrees of wrong. To say that the abortion of a week-old blastocyst is the murder of a person, in the same league with the assassination of a president, is tantamount to saying that swatting a fly is the same as shooting a baboon, or that smashing an acorn underfoot is the same as cutting down a large oak. It is ridiculous to argue that a teenage son who stabs his mother to death and a doctor who does a menstrual extraction of a week-old embryo are equally guilty of the crime of murder. Such overzealous extremism discredits the pro-life cause: the best way to undo is to overdo.

However, there are crimes other than murder. While abortion may be justified in some cases of rape, incest, abnormality, etc., such cases account for only one or two percent of all abortions. Rape pregnancy is very rare. The number of pregnancies in any given year in the United States as a result of rape is probably under 100. In Czechoslovakia, a careful study was made of 86,000 consecutive induced abortions, and it was found that only 22 were done for rape.[22] The vast majority of abortions are elective. As to these, I share the feelings of Mary Meehan:

> Often, in debates over ethics, people torture themselves with cases that are highly unlikely to occur. We ask, "Would I tell a lie to save the world?" when we are far more likely to face the question, "Will I tell a lie to stay in someone's good graces?" We ask, "Would I have an abortion to avoid having a severely retarded child?" The question is more likely to be, "Will I have an abortion to avoid social embarrassment or interference with my career?"[23]

I consider myself to be pro-choice in this sense: a woman may freely choose to have intercourse or not. If intercourse has been forced upon her, she should not be forced to continue a resulting pregnancy. However, once a man or woman has freely chosen to enter into a sexual relationship, he or she cannot freely choose to reject the responsibilities that come with that privilege.

Even though I find it impossible to accept the idea that the embryo is a person immediately after conception, I oppose all abortions of convenience at any time after conception. Why? For a similar reason that I oppose showing disrespect for the American flag or wearing a swastika. When someone tramples on a flag or wears a swastika, no rule of Scripture is being violated and no individual is being directly injured, but, from a symbolic standpoint, something important, perhaps even sacred, is being degraded. Again, why do civilized people go to such lengths to dispose of a dead body in an honorable way? Why not toss it out with the garbage? Because there is a symbolic content that goes well beyond the literal content. To treat a corpse—or a fetus—with casual disrespect is to cheapen and debase humanity. We sink to the level of savages.

Intuitively, mothers know this. In one study of 30 women dealing with the long-term manifestations of abortion 72 percent did not claim to be particularly religious at the time they had the abortion, but 96 percent afterward felt that abortion was "the taking of a life" or "murder." Eighty-five percent were surprised at the intensity of their emotional reaction, while 81 percent felt "victimized by the abortion process."[24] One gynecologist-obstetrician put it this way:

> Mental illness does not automatically follow an abortion. Often the trauma may sink into the unconscious and never surface in a woman's lifetime. But it is not as harmless and casual an event as many in the pro-abortion crowd insist. A psychological price is paid. I can't say exactly what. It may be an alienation, it may be pushing away from human warmth, perhaps a hardening of the maternal instinct. Something happens on the deeper levels of a woman's consciousness when she destroys a pregnancy. I know that as a psychiatrist.[25]

Thus psychic trauma to the mother is probably more likely to result from an abortion than from a birth.[26] And other than harm to the mother, I cannot imagine any financial or emotional consideration (embarrassment of mother, resentment of fetus, etc.) which would be sufficient reason for taking the life of this potential person. With regard to the mother's feelings toward the fetus, several studies have found that most pregnant women who initially reject their pregnancy end up wanting it.[27] And even if the parents do not want the child, there are thousands of barren couples who would cherish it.

While I am opposed to the black-and-white, all-or-nothing position, I believe that the vast majority of abortions done today are wrong. I do not believe church institutions should have any part in this cheapening of life. I hope the church will take a stand against elective abortion, and cease to impair its credibility by ignoring the moral climate regarding such issues.

Endnotes

[1]Ellen G. White never used the word "abortion." A brief passage on abortion found in her book *A Solemn Appeal* (p. 100) was not authored by her. Some have used Ellen G. White's statements against irresponsibly bringing children into the world as a justification of abortion; it is highly unlikely Ellen G. White would have approved of such interpretation in the light of something she wrote in 1861:

> "Hoops, I saw, should be discarded from the ranks of Sabbath keepers. Their influence and practice should be a rebuke to this ridiculous fashion which has been a screen to iniquity. Its first rise was from a house of ill fame in Paris. Never was such iniquity practiced as since this hoop invention; never were there so many murders of infants and never were virtue and modesty so rare" (Lt 16a, 1861).

Conclusions drawn on the basis of this one statement may be hazardous, but we can at least conclude that Ellen G. White opposed practices that resulted in the needless death of fetuses.

[2]Michael J. Gorman, *Abortion and the Early Church: Christian, Jewish, and Pagan Attitudes in the Greco-Roman World* (Downers Grove, IL: InterVarsity Press, 1982), 21.

[3]Josephus, *Against Apion*, 2:202.

[4]Gorman (p. 48) suggests that references to *pharmakeia* in Galations 5:20; Revelation 9:21; 18:23; 21:8; 21:15 may be an implicit reference to abortion. The word may refer to poisons and mind-disturbing drugs, potions supplied by a sorcerer or magician, or abortifacients.

[5]Gorman, 41.

[6]Gorman, 35ff.

[7]Josephus, *Antiquities*, 278. Similar understandings of Exodus 21 are found in TB *Sanhedrin* 74a and *Baba Kamma* 5:4.

[8]Bruce K. Waltke, "The Old Testament and Birth Control," *Christianity Today* (November 8, 1968):3

[9]Clifford E. Bajema, *Abortion and the Meaning of Personhood* (Grand Rapids, MI: Baker Book House, 1976).

[10]Norman L. Geisler, "The Bible, Abortion, and Common Sense," *Fundamentalist Journal* 4, no. 5 (May 1985):25.

[11]Paul K. Jewett, "The Relation of the Soul to the Fetus," *Christianity Today* (November 8, 1968):6.

[12]Ronald M. Green, "Toward a Copernican Revolution in our Thinking about Life's Beginning and Life's End," *Soundings* 66 (Summer 1983):171.

[13]Landrum B. Shettles and David Rorvik, *Rites of Life: The Scientific Evidence for Life Before Birth* (Grand Rapids, MI: Zondervan, 1983), 56.

[14]James J. Diamond, "Abortion, Animation, and Biological Hominization," *Theological Studies* 36 (1975):305-24, cited in Carol A. Tauer, "The Tradition of Probabilism and the Moral Status of the Early Embryo," *Theological Studies* 45 (March 1984):3-33.

[15]Henri Leridon, *Human Fertility: The Basic Components* (Chicago: University of Chicago Press, 1977), 81, cited in Tauer, *op. cit.*

[16]J. D. Biggers, "In Vitro Fertilization, Embryo Culture and Embryo Transfer in the Human; Appendix to Report and Conclusions of the Report of the Ethics Advisory Board: HEW Support of Research Involving Human in Vitro Fertilization and Embryo Transfer," *Federal Register* 44:118:35033 (June 18, 1979).

[17]The word "image," as used in the Old Testament, has to do primarily with physical, not psychological, resemblance (Gen. 5:3; Ex. 20:4; Ps. 106:19; and Isa. 40:19-20; 44:9,10,15,17).

[18]Ellen G. White, *Education* (Mountain View, CA: Pacific Press Publishing Association, 1903), 17.

[19]The issue of attendance at pagan shows and dramas is, like abortion, discussed by religious writers who were contemporary with Scripture. For example, Philo of Alexandria writes:

> For what other reasons do we imagine that the theatres all over the world are filled daily with innumerable multitudes? The people who are slaves to musical performances and spectacles, allowing ears and eyes to be borne about unbridled; honoring lutists and the singers that accompany them, in every form of unmanly and effeminate music; favoring dancers and other actors, because they execute and hold effeminate poses and movements; applauding the insistent warfare on community, but, wretches that they are, overturning through eyes and ears their own life (Philo, *De Agricultura*, 35).

[20]In Deuteronomy 14:26, the Israelites are allowed to drink "wine and strong drink." Strong drink is regarded as undesirable for men in positions of authority, but it has its legitimate uses for the depressed and afflicted, according to Proverbs 31:4-7. Indeed, wine which "makes man's hearts glad" is said to be one of the gifts of God (Ps. 104:15). Even Daniel, after refusing the king's wine (Dan. 1), mainly because it had been offered to idols, may have later drunk it (Dan. 10:3), presumably because in his position of authority he could obtain wine which hadn't been offered to idols.

In the New Testament deacons are forbidden to overindulge in wine (1 Tim. 3:8), but total abstinence was not required. It is drinking to the point of intoxication which is forbidden in the Bible (Ps. 20:1; 21:17; Isa. 5:11,22; 28:7-8; 56:11-12; Hos. 4:11; Eph. 5:18). The strongest injunction against drinking, in Proverbs 23:29-35, refers to a particular kind of spiced wine (cf. Cant. 8:2) also called mixed wine (Prov. 9:2; 23:30) which was prepared with herbs after the manner of the heathen nations and served at a banquet. This wine, being especially intoxicating, was forbidden. Otherwise the principle seems to be one of moderation.

In biblical times it was customary to mix the fermented wine with water, one part wine to two parts water. The resulting beverage was quite weak and relatively innocuous; it would take a lot of it to make a person drunk. And when fresh water was not always available, the alcohol in wine served a useful function in purifying the water by killing the germs in it.

[21]Several writers have documented a clear movement toward the pro-life position since 1975: Helen Rose Fuchs Ebaugh and C. Allen Haney, "Shifts in Abortion Attitudes: 1972-1978," *Journal of Marriage and the Family* 42, no. 3 (August 1980):491-99; Carol E. Neumann and Colin G. McDiarmid, "Changes in the Feminist Perspective: From 1970-1980," Paper presented at the eighth annual convention of the Association for Women in Psychology (Boston, MA, March 5-8, 1981); Jeanne E. Manese and William E. Sedlacek, "Changes in Religious Behavior and Attitudes of College Students by Race and Sex over a Ten Year Period," Counselling Center, University of Maryland (College Park, MD 20742, 1983).

It is clear that we are undergoing a paradigm shift on this issue in the Adventist Church as well, for at the recent symposium on abortion held at Loma Linda University in November, 1988, the position of the presenters tended to correlate with their age. The younger scholars took more extreme positions against abortion.

[22]Vance Farrell, *Pilgrim's Rest*, Waymarks 71 (September 1, 1983).

[23]Mary Meehan, "More Trouble Than They're Worth?" cited in Sidney Callahan and Daniel Callahan, *Abortion: Understanding Differences* (New York: Plenum Press, 1984), 168.

[24]Anne Catherine Speckhard, Ph.D., "The Psycho-Social Aspects of Stress Following Abortion" (Study, University of Minnesota), cited in Ardyce Sweem, "Laura's Question: Three Perspectives on Abortion," *Adventist Review* (September 25, 1986):12.

[25]Dr. Julius Fogel, quoted in the *Colorado Right to Life Committee Newsletter* 2, no. 10:3.

[26]According to Dr. Vincent M. Rue, psychotherapist and executive director of the Sir Thomas More Clinic of Southern California, women who have had abortions are at far greater risk for psychiatric hospitalization than are women who allow their babies to live. Post Abortion Syndrome (PAS), a stress disorder similar to that suffered by many Vietnam veterans, afflicts up to half of all women who have abortions, often leading to other problems such as substance abuse and suicide. A study cited by Paula Vandergaer, editor of *Living World*, has documented that sixty percent of the 3,000 women calling a suicide hotline service in Milwaukee had undergone abortions (*Signs of the Times* [July 1988]:6). On the other hand, the very recent survey by Surgeon General Everett Koop, himself pro-life, finds the evidence on this point ambiguous. Perhaps it is safe to say that a large minority of those who undergo abortion experience very painful emotional reactions.

[27]"There is a contention that unwanted conceptions tend to have undesirable effects... [but] direct evidence for such a relationship is almost completely lacking.... It was the hope of this article to find more convincing systematic research evidence and to give some idea of the amount of relationship between unwanted conception and undesired effect on children. This hope has been disappointed." (E. Pohlman, "Unwanted Conception, Research on Undesirable Consequences," *Eugenics Quarterly* 14 [1967]:143.)

It is clear that mothers who initially believed their pregnancy to be 'the worst thing that ever happened to them' came to feel about the same degree of affection for their children as the mothers who were initially 'ecstatic' about the pregnancy.... Most women who were most regretful of the pregnancy now claim they would have the child again if given the opportunity" whereas "one of every six mothers who were initially pleased with pregnancy would choose not to have the child again." (P. Cameron, et al, "How Much Do Mothers Love Their Children?" *Rocky Mountain Psychological Association* [May 12, 1972].)

The View of John Harvey Kellogg on Abortion

Dalton Baldwin

Kellogg on Abortion

As John Harvey Kellogg developed the Battle Creek Sanitarium into an internationally known health institution he became the best known Seventh-day Adventist in the world. Since he was the dominant influence in the early development of Seventh-day Adventist medicine and had strong convictions about abortion, an analysis of his views will be helpful for an understanding of abortion in the denominational context.

In his book, *Man the Masterpiece*, Kellogg devoted fifteen pages to a section entitled "A Chapter on Ethics."[1] Equating ethics and morality, he wrote, "The essence of morality is right doing, or the practical recognition of the obligation to law."[2] When he referred to "law," he had something much more comprehensive in mind than codified law such as the ten commandments. He held that a "view which regards man as a natural object, governed only by natural laws, and which defines right doing as being simply obedience to law, gives to the term *morality* an immensely broader scope, and makes it include all those laws and principles by which his entire being is governed."[3] He sometimes quoted the Bible to drive home a point, but he based his system of "biologic living" on the divine laws revealed in the scientific analysis of nature.[4]

One side of Kellogg's ethical foundation was rooted in the quest for harmony with nature that was dominant in the nineteenth-century health-reform movement. Larkin B. Coles summarized this position when he said that "it is as truly a sin against Heaven, to violate a law of life, as to break one of the ten commandments."[5] The other side of Kellogg's ethics of abortion was rooted in the "regular" branch of American medicine.

Crusade Against Abortion

James C. Mohr, in his book *Abortion in America*, describes three reasons why a number of activist physicians in the newly organized American Medical Association launched a "crusade against abortion" between 1857 and 1880. First, they could use the cause as a means to secure legislative help in eliminating the competition from "irregular" practitioners who were performing abortions and other medical procedures without adequate medical education. Second, they could use the abortion legislation to aid their own professional organizations in the discipline of members. Third, participation in the crusade would aid the medical profession to regain its sense of mission to society.[6] The most prominent leader in the crusade was Horatio R. Storer.

Kellogg graduated from Bellevue Hospital Medical College in New York City in 1875, near the end of the crusade, when most states had enacted restrictive abortion legislation. He became medical superintendent of the Health Reform Institute in Battle Creek in 1876,[7] and by 1877 succeeded in getting the Michigan State Medical Association to hold a meeting at the renamed Battle Creek Sanitarium where he reported that they declared the institution "entirely rational and 'regular.'"[8] In his drive to be recognized as a "regular" physician, Kellogg seemed to have joined the physicians' crusade against abortion.

Abortion Is Murder. Kellogg quoted the leading abortion crusader, Storer, when he made abortion "a crime of the same nature, both against our Maker and society, as to destroy an infant, a child, or a man."[9] Kellogg included this statement in his most widely circulated book, *Plain Facts*, an early sex-education manual which went through many editions and expansions and reached a half-million buyers.[10] He also included discussions of abortion in a book for women, *Ladies' Guide in Health and Disease, Girlhood, Maidenhood, Wifehood, Motherhood*, and in a book for men, *Man, the Masterpiece: or, Plain Truths Plainly Told, about Boyhood, Youth and Manhood.*[11]

Kellogg wrote the first draft of *Plain Facts* in fourteen days.[12] In the white heat of his own crusade he used, among others, the following graphic terms to express his total rejection of abortion: "ante-natal murder,"[13] "awful crime of murder,"[14] "enormously common crime,"[15] "heinous crime of criminal abortion,"[16] "horrible crime,"[17] "the most revolting of all crimes against human life,"[18] "terrible crime,"[19] and "unnatural crime."[20]

Kellogg had the temperament of a crusader, and the following paragraph is a good example of the emotional power of his appeals:

Often as we pass along the street we meet a little fair-haired boy who does not know how narrowly his mother escaped the commission of the awful crime of murder, how earnestly we pleaded for his life when he was a helpless, yet undeveloped, and, unfortunately, unwelcome child. Would to God that we could place before the mind of every woman in the land a picture of the evils of this awful crime, the sacrilege, the profanity, the worse than brutish cruelty of this crime against God, against the race, against nature, and against the perpetrator, a picture so vivid in coloring, so horrifying in its hideousness, that it would make an impression ineffaceable by any of the selfish and frivolous considerations usually urged as reasons justifying the act.[21]

No Adequate Reason. Kellogg listed a number of reasons why women seek abortions. They include the desire "to conceal the results of sin, to avoid the burdens of maternity, to secure ease and freedom to travel, etc., or even from a false idea that maternity is vulgar."[22] Sometimes women explain that "they do not wish to endure the inconvenience and trouble of pregnancy and childbirth, or that they 'do not want to have children,' or they 'have children enough,' or some other equally frivolous excuse."[23]

While Kellogg held that none of the reasons advanced by women justify having an abortion, he maintained that men are the "primary cause" of this crime. He complained that the most "scathing invectives" are hurled at the mother who seeks an abortion while nothing is said about the man who "forced upon her the circumstances which gave the unfortunate one existence."[24]

The Victorian convicton that sexual desire is primarily a male characteristic no doubt encouraged Kellogg to put the most blame on men. He quoted with "pleasure" the explanation of Prof. T. Parvin, M.D., of Jefferson Medical College, Philadelphia, saying, "I do not believe one bride in a hundred, of delicate, educated, sensitive women, accepts matrimony from any desire of sexual gratification; when she thinks of this at all, it is with shrinking, rather than with desire."[25] The male monopoly on sexual desire was again emphasized in a quote from Dr. Acton:

The best mothers, wives, and managers of households know little or nothing of sexual indulgences. Love of home, of children, of domestic duties, are the only passions they feel. As a general rule, a modest woman seldom desires any sexual gratification for herself. She submits to her husband, but only to please him; and but for the desire of maternity, would far rather be relieved from his attention.[26]

Kellogg concluded that sexual excess is the basic cause of abortion. Since sexual desire is primarly a male quality, males are most responsible. "This evil," he said, "has its origin in 'marital excesses,' and in disregard of the natural law which makes the female the sole proprietor of her own body, and gives to her the right to refuse the approaches of the male when unprepared to receive them without doing violence to the laws of her being."[27]

Natural-Law Rationale

Kellogg explained his abortion policy with natural law arguments. Violation of natural law causes unwanted pregnancies. The way to avoid unwanted pregnancies is to obey natural law.

Highest Human Function is Procreation. Kellogg gave high priority to sex and procreation among human functions. He argued that since perpetuation of the race is more important than any individual, "the organs of reproduction may in a certain sense be said to rank higher than any other organs." The production of human beings is "the most marvelous of all vital processes." "The *use* of the reproductive function is perhaps the highest physical act of which man is capable."[28] Semen is "the most vital of all fluids."[29] Everyone should respect the "sacredness of the reproductive function."[30] He had a high view of the value of sex and reproduction.

Reproduction is the "natural" purpose of the sex organs. Kellogg derived his natural law norm about the exclusive purpose of sex from the observation that the females of lower animals "resolutely resist the advances of the males except at such times as the reproductive act may be properly and fruitfully performed."[31] He admitted that the majority will not "accept the truth which nature seems to teach, which would confine sexual acts to reproduction wholly."[32] "Physiology recognizes one object for the institution of marriage, namely, the preservation of the species." Although there are other "ends" which marriage accomplishes, the "opportunity for the gratification of the animal passions is no part of the function of marriage."[33]

The term "animal passions" seems to refer to any pleasure involved in sexual function. Kellogg held that the better pleasures of married life do not include sexual function. "Connubial happiness may be perfect without the passionate embrace. Its purest pleasures may be thoroughly enjoyed without those grosser excitements which, while necessary for the perpetuation of the race, are not essential either for the health or the happiness of the individual."[34] The pleasure of companionship is appropriate at any time in marriage, but the unavoidable pleasure of sex in reproduction should be limited to procreation.

What makes abortion a violation of natural law is that it obstructs reproduction which is the natural purpose of sex. Kellogg seemed to think that recognizing any other purpose for sex would exclude the realization of its primary purpose. He did not seem to recognize the value of sex in marriage as either a means of bonding or for the expression of affection.

Kellogg held that natural law excludes all methods of contraception other than continence. He rejected the "numerous devices" which result in "cheating nature."[35] Speaking of sponges, shields, or even cold water, he held that "all are injurious in character."[36] He quoted Gardner: "It is undeniable that all the methods employed to prevent pregnancy are physically injurious."[37] He claimed that "various filthy maneuvers" in an attempt to subvert "natural processes" are among the "most common causes of malignant disease."[38] The "prevention of conception" is the "same crime" as the crime of abortion.[39] When someone objected that insisting on continence as a method of limiting pregnancy might lead to divorce, Kellogg suggested that in such a situation divorce would be preferable.[40] Even the "rhythm" method of avoiding pregnancy is "unnatural."[41] For those who follow the "teachings of nature" the only acceptable method of limiting pregnancy is "total-abstinence."[42]

Kellogg concluded that natural law excludes abortion because it prevents the fruition of the purpose of sex which is reproduction and the maintenance of the species. All methods of contraception are wrong because they also interfere with the natural purpose of sex. The highest human function is procreation; nothing should interfere with its fulfillment.

Destructive Consequences of Abortion. Abortion is not only wrong because it is murder, but it also produces other tragic results. The mother receives the greatest damage. Kellogg reported, "All medicinal agents used for this purpose are powerful poisons, and quite as likely to produce the death of the mother as the expulsion of the fetus."[43] "The violence done the delicate tissues of the womb often sets up most terrible inflammations, the results of which can never be wholly effaced."[44] Having had an abortion threatens subsequent pregnancies, sometimes making pregnancy impossible, increasing the "liability to miscarriage," or resulting in a "weak" or "puny" child.[45] Kellogg held that the attempt to produce abortions is "one of the most prolific causes" of cancer.[46] He claimed that it "had been proven by statistics" that the danger of "immediate death" from abortion is "fifteen times as great as in natural childbirth."[47]

If efforts to produce an abortion are unsuccessful, there is great damage to the child. Attempts to produce an abortion by mechanical means run the risk of producing "an eyeless or crippled child, or a headless monster."[48] "It is fair to consider abortion to be 'the cause of some of those terrible monstrosities which have sometimes been attributed to some demonic agency and which may still be charged to motives that are certainly something less than human,—may we not say devilish?"[49] Even if there is no physical damage, "Who can doubt that the murderous intent of the mother will be stamped indelibly upon the character of the unwelcome child, giving it a natural propensity for the commission of murderous deeds?"[50]

Sometimes Kellogg spoke of the damaging results of interfering with the natural progression of reproduction as punishments meted out by nature. He spoke of a "weak" and "puny" child born after an abortion attempt as the "silent witness of the mother's criminal attempts."[51] "The penalty of disease is certain to follow sooner or later, no matter what subterfuge is employed."[52] Kellogg quoted Black who said that even if the guilty person escaped the punishment of civil law, "there is a surer mode of punishment for the guilty mother in the self-executing laws of nature."[53]

Kellogg told about one of his patients who had sought an abortion, and he persuaded her to give up the plan. She later gave birth to an emaciated child.

> The eyes were sunken back in their sockets, the cheeks fallen in, the nose pinched, and the whole countenance presented the appearance of infirm old age, just on the verge of the grave, from consumption. The fingers resembled most those of a skeleton. Horrible sores began to make their appearance, first on the hands, then about the head and eyes. The bones began to decay and drop out one by one, and yet the poor little creature clung to life week after week, becoming more wretched and miserable, the constant moaning and crying day and night indicating the intense suffering which it endured. Horrible spasms now and then deprived it of the power to breathe. Again and again the mother thought it was dying, and even dead, but still it survived month after month, lingering on literally a living, breathing putrifying corpse. During all these days and weeks and months of weary watching, day and night, what must have been the mother's thoughts! What pangs of bitter self-reproach, and what remorse of conscience must have burned in her heart, as during the long night watches she sat beside her dying babe, and listened to its piteous moans!

> And still the wretched infant lingers on. Its little flickering flame of life still faintly burns, and still the mother tends it day and night, dressing its festering sores, and soothing its feeble cry. Vain is her effort to undo the wrong she has done her little one; but let us hope that by genuine repentance and the many months of faithful and patient watching she has made a full atonement for her sin.[54]

This account dramatically emphasizes the punishment meted out to those who violate natural law.

No Gradations of Fetal Value. Kellogg held that from conception to birth there are no gradations of human value which confer an increasing right to life.

He rejected the common belief that "quickening" represents a significant change in the status of the conceptus. At this point the "movements of the little one become sufficiently active and vigorous to attract the attention of the mother." At conception "a new human being has come into existence,—in embryo, it is true but possessed of its own individuality, with its own future, its possibilities of joy, grief, success, failure, fame, and ignominy."[55] The ancients who justified infanticide contending that "no distinct life was present until after birth" had "just as much reason" in support of their position as those who claim that life is not present until quickening.[56]

Kellogg held that at the "instant" of contact between the ovum and the sperm "individual life begins":

> From that moment until maturity is reached, years subsequently, the whole process is only one of development. Nothing absolutely new is added at any subsequent moment. In view of these facts, it is evident that at the very instant of conception the embryonic human being possesses all the right to life it ever can possess. It is just as much an individual, a distinct human being, possessed of soul and body, as it ever is, though in a very immature form.[57]

The fertilized egg has just as much right to life as the mature adult. There is no point a certain number of days after conception of the physiological organism when the soul or spiritual substance of a human person is added. The gradual development from a single cell to a complex person does not increase the value of the conceptus with regard to its right to life.

Therapeutic abortion, which sacrifices the life of the fetus if necessary in order to save the life of the mother, implies that the value of the undeveloped fetus is not as great as that of the mature mother. Kellogg did not discuss therapeutic abortion in his widely circulated books. In 1756 a London medical convocation decided that the sacrifice of an unborn child is medically and legally acceptable, if necessary in order to preserve the life of the mother.[58] England and America prevailingly followed this precedent, and the "therapeutic exception" was explicitly stated in the New York Criminal code which went into effect in 1830.[59] The Michigan abortion law of 1846 granted therapeutic exceptions where "the same shall have been necessary to preserve the life of such mother, or shall have been advised by two physicians to be necessary for such purpose."[60] Kellogg was probably aware of the provisions of the Michigan statute.

In 1869 a council of Roman Catholic bishops developed and Bishop Spaulding issued a policy which rejected the therapeutic exception. "The murder of an infant before its birth is, in the sight of God and His Church, as great a crime, as would be the killing of a child after birth. . . . No Mother is allowed, under any circumstances, to permit the death of her unborn infant, not even for the sake of preserving her own life."[61]

Kellogg neither explicitly rejected nor adopted the therapuetic exception. Since he mentioned incidents where mothers requested abortions from him, it would be very strange if his large surgical practice never included a case where he had to decide to save either the life of the mother or the fetus. The Catholic rejection of therapeutic abortion would seem to be more consistent with his contention that there are no adequate reasons for an abortion and that at conception the fetus has as much right to life as a mature adult. Why did he not openly reject therapeutic abortion, as the Catholic position did?

Strategies Against Abortion

Although Kellogg doubted whether the "gigantic evil" of abortion could ever be eradicated, he threw the full weight of his persuasive powers into a campaign to reduce the incidence of the crime. He recognized that it would be necessary to "revolutionize society" in order to be successful.[62] His international reputation as a crusader and health educater were invested in the cause.

Legislation Ineffective. Kellogg held that laws prohibiting abortion "are of no consequence, or at any rate are of little avail."[63] In the first place, it is difficult to obtain evidence. Usually the only witnesses are both criminals and desire to conceal the event. In the second place, convictions are difficult. In Massachusetts between 1849 and 1857 only thirty-two cases against abortion came to court and none were convicted.[64]

Kellogg expressed his own personal frustration with using legal processes to stem the tide of abortion:

> We have had some experience in attempting to bring these human fiends to justice, but not such as to encourage us in repeating the effort. Though evidence may be as clear and conclusive as possible, shrewd and unscrupulous lawyers will find some means for befogging the average jury to such an extent as to cause a disagreement if not an out and out acquittal.[65]

Because of the "evident inefficiency of any civil legislation,"[66] he turned to other methods of attack.

Education. Kellogg declared that the "only hope" for any progress against abortion would come from the "education of the people. Women must be educated concerning themselves, and a wholesome respect for the sacredness of the reproductive function must be cultivated. Women must be informed of the perils which they incur in resorting to instrumental or medicinal means for producing abortion."[67]

Kellogg advocated the use of social pressure. Every woman who commits or attempts to commit an abortion and every man who "encourages or even assents" should "be treated as criminals, and ostracized from society." He argued that the frequency of abortion will increase as long as it is condoned as a trifling offense. "The crime must be made odious, and the perpetrators condemned in unstinted terms."[68] Those who are known to have obtained an abortion should be "looked upon as murderers, as they are; and let their real moral status be distinctly shown."[69]

Power of the Pulpit. Kellogg held that religious institutions have an important role in the crusade against abortion. "From every Christian pulpit let the truth be spoken in terms too plain for misapprehension."[70] He hoped that every preacher would "send out in stirring and unmistakable tones, warnings against the gross immorality of this practice, drawing vivid pictures of its cruelty and unnaturalness, and pronouncing anathemas upon its perpetrators." When members become aware of an abortion they should not maintain secrecy, and the church should disfellowship members who obtain abortions.[71]

Physicians as Crusaders. One of the primary methods of crusading for "biologic living" was the presentation of public lectures. One scholar estimated that Kellogg gave five thousand public lectures during his lifetime.[72] Kellogg held that physicians have a responsibility to educate the public about abortion. "Physicians must warn women of the physical as well as the moral calamities which follow in the wake of this inhuman practice, and the certainty of retribution in this life, as well as the next."[73]

Kellogg also actively opposed abortion in office visits. He published the following account of a conversation he had with a woman who came to him requesting an abortion:

"Why do you desire the destruction of your unborn infant?"

"Because I already have three children, which are as many as I can properly care for; besides, my health is poor, and I do not feel that I can do justice to what children I now have."

"Your chief reason, then, is that you do not wish more children?"

"Yes."

"On this account you are willing to take the life of this unborn babe?"

"I must get rid of it."

"I understand that you have already borne three children, and that you do not think you are able to care for more. Four children are, you think one too many, and so you are willing to destroy one. Why not destroy one of those already born?"

"Oh, that would be murder!"

"It certainly would, but no more murder than it would be to kill this unborn infant. Indeed, the little one you are carrying in your womb has greater claims upon you than the little ones at home, by virtue of its entire dependence and helplessness. It is just as much your child as those whose faces are familiar to you, and whom you love. Why should you be more willing to take its life than that of one of your other children? Indeed, there are several reasons why, if one must die because there are too many, one of these already born should be sacrificed instead of the one unborn. Your other children you are acquainted with. Some of them have serious faults. None of them have very marked mental ability, or give very great promise of becoming specially useful in the world. This one that is unborn may, for aught you know, be destined to a career of wonderful usefulness. It may be a genius, endowed with most remarkable gifts. It may be a discoverer of some new truth or new principle, which will be of great service to the world. It may be of all your children the most talented and the most lovable, and in every way the most desirable. Again, you cannot destroy the life of this innocent child whom you have never seen, without endangering your own life as well, and certainly not without incurring the risk of life-long suffering and disease. This could all be avoided by the sacrifice of a child already born."

"But that would be too horrible! To think of taking one of my little boys and cutting his throat, or throwing him into the river! I could not."

"The act would be in no sense more wicked than what you have come here to request me to do for you. Certainly, you do not think that I advise you to take the life of one of your little children. I only wish to present the matter to you in such a light that you will see the enormity of the crime which in your heart you have proposed to commit. My most earnest advice to you is that you put such thoughts far from your mind, and endeavor to make the best of your present circumstances. Employ all such means as will build up your health, and fortify yourself for the ordeal through which you must pass, and which will conduce in every way to the development of a vigorous and healthy child."[74]

As a physician Kellogg exemplified the righteous zeal which he required of preachers in the defense of the fetus, which has as much right to life as any mature human being.

The Individual Crusade. The crusade against abortion would fail unless every individual rallies to the cause. Physicians and ministers are responsible for mobilizing individuals. Kellogg held that sexual excess was the basic cause of abortion. He sought to get at the root of the problem in his sex-education manual, *Plain Facts.* In the preface he wrote, "The prime object of its preparation has been to call attention to the great prevalence of sexual excesses of all kinds, and the heinous crimes resulting from some forms of sexual transgression, and to point out the terrible results which inevitably follow the violation of sexual law."[75]

The only method of limiting the size of a family which obeys natural law is continence. Kellogg cited "Sir Isaac Newton, Kant, Paschal, Fontenaille, and Michael Angelo" as men whose continent lifestyle was consistent with health and productivity.[76] He included a seven-page section in *Plain Facts* entitled, "Helps to Continence."[77] There were subsections on "The Will," "Diet," "Exercise," "Bathing," and "Religion." The entire program for "biologic living" would aid individuals to be successful in continence as the way to avoid abortion.

In his books Kellogg included scattered comments designed to help individuals bring their sexual life into harmony with nature:

> Many writers make another suggestion, which would certainly be beneficial to individual health; viz., that the husband and wife should habitually occupy separate beds. Such a practice would undoubtedly serve to keep the sexual instincts in abeyance. Separate apartments, or at least the separation of the beds by a curtain, are recommended by some estimable physicians.[78]

As suggestion for an exceptional case, *The Ladies' Guide* recommended the following treatment for nymphomania: "Cool sitz baths, the cool enema; a spare diet; the application of blisters and other irritants to the sensitive part of the sexual organs; the removal of the clitoris and nymphae, constitute the most proper treatment."[79]

In the first sentence in the section on religion as an aid to continence, Kellogg wrote, "After availing himself of all other aids to continence, if he wishes to maintain purity of mind as well as physical chastity,—and one cannot exist long without the other,—the individual must seek that most powerful and helpful of all aids, Divine grace."[80] For the reception of grace prayer is crucial:

> The struggling soul, beset with evil thoughts, will find in prayer a salvation which all his force of will, and dieting, and exercising will not avail; faith and works must always be associated. All that one can do to work out his own salvation, he must do; then he can safely trust to God to do the rest, even though the struggle seems almost a useless one; for when the soul has been long in bondage

to concupiscence, the mind a hold of foul and lustful thoughts, a panorama of unchaste imagery, these hateful phantoms will even intrude themselves upon the sanctity of prayer, and make their victim mentally unchaste upon his knees. But Christ can pity even such; and these degraded minds may yet be pure if, with the psalmist, they continue to cry with a true purpose and unwavering trust, "Create in me a clean heart, O God, and renew a right spirit within me."[81]

EVALUATION

Achievements

At least four advantages of Kellogg's position on abortion should be emphasized:

High Value of Marriage and Reproduction. Kellogg elevated the value and significance of the human participation in the creation of new human life. He recognized that marriage promotes health and longevity.[82] He also agreed that "the sexual relations of men and women determine in a great degree their happiness or misery in life."[83] The awesome privilege of participation in the creation of new human life and the responsibility to do nothing that would frustrate that achievement was the foundation of his abortion policy. He made participation in bringing forth new human life a sacred privilege and responsibility.

Multidimensional Unity. Kellogg did not see the human being as a soul imprisoned in a body but as a multidimensional unity. He recognized that healthy physiology is an important aspect of sound religion. Both moral and physical laws are descriptions of right relationships created by God. He depended on grace and divine transformation in order to achieve desirable physical and comprehensively human goals.

Futility of Legislation. Kellogg recognized the futility of legislation of moral values which are not supported by cultural consensus. He saw that lack of cultural support facilitated secrecy and coverup. He recognized that a revolution was needed in the whole culture. Such a change cannot be produced by legislation.

Moral Persuasion. Kellogg dedicated his life to a massive campaign to educate the race to enjoy the present and future benefits of "biologic living." W. K. Kellogg cashed in on his brother's success in persuading Americans to live healthfully. We live in a healthier and happier world as a result of the moral persuasion of John Harvey Kellogg.

Potential Areas for Growth

Kellogg soaked up new ideas like a sponge. He was always reading and transforming visions of progress into reality. He launched the Adventist program of religious health on a trajectory that is still climbing. The following factors need reexamination in Kellogg's spirit of growth and progress.

Grace as Liberation. A child who is burdened with a guilty conscience may yearn for the release which occurred the last time it happened, and he was caught, punished and relieved from the burden of guilt. Hundreds of such experiences may write the connection between punishment and release into the depths of his soul. He may project the connection between punishment and release onto God and picture atonement as primarily the removal of a barrier by suffering punishment. If he does he may be worshiping a god who creates masochism.

When Kellogg dramatized the punitive actions of nature and encouraged the church to "ostricize," make "odious" and expose those who have fallen into the trap of abortion, he was giving expression to a misunderstanding of grace and liberation. The story of Jesus and the woman taken in adultery is a better model for this problem. The poor woman did not need to feel the impact of rocks or social stones. She did not need to be admonished to think about what she could have and should have avoided as she felt the pain. She needed to be severed from the bonds of her past by undeserved grace. She needed to feel the reality of disconnection from what she could have avoided but did not. She needed to hear, "Neither do I condemn you; go, and do not sin again" (John 8:11). The person caught in the trap of abortion needs shelter from vindictive stones, loving sympathy and the promise of liberation by grace to sin no more.

Gradations of Value. In the dramatic account of the mother who had one child too many, Kellogg used a calculus of gradations of value. He explained that there were several reasons why she should kill one of her existing children rather than the new baby on the way. The existing children were not very good, talented or creative; and the new baby might be all of these, and saving him might also save the life of the mother. Of course he was using *reductio ad absurdum* argument, and none of the children should have been killed, but he was arguing on the basis of gradations of value.

It is difficult to imagine Kellogg with a large surgical practice without doing a therapeutic abortion. Why did he not openly face this problem, and discuss gradations of value? When a physician decides to sacrifice a totally human baby for the benefit of the mother in a therapeutic abortion, he decides that the developing fetus does not have as much right to life as the mother. He decides

83

by comparing gradations of value. We need to recognize that decisions sometimes have to be made on the basis of gradations of value.

Purposes of Sex. When the Bible likens the relations between Christ and the church to the relation between bridegroom and bride (Rev. 19:7-9), the quality that is emphasized is intimate bonding. It is not true that the exclusive purpose of sex is procreation. Other purposes for sex are the expression of affection and bonding. Both of these purposes help to provide an enduring, stable home in which to nurture the children who are brought into the world. When God reveals the laws of physiology which permit achievement of bonding and expression of affection without jeopardizing the health of the mother with too many pregnancies, these should be used. Contraception is not the same crime as abortion, but a way to avoid the crime of abortion.

When we look at some of Kellogg's problems from the standpoint of his basic presuppositions, they can be solved. If we approach these unsolved problems with his enthusiasm, creativity, and faith, the forces of Life will triumph over denial and death.

Endnotes

[1]J. H. Kellogg, M.D., *Man: the Masterpiece: or Plain Truths Plainly Told, About Boyhood, Youth and Manhood* (Des Moines, Iowa: Condit & Nelson, 1886), 135-150.

[2]*Ibid.*, 135.

[3]*Ibid.*, 138.

[4]Richard William Schwarz, *John Harvey Kellogg: American Health Reformer*, Ph.D. Dissertation (University of Michigan, 1964), 96. Chapter III is entitled, "Biologic Living: The Kellogg 'Gospel of Health.'"

[5]Larkin B. Coles, *Philosophy of Health: Natural Principles of Health and Cure* (Boston: Ticknor, Reed, & Fields, 1853), 216.

[6]James C. Mohr, *Abortion in America: The Origins and Evolution of National Policy, 1800-1900* (New York: Oxford University Press, 1978), 60-164.

[7]Schwarz, 175.

[8]Dores E. Robinson, *The Story of Our Health Message* (Nashville, TN: Southern Publishing Association, 1935), 215. *Health Reformer* (June 1877).

[9]John Harvey Kellogg, *Plain Facts for Old and Young: Embracing the Natural History and Hygiene of Organic Life* (Burlington, Iowa: I. F. Segner, 1890), 511 (cited as PF in the following).

[10]Schwarz, 237.

[11]John Harvey Kellogg, *Ladies' Guide in Health and Disease, Girlhood, Maidenhood, Wifehood, Motherhood,* (Des Moines, Iowa: W. D. Condit & Co., 1884), 672 (cited as LG in the following) and *Man, the Masterpiece: or, Plain Truths Plainly Told, About Boyhood, Youth and Manhood* (Des Moines, Iowa: Condit & Nelson, 1886), 604 (cited as MM in the following).

[12]Schwarz, 233.

[13]LG (1901), 352.

[14]LG, 359.

[15]PF, 477.

[16]MM, 423.

[17]LG, 352.

[18]MM, 425.

[19]MM, 423.

[20]MM, 424.

[21]LG, 359f.

[22]PF, 511f.

[23]LF, 355.

[24]PF, 512.

[25]PF, 472.

[26]PF, 474.

[27]PF, 512.

[28]PF (1882), 116.

[29]PF (1882), 229.

[30]LG (1901), 364.

[31]LG, 342; cf. PF (1882), 217-225, 486, 504; MM (1886), 418.

[32]PF (1890), 502.

[33]LG (1902), 419.

[34]MM (1886), 419.

[35]MM, 426.

[36]LG (1901), 349.

[37]PF (1890), 493.

[38]LG (1901), 350.

[39]PF (1890), 507.

[40]PF (1890), 501.

[41]PF (1980), 503.

[42]LG (1901), 348.

[43]LG (1901), 365.

[44]MM (1886), 424.

[45]LG (1901), 363.

[46]LG (1901), 360f.

[47]PF (1890), 516.

[48]LG (1901), 362

[49]MM (1886), 424.

[50]PF (1890), 515.

[51]LG (1901), 363.

[52]MM (1886), 427.

[53]PF (1890), 510.

[54]PF (1890), 519f.

[55]MM (1886), 424f.

[56]PF (1890), 509.

[57]PF (1890), 498.

[58]Mohr, 30.
[59]*Ibid.*, 26-27.
[60]*Ibid.*, 129.
[61]*Ibid.*, 186.
[62]PF (1890), 520.
[63]LG (1901), 364.
[64]Mohr, 122.
[65]LG (1901), 364.
[66]PF (1890), 520.
[67]LG (1901), 362.
[68]LG (1901), 365.
[69]PF (1890), 520.
[70]PF (1890), 520.
[71]LG (1901), 365.
[72]Schwarz, 199.
[73]LG (1901), 365.
[74]PF (1890), 516-518.
[75]PF (1879), v.
[76]PF (1890), 161.
[77]PF (1890), 162-168.
[78]PF (1890), 503.
[79]LG (1901), 550.
[80]PF (1890), 166.
[81]PF (1890), 67.
[82]LG (1901), 291.
[83]PF (1882), 116.

Part III

Theology and Ethics

6 Immortality of the Soul and the Abortion of the Body

Sydney Allen

The Sanctity of Life

What kind of life is to be treated as sacrosanct, holy, and deserving of reverence and all our efforts to extend, preserve, and enhance it? Microbial life? Cellular life? Botanical life? Zoological life?

There are good reasons to take away the life of some creatures, good reasons to treat some of them as means to an end—a human end—rather than as ends in themselves. It is proper to deprive polio viruses of life in order to prevent disease in our children, to deprive cancer cells of life in order to prevent the pain of metastasis, and to eat tomatoes for their ability to delight and nourish us, but it is nearly always wrong to destroy a human life, especially an innocent one, at any state of its existence.

Human societies have made exceptions to this rule from time to time, holding that general human ends can be threatened by some persons and, that it is more important to serve those general ends than to preserve the life of those threatening human beings. When faced with the option of either (a) seeing innocent persons destroyed or (b) trying to destroy their persecutor first, nearly everyone would agree that (b) is justified in some cases.

Even in the case of a Hitler, a Stalin, or a Pol Pot, however, depriving the culprit of life is not always even prudent, let alone moral. Violence has a way of begetting violence, and a behavioral loop can be formed that is almost impossible to stop. Thus we have the teachings of Jesus against vengeance.

No innocent human being should ever be killed or allowed to die prematurely or unnecessarily. Innocent people, however, may get involved in movements and projects that are not innocent. A certain fetus may, if born into certain situations, cause more pain than pleasure to himself or herself, the parents and siblings, and to mankind in general. A soldier, drafted without his consent, informed or otherwise, may find himself fighting on the wrong side in a wicked, unjust war that his aggressor nation started. An infant whose innocent crying would give away the hiding place of a persecutor's intended victims, may, tragically, be less important to keep alive than the group.

A fetus with a firmly and conservatively diagnosed major defect in the neural tube and its resultant nervous system is plainly innocent. Whether this fetus is a person in the full sense is not so clear. Whether this fetus has the same human rights as a fully developed person is easier to determine. Personhood means more than mere physical viability, actual or potential. To be a person involves having a body, and the fetus obviously has a body; but to be a person also involves certain spiritual qualities such as a normal degree of will, feelings, and intellect. The fetus of a child certain to be born with a body misshapen and caused to malfunction by a neural tube deficit often lacks both these personal qualities and the potential for achieving them.

Some adults, who are breathing and circulating their own blood, are dead mentally and spiritually. I refer not to the brain-dead but to the mind-dead. If their continued life causes them and mankind in general more loss than enhancement of well-being, is it morally justifiable to help them die or even kill them?

No. I answer this way, because I do not believe any of us is in a position to declare that such a person is causing them and us more loss than enhancement of well-being. Why not? Because these people have been active; they have made a personal contribution to the general well-being of family, institution, community, nation, and world, and may be continuing to make such a contribution, by proxy, through the memories they evoke and the example they invoke in the minds of those friends and loved ones who remember them as they once were. This is an intangible but real consideration. It may be an insult to life itself either to help them die or to kill them because, although they have lost nearly all of their intrinsic worth, they still retain enough extrinsic and symbolic worth to obligate us to preserve and enhance their comfort as long as this is feasible (I repeat, I am not speaking of the brain-dead, and especially not the brain-dead who are only breathing and circulating their blood with the help of an appliance).

None of the obligations mentioned in the previous two paragraphs pertain in the case of the rare fetus whose birth poses a threat that is likely to be disastrous to a family.

Human beings are probably the only species with a culture that can be passed on from generation to generation. This is possible for people, because they have a remarkably capacious memory which has been enormously enhanced over the last five millenia by the technologies of writing, printing, and the preservation of documents.

Even though a corpse, or a physically alive but spiritually and mentally dead person, may no longer be capable of thinking, willing, and feeling humanly on his/her own, both the corpse and the mentally dead person are, at least, remembered symbols of a person who once felt, loved, decided, and thought, and this capacity to trigger such memories is precious to the well-being of mankind —indeed, it may be most of what human well-being consists of. It is this capacity that obligates us to treat both the corpse and the mentally dead person with reverence and respect. If we fail to show this respect (if it is feasible), we harm both ourselves and mankind as a whole.

When the bell tolls for any human death, it tolls for us, as fellow image bearers of God. If we treat the dead—whether mentally dead or physically dead or both— with any kind of disrespect, we are depriving ourselves and humanity and God of part of the well-being we and they deserve.

The part of life that we are obligated to treat as sacred, sacrosanct, holy, and with reverence is human and personal life. The part of human, personal life that deserves this tender regard is primarily the spiritual part. When the physical part dies, it disappears, sooner or later, but the spiritual part, in many cases, plainly does not totally disappear from our memories—whether those memories be enhancing or degrading.

Even if one denies the eventual survival of personal, integrated identity, one must admit that when our friends, parents, loved ones, and even enemies die, the spiritual side of their lives continues, somehow, to exist, at least in our memories, and in whatever we want to call the stuff of dreams. In the case of persons whose spiritual lives were beneficent or maleficent enough to trigger their mention in any of our forms of memory—oral, written, folktale, history, or secret personal memory— their reality as influence can actually increase with time.

This is not the case with animals, and it is not the case with fetuses, who are, certainly, less than persons. I say this with all the respect I can muster for them and the feats of which they are capable.

Although the position that (a) allows the abortion of fetuses that are (1) the result of sexual intercourse entered into through rape or incest, or (2) that have been firmly and reliably diagnosed as the bearers of serious, crippling, and care-demanding congenital defects, but that (b) disapproves of abortions for (1) convenience, (2) birth or population control, or (3) cowardice or sloth toward parenthood, may, indeed, be the majority position in this society, it is not the only one, and we must take into account the contrary position.

The Basis for the Absolutist Anti-Abortion View

It is the contention of this paper that the absolutist position that would ban all abortions is based, philosophically, on the shaky notion of the innate immortality of the human soul.[1]

We are speaking here primarily of certain Roman Catholic, Mormon, and other Christian believers who, either consciously or by default, go back to a decree of the Fifth Lateran Council in the Roman Catholic Church from 1512-1517.

An Italian Renaissance philosopher, Pietro Pomponazvi (1462-1525), claimed (correctly, I think) that the arguments of Plato and others attempting to prove the dogma of human immortality were fallacious. If, he argued, one wished to believe in immortality, one had to base that belief on Scripture.

The Pope at the time of the Fifth Lateran, the famous Leo X of the Florentine banking family of De Medici, soon to excommunicate Martin Luther, labeled teachings similar to Pomponazvi's an error at the Fifth Lateran Council and decreed that innate immortality was to be taught as a philosophically necessary dogma to all Catholics. In this he got his way.

In line with this tradition, today's Roman Catholics and, increasingly, fundamentalist Protestants, can be heard to assert that from the first moment of conception a human life contains an immortal soul, that is, a crucial, non-bodily, separable element of human personality which is divinely infused into the body at the moment the sperm penetrates the egg.

Starting from this dogma, aborting a human conceptus or fetus at any point has to be seen as wrongful. On that premise the situation and consequences that precede and follow the abortion cannot change its moral status.

Protestant fundamentalists, whose religious roots go back to the Puritanism of 1540-1660 in Great Britain, may not be aware that "mortalism," as Professor Christopher Hill describes it, was taken seriously by many of the ancestors of today's Baptists, Congregationalists, and Presbyterians. How did this happen?

A central controversy in the religious turmoil of the period before and after the English Civil War (1640-1660) swirled around the question of what kind of church the Church of England should be.

As a result of decisions arrived at in the Lambeth Articles of 1595, confirmed in 1618 by the acceptance of the articles of the Synod of Dort, the Church of England was firmly on record as having embraced John Calvin's theology. In the name of that theology and the egalitarian clergy and polity exemplified by the Calvinist Church of Scotland, the English Parliament went to war and temporarily won control of England from King Charles I and his pro-episcopal supporters. And, as we know, Parliament (unwisely we now see) executed both the Puritan-eating Archbishop Laud and King Charles I.

Winning a revolution is one thing. Deciding who is going to run things afterward is another. The army ran things in England and Wales for years after the English Civil War, and the General who most frequently commanded obedience from that army on military matters was Oliver Cromwell.

The Puritan armies had been, between battles, a gigantic series of Bible camps—John Bunyan was one of the campers—that fostered discussion of every aspect of Church life. Out of these furious conferences came parties that favored reforms far more radical than the mere egalitarianizing of clergy and abolishing of bishops.

Cromwell allied himself with one of these radical groups, the Independents, whom we know as Congregationalists. As his Latin Secretary he appointed the greatest of the English evangelical poets, John Milton, and held conferences with the likes of Roger Williams of Rhode Island, when that gentleman was in London. As is well known, Milton was a mortalist, and not alone in that persuasion. What is sometimes ignored is the story behind the story of the split that rent the Congregationalists both in England and America over who was qualified to be a member of a true Church.

Under standard Roman Catholic, Episcopal and Calvinist arrangements, every child born to Christians had to be baptized as an infant and thus became a potential communicant. In the Catholic view the matter and form of baptism were believed to act savingly, *ex opere operato,* on the child's immortal soul, largely bypassing his/her will, feelings, and intellect, such as they are during the first weeks of life.

Whether this ancient but dubious practice of infant baptism was scriptural, wise, or evangelistically productive was argued far into the night, endlessly, in all the territory controlled by Roundhead forces. Argued, we might add, by people who were frequently being called to put their lives on the line for the difference between their opinions and those of the King and the Church of England's bishops.

Some of the Congregationalists in America and England—whose party became the Baptists—were passionately opposed to the inclusion of nominal Christians, whose beliefs and behavior were often openly less than devout and observant, in Church of England membership. In their view, the inclusion of such people bred hypocrisy, and they argued that this sort of thing was inevitable as long as the decision on whether to join the church was made (a) before a baby was born and (b) before the baby could possibly have a religious experience and (c) by someone other than the baby.

Roger Williams of Rhode Island was one of the most eloquent of these, although he paused only briefly at the position around which the Baptist offshoot of Congregationalism clustered. He became so radical that he taught, for most of his life, that there were no true churches on earth and that there would be none until the Second Advent.

This Baptist position, namely, that no one should have his or her religion marked on his or her forehead as a newborn, and that only an informed consent gives meaning to church membership, has become one of the most influential ideas in subsequent religion. Martin Marty has spoken of the "Baptistification" of modern religion. In my opinion the ban on infant baptism contains within it the seeds from which have grown the non-absolutist position on abortion that seems to be accepted by most Americans these days.

The Baptists and their theological cousins symbolized their notion that churches ought to be self-gathered adults, not legally franchised parishes, by banning all modes of baptism except immersion, a mode that was not practical for infants. The Baptists went on to argue that it was ludicrous to imagine that the duties and obligations of church membership were possible for infants.

Wait until the child knows what she or he is doing, they argued, and then baptize only those who, with convincing sincerity, petition the minister for the rite.

The key appeal the Baptists made was that by becoming a Baptist you joined a church where membership meant something. It meant that you had joined freely and without duress, that you had given your consent after pondering the evidence (the Enlightenment rejection of arranged marriages, and preference for "marriages of love" without parental intervention, followed the same logic with—alas!—less praiseworthy results).

The Decline of Innatism

The doctrine that confines baptism to responsible persons implies that fetuses—occasionally baptized even when dead by Roman Catholics—as well as neonates and children whose cognitive development is not up to choosing for or against a lifetime commitment have, at those early stages of life, fewer human rights than full persons. This position makes one more amenable to an argument that, for instance, the abortion of the fetus known to bear the phenotype for Tay-Sachs disease, while tragic and not to be entered into lightly, may well be within the will of God.

Belief in an immortal soul divinely infused into the blastocyst supports the conclusion that causing or allowing such a life to die is wicked even if that life is structurally flawed by a blurred, Tay-Sachs genetic map that leads nowhere but to death.

God may not intentionally make garbage, and it would be both misanthropic and ugly to describe any fetus or neonate as such, but the genetics and physiology of reproduction plus the sometimes-bad fortunes of life result in the production of a certain percentage of malformed fetuses. Built-in devices naturally and spontaneously discard these fetuses in considerable numbers. If God is Creator, He must be responsible for having installed such devices in His imagebearers.

If, with our current ability to predict phenotypes of genetic disorders that virtually guarantee mental and physical disabilities for the child that can, in turn, create a kind of prison for the child's parents and siblings, people in the tradition of latent but unrealized immortality can, without holding contradictory views, support the mother, the father, and the physician who intentionally abort that fetus so the couple can try again to produce a whole and healthy child.

I believe that nearly all biblically informed Christian hearts are warmed by the hope of immortality, but not all of them take this to be something infused at conception.

There are, of course, people, even Christians, who do not believe in life after death. To them the difference between innate immortality and the view I am espousing may seem trivial.

It is probably too late to do anything about one conventional terminology for our brand of "mortalism," namely "conditional immortality." An objection might well be made to turn this phrase on the grounds that it makes it seem as though one's obedience to the law of God is the chief cause of one's getting immortality. To avoid giving this impression, one can speak of "latent immortality" which becomes actual after the resurrection of the saints at the second Advent.[2]

Resurrection, Not Innate Immortality

A little-known achievement of biblical scholarship in the last century has shown that the notion of innate, but not latent, immortality has weak foundations in the Judaeo-Christian tradition.

The Old Testament is practically silent on the subject. Its view has to be deduced more by the methods of the anthropologist than from any explicit didactics on the subject.

Although the New Testament contains many references to the resurrection of the body, and fixes it at the core of the church's beliefs, it contains two or three passages in which the Pauline writings wobble off in a semi-Platonic direction.

The weight of evidence in the whole Pauline corpus is that these latter Platonic passages are mere noddings or oversights, and that the tendency of his thought is in the opposite direction, namely toward resurrection into immortality, not lifelong possession of it.

The popular notion that the Bible teaches the innate immortality of the soul seems indelibly written on many minds. This makes Christians and Jews a people divided against themselves on abortion at a time when those who are misusing *Roe v. Wade* as a license for unwarranted prophylaxis need to be dealt with by united ranks of Christians who are determined to save whatever is left of the family and decent human community life from this and other threats.

To try to deal with abortion problems without dealing with the stumbling block of innate immortality would be like trying to deal with a plague of moths while ignoring their caterpillars. I confess to being pessimistic about the chances of changing many minds on this subject.

People falsely think that one must either believe (a) that the soul is immortal from conception onwards or (b) that the human body is just tissues that disappear with decay.

We need not be caught on either horn of this false dilemma. We can pass through them with an intermediate position. Rather than a separable soul, it is consistent both with Scripture and with reason to hold that man possesses a unique potential for responsible and loving addressability by God and his fellow human beings that can be appropriately called "latent," not "innate" immortality.

The picture on the film inside the camera is latent until the developing chemicals bring it out. The immortal person is latent in the fetus, but the fetus is not yet a person. Because it is latently immortal we must treat the fetus with great reverence, respect, and protectiveness, but this does not give it the same human rights as its mother or father or siblings.

The latency view has no need for the hypothesis of infusion of some entity at conception. Neither is it necessary to claim that some part of the person escapes at death. Both of these adjuncts to the innatist view probably had something to do with anxiety over maintaining the monopoly position the medieval church held over religious life.

The latentist view prizes the human conceptus, from its inception, above every other earthly object save a human person, and teaches that the virtues developed in the person during his or her earthly life are the result of God's gracious gifts that can qualify the receiver for immortal life, and save him or her both from annihilation and nihilism.

But immortalists from both the Christian and the Enlightenment viewpoint

(Kant) have argued that, without the notion of quick judgment in either heaven or hell soon after death, people will not take moral imperatives seriously. One strongly suspects that many of the advocates of a quick heaven/hell journey are less convinced of its truth than they make out to be. They seem, at times, to be mouthing the belief in the hope that it will keep the servants out of the silver. It is a kind of leash to keep the infantile from straying.

The latent immortality tradition's reply to that claim unites many Christians with some secularists. What, we ask, happens to the morals of the poor, scared peasant if and when he stops to ponder the morals of a God who puts people into everlasting torture to pay them for a few decades of imperfect living?

Thomas Hobbes, who looked at the Puritans of his time the way Joseph McCarthy looked at the Ivy League Socialists of his, said that "it is natural and so reasonable, for each individual to aim solely at his own preservation or pleasure" (*Leviathan*, chapters 14 and 15). Unscrupulous religious leaders have always known how to take advantage of this real, but not universal, tendency to selfishness.

The Enlightenment centered one of its most passionate critiques of folk Catholicism on the proneness of great world religions to degenerate into a funeral racket.

Nowhere is the irrelevance of a mere fire escape to a deeply moral religion to be seen more clearly than in the myth of Don Juan, the lecher who laughs in the face of moralists, and hops, gleefully unrepentant, into the flames of hell with the same huge laugh that had disgraced the bedrooms of his thousands of paramours.

Mozart reflects this Enlightenment critique when, in "The Magic Flute," he has his chief pair of characters tested to see whether they are more afraid of passing through flames than of doing wrong. They show themselves more afraid of doing wrong and are found worthy.

Time has proven, I believe, that the doctrine of innate immortality and its entailments such as original sin and everlasting hell have done more to discourage than to encourage Judeo-Christian faith.

How could one possibly bring oneself to worship and show gratitude to a great Torturer in the Sky who keeps his victims alive so they can feel the pain forever?

Along with that wonderful Catholic, Evelyn Waugh, I would argue that the notion that God is some kind of horrible torturer is self-contradictory. To assert that the constitution of the universe is malignant is meaningless. Malignant compared to what?

The moral liability entailed by the notion of God as Everlasting Torturer does not afflict the latent immortality view.

But does the latent immortality view enforce morality and encourage virtue in common folk? Yes, it does. As evidence I put forth the works of John Bunyan, one of the sweetest, most heaven-enraptured souls this world has seen, but not a man his acquaintances could fairly describe as overly permissive or naive. He and we hold that God is just and that, because of this, anti-human conduct will be punished proportionately and finally, and the virtue that is the product of faith will also be rewarded proportionately.

God is just, but He is also compassionate, not in some watery and predictable way, but in the way Wolfgang Mozart, Giuseppe Verdi, and Louis Hector Berlioz portrayed in their Requiems. He is too just and too compassionate to sentence a malefactor to an eternity of pain for a few decades of misbehavior, and for the same reason He will not let malefactors go scot-free.

Both Plato and Kant came down on the side of belief in immortality, but, insofar as I understand them, do not insist on the innateness view. So they are neither help nor hindrance to our choice between the latent and innate positions.

Nothing in what we have said can be correctly construed, so far as our intentions are concerned, as justification for lighthearted abortions for the sake of birth or population control, economy, or mere convenience.

The awful choice between outlawing all abortions, as the innatists wish us to do, and a laissez-faire attitude toward all of them need not be taken by the latent immortalist believer. It is consistent with this position to open a middle way for abortions in cases of rape, incest, and firmly diagnosed disabling defects, while continuing to oppose the misuse of this seldom justified fail-safe.

Endnotes

[1]John Locke may have been influenced, consciously or unconsciously, toward his empiricist epistemology that denied the existence of innate ideas by the arguments pro and con of the Baptist position which had to deny the existence of an innately immortal soul susceptible to religious change by the waters of infant baptism without the conscious acceptance or compliance of the subject.

[2]The Adventist tradition acquired the doctrine of conditional immortality through the ministry of a Millerite preacher, George Storrs, who got the belief out of a tract written by Henry Grew. I have not yet learned who the principal patron of the doctrine among the SDAs may have been. Ultimately, one imagines, the roots of the teaching go back to John Milton and his companions, and, one further imagines, to Pomponazvi.

7 Abortion and Adventist Interpretation: Significant Theological Themes

Ginger Hanks-Harwood

Abortion

Few issues in the field of bioethics elicit as much concern, conflict or consternation as does abortion. Both the degree of emotional intensity which permeates the discussion and the epic proportions of its incidence earmark abortion as a topic worthy of meticulous, conscientious consideration. Most significantly, the human anguish surrounding each incident represented in the statistics mandates the engagement of Christian ethicists in the issue.

The mere numbers of abortions performed in the United States in the last five years indicate that our society has engendered a situation necessitating principled reflection and scrupulous remediation if what is being referred to in some quarters as "the American Holocaust" is to cease. For the morally sensitive, the current situation reflects enormous tragedy. The tragedy, however, is not confined to the loss endured by the individuals who are denied the privilege of birth, but rather extends and is magnified in those who inhabit this culture.

The tragedy begins when women are socialized to view their own sexuality passively and naively, believing that the assumption of contraceptive responsibility indicates promiscuity. It is magnified in those who do not take their own personhood seriously enough to perceive the emotional and spiritual damage done by permitting sexual intimacy without the benefit of emotional commitment and support. It is certainly heightened when women become pregnant carelessly, not caring sufficiently for themselves either to define their own boundaries protectively (to refuse sexual intimacy with partners unwilling to take mutual responsibility for birth control and the parenting that potentially arises from intimacy) or to appreciate women's unique ability to procreate. The focus of the tragedy shifts only slightly when it involves women who have been contraceptively responsible, or those who have been the victims of unwilling sexual violation, and have become the carriers of a life they feel they cannot support.[1]

Ultimately, women involved in abortion carry the physical, spiritual and emotional scarring associated with the process. While for some, the grief, loss and guilt may be more sublimated than for others, the decision to abort has long-term consequences for women.

At this juncture, our society has scarcely begun to consider the scope and magnitude of the tragedy. The complexities of the abortion question require that we as ethicists employ the full range of our resources (careful reasoning, moral sensitivity and theological reflection) if we are to shed light on the current dialogue.

If abortion is apprehended as the augury of tragedy in the universe, then the woman in this decision-making position must be regarded as a key figure within a morality play. As such, her struggles personify the human predicament, the search for the human and redemptive response to the tragic. While her role in this drama cannot be abrogated, nor the cup removed, the art of the ethicist may be beneficially employed to ameliorate some of her existential anguish. The church, adopting a posture reminiscent of Aaron supporting Moses' arms, may identify theological and spiritual resources that will strengthen and nurture the protagonist.

The Seventh-day Adventist Church, with its deep regard for the Bible as the revelation of both sacred history and divine intent towards humanity, is not without ground on which to stand while endeavoring to serve as a vehicle of love and grace to men and women faced with moral dilemmas. In the past, the church has addressed moral quandary (i.e., issues of slavery, participation in war, etc.) boldly, based on faith in the applicability of scriptural principles and the continued revelation and presence of God in the midst of the church community. It has been our practice to address moral concerns after a diligent review of relevant Scriptural texts. The Adventist exegetical style and practice has ever been to understand the Scriptures in their original integrity, and then to apply their great spiritual lessons to current situations. In conformity to this tradition, this chapter will attempt to probe the question of abortion.

Identification of Pertinent Biblical Themes and Motifs

A substantial part of the moral landscape of the Adventist world view is established by the serious manner in which we regard the Genesis rendition of our beginnings and high calling.[2] The book of beginnings clearly provides the foundation for essential themes which are replayed, explored and amplified throughout the rest of Scripture. The first three chapters of Genesis are particularly crucial as they introduce the human actors into the drama as children springing from the hand of God, enspirited and gifted by God's own breath and intention, as well as being a record of the memories of our earliest interactions with God and each other.

Within the narrative of those chronicles we find the story of God's gifting of humanity: the sacred bestowal of a set of rights and privileges that set human beings apart from all other created orders. In essence, the gifts given defined the nature of human existence and translated into the commission and authorization to inhabit and oversee the creation. These bequests, dispensed over an unspecified period of time, included the gift of life, the gift of stewardship over creation, the gift of moral choice, the gift of responsibility, the gift of death and the gift of redemption. These endowments were the legacy and inheritance of the children of God, given to equip and empower them for a difficult and uncertain journey. The meaning and implications of these gifts provide not only the preeminent motifs woven through the rest of Scripture (a collection of narratives focusing on the human struggle to find meaning and wholeness in the face of chaos and grief), but the resources to be utilized when we face situations which tax our ability to generate moral clarity.

The Gift of Life

According to the Genesis account, the intrinsic value of human life derives from our origin as the children of God.[3] Designed with a distinctive incarnational form characterized by a coalescence of physical, psycho-emotional, social and spiritual components, humans were bequeathed time and space and being. The gift was to allow us to experience the being of God as we encountered the cosmos and became collaborators with God in defining and structuring the world through our own creativity, community and procreation.

The gift of life was a sacred gift, because it directly reflected the will of God for humanity. In accordance with that will, life was never a behest meant to benefit some passive "recipient," but to provide the basis for active engagement with the creation, that by being gifted we might in turn gift.

The Gift of Stewardship

The story records that the gift of stewardship was given at the very inception of our habitation.[4] We were adjured to exercise guardianship over the creation, to become conversant with every creature that we might know both its name and its necessities, to be ready to intervene on the behalf of that which has no voice. The commission of stewardship endowed us with lordship, the right and the responsibility to determine how the limited resources of a finite planet could be utilized most responsibly to protect, preserve and augment the quality of life. Christ's parables imply that the duty of the steward goes beyond the mere conservation of the original trust to the actual enhancement and augmentation of the award. The gift of stewardship, and our satisfaction of that commission, was designed to give structure and meaning to our occupancy of the planet and assist us in experiencing the character and nature of God. By exercising God's duties after God, we were to be brought into closer communion with God.

The Gift of Moral Choice

Genesis 2 indicates that moral choice was a gift accorded to humanity from the very beginning. The tree of the knowledge of good and evil was placed with the tree of life in the very center of the garden, as continual choice was a central part of being morally free, and being morally free was essential to our design as image of God. The unfathomable import of freedom to choose was demonstrated by God's maintaining its necessity at the cost of the life and death of Jesus Christ.[5] While eating from the forbidden tree opened our eyes to the destructive potential of our power, the right to choose our life was not rescinded. Knowing the end from the beginning, God chose to suffer the consequences of misused freedom rather than to abrogate humanity's moral agency.

The Gift of Responsibility

In essence a corollary of moral choice, the gift of responsibility was evidenced by the real results of the human decisions and actions recorded in the Genesis story. Our choice of conduct has future implications; the reverberations released by each action come back to us. As beings who make decisions, we are both blessed and afflicted by responsibility. As Joseph Pieper once noted, "No one can be deputized to take the responsibility which is the inseparable companion of decision."[6]

Ellen G. White speaks of the noticeable cooling of the atmosphere, the drooping flowers and the falling leaves as the first signs of the decay that set in after the fall: the earnest of the consequences of the catastrophic decision.[7]

She records their sincere desire to return to the original state, yet the impossibility of turning back the clock: the results were real. Once they had acted, the actions were not subject to recall. They tasted the savor of the amalgam of power and impotence that is the essence of human action: the power to affect and sculpt the future by our choice of actions and simultaneously consequences of those actions. From each action emerge new patterns and forms which inhabit the moral landscape of our existence: new decisions are needed to deal with the issues from previous choices.

The Gift of Death

In a creation marred by sin, death was the generous gift of a loving Creator who provided limits on what any one person or being might be asked to endure. It addressed the temporary nature of the hold sin had gained over the creation, denying and defying those malevolent forces which would assault the spirit by taking captive and torturing the body. It established bounds on the amount of time any individual suffered the consequences of even his or her own destructive actions.

The Gift of Redemption

The plan laid "before the foundation of the world," redemption was God's active grace interceding in the lives of individual humans.[8] This plan recognized the essentially flawed character of post-fall humanity, its limitations, fallibility, proclivity towards myopic morality, propensity towards self-deception and spiritual amnesia, and extended a salvific response. Without discounting the odious character of sin, God provided hope for the sinner (i.e., the human race). Taking on himself the final consequences of sin, Jesus offered the certitude that His grace is sufficient answer to our condition. We have the assurance of God's presence with us in the midst of our struggle to identify the appropriate course, striving to reveal the secrets of the heart. While human judgment fails to discern the good, the right and the fitting in many cases, we also have God's grace and forgiveness. Only this allows a race of sinners who retain the vestiges of moral sensitivity to act boldly in the face of ethical quagmires and incomplete information.

We have no guarantees that even the most deliberate application of our principles and values to our life situations and our moral dilemmas will generate adequate or sufficient responses. Humility mandates that we recognize that we know only in part, that we see through a glass darkly, that we are culturally, socially and personally deceived. Faith mandates that we recognize God's response as sufficient to cover the gap. In essence, it is the gift of redemption that frees us from the paralysis of inadequacy and guilt that would overtake us and render us incapable of exercising the moral agency accorded to us. It is, in fact, this gift that frees us to enjoy all the endowments bequeathed to us in those early days.

Application

As Seventh-day Adventists begin to meditate on these scriptural themes, each one of which has been richly developed within the Spirit of Prophecy and denominational literature in general, a faith response to the phenomenon of abortion can be generated. It must be as many-faceted as the issue itself and as true to our ecclesiastical charge to participate in the healing of the nations as the building of hospitals and medical-education facilities has been. Most crucially, it must reflect the role the church has been given in the great controversy: it must reveal the presence and goodness of God, the love of God for the beleagured human race.[9]

The approach we make to the question must be that of the Great Physician, the great Lover of souls. As such, the motivating impulse behind any church statement must be to articulate to the community the concern of God for those touched by this issue. It is for us to express the necessity of remembering the great value God places on human beings and God's passion for our wholeness and well-being. We must reflect the singular objective manifested by Christ's life: the incarnation of the good news of God's healing presence in our midst. Our mission, in continuity and congruence with Christ's, is to bring healing to a fractured and aching world. We participate in this process by articulating the necessity of church response to the situation, assisting in the formulation of the response, and providing advocacy for those who might become faceless or voiceless during the formulation process.

Our first premise must be that human life, as a gift of God, is always precious and sacred.[10] This will be the first principle to be consulted before any ethical decision is made. Is a certain decision harmonious with respect to both the giver of life and the gift? How may the principle of sanctity of life best be ratified in this situation? Ultimately, however, this argument will only be as convincing as we are: If we do not treat the poor, the despised, the handicapped, and the criminal as a valued part of our community, then the rest will be regarded as rhetoric. Only a consistent program of exertion to extend grace to the undervalued and to augment respect for the living creatures of the earth will render us credible witnesses with a right to pontificate on the inviolability of the gift.

The emphasis on the sanctity of life will lead us to a position of marked conservatism vis-a-vis the practice of abortion.[11] It will be our underlying premise that abortion is a sign of failure within the human community, a cipher attesting to the tragedy of our fallen state and the plight which has subsequently evolved. As Jesus once observed concerning divorce, "In the beginning, it was not so." We cannot help but be moved to sadness and compassion for both the fetus and the mother. We cannot help but abhor the situation. Moral sensitivity and Christian compassion dictate that we mourn the great loss represented by each abortion and be prepared to intervene where we may to prevent such tragedy and to facilitate healing among its survivors.

At the same time, we must also recognize the duty of stewardship granted as a right and obligation, as an essentially defining quality, and our duty to respect the divine charge given to each human. Every woman—and every man—has been made steward over his or her own physical resources. Both humility and faithfulness to the creation story require that we acknowledge the integrity of each individual, that we do not abrogate their stewardship by attempting to enforce our perspective on them.[12] Rather, we must defer to each person's sovereignty within his or her own domain, and assign to God the right to censure and convict of wrongdoing in cases of abuse.

For the woman who is considering becoming pregnant or the woman for whom pregnancy has catastrophic overtones, stewardship is exercised through a careful examination of the resources which she has at her disposal to bring the pregnancy to successful culmination and the baby to spirit-filled adulthood. While crystal balls are anathema (to say nothing of unreliable) and Christianity is a walk of daily revelation rather than oracle, a woman is not without capacity to weigh the judiciousness of a particular pregnancy. While she may not know the calamitous (or serendipitous) events which may unfold in the future, she can assess her present condition. She may well be able to ascertain whether she has the physical health to sustain a pregnancy, and have outlined to her the impact a decision to gestate a child or take care of it after it arrived would have on her body. She may have the information as to her own psychological stamina, and the effect (or risk) that a pregnancy (or additional child) would have on her ability to function productively. Finally, far better than anyone else in the situation, she may consciously or intuitively know the reverberation the pregnancy would have on her familial and social community. She may be able to evaluate the support she will receive both during and after the pregnancy, and whether that will be sufficient to bring a sacred being into the world and guide it.

As female physiology designates women as the door to human embodiment, it is women to whom the stewardship of population has ultimately been assigned. While this does not nullify male procreative responsibility, the final decision has been placed with women. In this way women, just as they must appraise their personal, familial and spiritual resources and how those need to be allocated, must also evaluate the capacity of the society and the earth to welcome new additions to the human population. The conduct of stewardship will necessitate painful decisions as women realistically survey the finite resources of the community and the demands that specific additions (i.e., children with severe physical handicaps) would make on those resources, as well as the impossibility of providing for a limitless potential number of new humans. Women, through the execution of their role in procreation, assume a distinct and peculiar custodianship of the earth.

The moral mandate of choice decrees that women cannot be passive observers in the grand drama. Rather, each woman must make the choices (and bear the ensuing responsibility) with respect to her generativity as well as to everything else. Whether she comes to the threshold of maternity after intentional assessment of her desire and ability to embrace parenthood only to be confronted with a pregnancy which threatens her life or exceeds her capacity to provide care, or as a result of violation, self-abasement or neglect, each woman must make a choice, exercise her obligation as an endowed moral agent. In making that choice, whatever the actual choice is, she reflects the will of God towards her as a human being in that she has functioned as a moral actor, she has assumed agency for her destiny and procreativity.

It is easy to critique the obvious lack of self-awareness and personal respect demonstrated by the woman who approaches abortion as a "quick fix" to a situation engendered by delinquent sexuality. Neither her attitudes nor her actions seem congruent with sensitivity to the moral dimensions involved. While she may seem an unlikely candidate for adequately processed ethical decision-making, the gift of choice remains hers to exercise. With her alone stands the final decision on how she will utilize the temple given, whether to her glory or her destruction, as a stronghold of the Spirit or the defiled shell of a dwelling place.

Perhaps it is central to God's plan that those who make the choices bear the consequences, as women most certainly do in the case of abortion. Abortion, while posing less physical risk (if done under proper medical circumstances) than full-term pregnancy and delivery, still poses several threats to the well-being of women. The first is that of possible infection and other gynecological complications which may result in future sterility. Repeated abortion, even without infection, significantly increases the chances of sterility or miscarriage in a future, planned pregnancy. The elimination of one's potential to reproduce and thereby effect biological continuation of their family line, to create a concrete expression of the love shared between a man and a woman, or to participate in the wonders of gestational development is a heavy price many women pay for choosing abortion.

The physical scarring is only a material manifestation of the emotional and psychological scars borne by women who have taken this path. Awareness of the intense need for grief counseling for women who have been through this trauma is just beginning to dawn within the therapeutic community. Anorexia and suicide are only the more dramatic manifestations of the depression, anxiety, grief and sense of loss that are typical residual effects of abortion.[13] The loss of any child is a significant event in the life of a woman, and in the case of abortion the death is not simply mourned; it is complicated by doubts as to the ultimate validity of the decision, its reflection on a woman's maternal qualities, its impact on the woman's position within her faith community and with God, and the goodness of intimacy. Whatever else abortion is, it is not "an easy way out" or "a way to escape the consequences of sexuality" any more than pregnancy itself is a punishment for sexual expression.

Women's lives are shaped and permanently sculpted by their generativity and the decisions they must make around it. Pregnancy, whether one's first or fifth, always augurs change, transition and peril for women. For those who receive the news in circumstances where we cannot provide adequate prenatal care (those addicted to drugs, who are alcoholic or diseased, or simply too poor or ignorant to access proper nutritional and medical input), the jeopardy is immediately transferred to the child. In many of these cases, there is no opportunity to gestate a holy thing in the image of God. The only thing we can produce at such a point is formed in the image of our own brokenness, suffering and shame.

Pregnancy finds some of us outside of a committed relationship, or in a relationship marked by abuse, degradation and violence. Our resources are consumed by efforts to survive or to protect other family members (perhaps even other children). We have not discovered enough love for ourselves to nurture even the holy within ourselves, and are not likely to bring the baby into the world enveloped in a wrap of love. We know that any child we bear will have received nine months of trial, trauma and distress that may have chemically altered the very physiology of its existence.[14] For others of us who have carefully stewarded our own resources and would seem to be ideal candidates for maternity, the pregnancy of our dreams is transformed into a nightmare when it is discovered that the baby we carry is incompatible with life.

In addition to these cases, there are those of us who become pregnant because we are small or very young and do not know of our right to say no to a stepfather, brother, uncle, or family friend, or have a brutal and forced sexual encounter with a stranger or former friend. While these situations are very dissimilar in many ways, they have at least two things in common: each points to the great discrepancy between God's intention for humanity when procreativity was given as a gift and the circumstances we experience in the fallen creation, and in the wounding nature of the experience.

The gift, once bequeathed so that we might experience the joy of creating new physical life, has transmuted into a curse. That which was given to put us in communion with God alienates us not only from God but from our lovers, our families, our community, and even ourselves. The choices we are confronted with are not between good and evil, but only between bad and worse.

It is to this situation that redemption, the one gift that cannot be perverted to work our destruction, must be applied. Where human beings are required to make moral decisions that exceed our ken, where it is impossible to know fully the ramifications of the choices involved, we are left with the mandate to assume our responsibility and make a choice, and let God assume responsibility for bringing something salvific out of the experience. The promise "My grace is sufficient unto thee" functions to allow us to retain the vestiges of God's original plan for humanity: we utilize the agency given so that we remain moral actors in the universe.

When a decision whether or not to disrupt a pregnancy must be made, or has been made, there is always opportunity for self-doubt and recrimination, as the possibility of misjudgment or self-deception is an ever-present side effect of human fallibility. Without the intervention of divine grace, the mediation of the Spirit, the wounding of the soul may occur continuously for many years. The recognition of our own inadequacy to preside over such decisions, and the verity that our decisions are frequently the product of myopia, confusion and pain, may be the first step in healing the wound. The knowledge that our insufficiency has been compassionately recognized and provided for by the Creator gives us permission to forgive ourselves for the fallibility that characterizes our fallen state.

The Specific Case

In most cases, women come to the church for support and counsel long after the decision has been made as to whether or not to bring a pregnancy to term.

In those cases we can listen to the story and act as a witness against that which has brought pain and injury into the woman's life. We can provide her with a new framework from which to view her story, reacquainting her with the biblical themes that might bring clarity and offer salvation. Most significantly, we can stand in the place of Christ, pointing her to the great Lover of souls, the master plan for wholeness, and the unfathomable value of her own life.

In those rare opportunities which present themselves where a decision has not yet been made, we can stand with a woman making her decision. In our presence she will see herself reflected as the treasured moral agent that she is. Without trying to abrogate her own process, we will provide information and appropriate questions to facilitate her examination of her options. As it has been labored throughout the chapter, the theme of the gifts will be helpful in our endeavor to furnish her with theological structure to support her as she formulates her response.

We may begin with helping her envision the significance of pregnancy itself: woman is a life-giver, a co-creator with God. As such, the decision to bring a person into the world is a sacred one and the pregnancy a sacred interval in which she is participating in a mystery with God.[15] The decision to participate in such a project is not to be undertaken lightly, and is not without serious and lifelong effects.

The decision to embrace maternity as a God-given gift is one which only she can make for herself, and needs to be done on the basis of realistic assessment of her own resources. Does she possess the reserves required to complete the project adequately, so that she is not like the poor stewards whom Jesus chided for not counting the cost before the project was undertaken and so ended up in disaster? What is her own situation, and what are the specific needs of the child she would carry?

As the woman gains clarity regarding the task at hand, and the range of her resources, she increasingly understands the significance of her choice. She faces the responsibility creation entails and the consequences of accepting or denying that privilege. She experiences herself as an actor, a moral agent in the universe, making decisions which shape not only her own temporal life but the eternal destiny of others. She samples divinity and humanity simultaneously, as she recognizes her human limitations and the enduring significance of the decision she must make. For many, the conflict would be unconscionable if it were not for the assurance of God's presence and grace with the decision-maker.

In all of this, the ethicist has been true to the calling to identify the good, the right and the fitting, as he/she has ever acted out of a paradigm which respects and declares allegiance to the Creator while facilitating the healing of creation. As compassion and esteem are evinced towards the human decision-maker, the nature of God has been revealed steadfastly. The ethicist has played his or her own role faithfully, ever loyal to the vision of humans as free and responsible moral agents. In assisting a woman to work through the decision-making process, the ethicist has participated in her moral education and development.

The Ethical Challenge of Abortion

All too frequently we center a discussion of abortion around the question of whether or not it is moral to decide to take the life of a fetus and ignore the larger issue and context: Why are these large numbers of unplanned and disastrous pregnancies occurring, and why is abortion so often seized as the solution of choice? Without attention to these subjects, we can offer only "band-aid" solutions to women wounded by this choice.

If nothing else, the high incidence of abortion should alert us to the presence of a serious moral deficit within the community: life is not being perceived as sacred. If life is being handled callously, with little regard by women faced with an unexpected pregnancy, where is that attitude stemming from? What in our culture has prepared them to dismiss life so cavalierly? What is functioning to deaden our perceptions to the value and priority that is rightfully accorded human life? How may we bolster communal awareness of the inestimable value of human beings?

How does it happen that so many women are in a position where abortion seems to be the only viable response to their pregnancy? Are there environmental hazards that need to be alleviated so that fewer babies suffer from major birth defects? Are there economic conditions that make the assumption of the responsibility of a new life untenable for numbers of women? Are there social conditions and sanctions which actively discourage women from bringing a child into the community?

Where are the males who participated in these conceptions and where is their sense of responsibility for the financial, emotional and spiritual well-being of these children? Why is the outrage over the abortion question so rarely directed towards males for their lack of procreative planning and responsibility?

We must take another step behind these questions and begin to ask why there are so many unexpected pregnancies to begin with. Why are such large numbers of young women in particular demonstrating such profound neglect of personal stewardship? What is lacking in our preparation of these women for adulthood that they enter without the intuition or instinct to cherish themselves, to avoid facing maternity without adequate social, financial and emotional support? Why do they value their own persons so little that they fail to set appropriate boundaries? Where and how do we need to work to express the sacred value of women?

Finally, a concern for the sanctity of life that terminates its activism once the fetus has been gestated and entered the world has to qualify as something less than dedication to Divine principles. If we do not demonstrate our devotion to life through dynamic intervention wherever life is depreciated, our pro-life stance vis-a-vis fetuses will lack credibility. If our voices are not raised on behalf of the homeless, the victims of abuse or discrimination, the handicapped, the dispossessed and the social lepers, if our energies do not follow the articulated position of the value of every human life, then we have little clarity to share with the woman considering abortion.

The challenge of abortion is a challenge to the depth of our commitment to the sanctity of life, to the paradigm of the Creator for humanity, and to the message of radical grace in a fallen world. The epidemic proportions of abortion serve as a cipher: if we can read the handwriting on the wall, we can both diagnose and treat the malaise. It requires, however, a passionate desire to participate in the healing of the creation that includes but exceeds the practice of binding the wounds originating from unwanted or unworkable pregnancy and abortion. The task entails pushing back the cultural forces and attitudes which blind and enslave women to the very gates of hell: anything less will not disclose the high calling to which we were ordained.

Endnotes

[1]The essay best outlining these issues is one by Beverly Harrison, "Theology and Morality of Procreative Choice," in Stephen E. Lammers and Allen Verhey, eds., *On Moral Medicine: Theological Perspectives in Medical Ethics* (Grand Rapids, Michigan: William B. Eerdmans Publishing Company, 1987), 422-33.

[2]The writings of Ellen G. White stress the theme of the creation story and its significance to Christian understanding of our world. A prime example is *Patriarchs and Prophets* (Mountain View, California: Pacific Press Publishing Association, 1958), Chapter Two.

[3]*Ibid.*

[4]*Ibid.*, 50-51.

[5]White notes: "Our first parents, though created innocent and holy, were not placed beyond the possibility of wrongdoing. God made them free moral agents, capable of appreciating the wisdom and benevolence of His character and the justice of His requirements, and with

full liberty to yield or withhold obedience . . . . God might have withheld the hand of Adam from touching the forbidden fruit; but in that case man would have been not a free moral agent but a mere automaton." *Ibid.*, 48-49.

⁶Joseph Pieper, *The Four Cardinal Virtues* (New York: Harcourt, Brace and World, 1965), 28.

⁷White, 62.

⁸*Ibid.*, Chapter Four is based around this issue.

⁹*Ibid.*, 68.

¹⁰Daniel Maguire, in *The Moral Choice* (New York: Doubleday and Company, 1978), 58-99, discusses the meaning of morals and contends that morality begins in the discovery of the value of the self, others and the environment. In his words, "Is human life really sacred? I must answer that it is, self-evidently. Its sacredness is the most primordial of all experiences," 83.

¹¹Daniel Callahan, "Abortion: The New Debate," in *Primary Care* 13, no. 2 (June 1986):260, notes that "one does not lightly or without serious reason deprive the fetus of life."

¹²White, 48-49.

¹³Paul Fowler, *Abortion* (Portland, Oregon: Multnomah Press, 1987), 95.

¹⁴Ellen G. White in *The Ministry of Healing* (Mountain View, California: Pacific Press Publishing Association, 1905), 372-373, notes the influence of prenatal forces on the development of the child: "Thus, many children have received as a birthright almost unconquerable tendencies to evil."

¹⁵*Ibid.*, 377-378, declares that it is the work of the mother, "with the help of God, to develop in a human soul the likeness of the divine."

8 Reverence for Life and the Abortion Issue

Jack W. Provonsha

The abortion question when reduced to its simplest form has usually been a question regarding value. How much is a human zygote/pre-embryo/embryo/fetus worth? This question can be further divided into two derivative questions. What is the source of its value, and when and under what circumstances does it possess it?

For the most part, the latter of these two sub-questions has dominated the discussion. The controversy has largely revolved around the stage or "moment" when this specialized organism comes to impose human claims upon us—at the moment of conception, at implantation, at some developmental point along the way such as at the time of transition from embryo to fetus, at quickening, at viability, at parturition, or even at the initiation of independent respiration. No one that I know of would extend full human meaning to pre-conception gametes or delay the definition to early childhood when functions of the human "self" such as reason, self-awareness, and self-determination come into active play.

That the usual focus of the argument was misplaced is suggested by the fact that the controversy continues unabated. No consensus, the *sine qua non* of social legislation in a free society, is presently possible. Partly the difficulty has arisen from the fact that none of these moments, with the possible exception of conception, the time when the two gametes unite, is precise enough, or the changes radical enough, to be formally useful. Certainly, later moments such as spacial separation from the mother, or the alterations in cardiopulmonary physiology that go with respiration in the newborn do not involve changes that specifically affect its "humanness." Viability's moment, the time when independent existence is possible outside of the womb, the only "moment" currently enjoying legal sanction in most states, itself depends to a great extent on whether natal care is being rendered in Appalachia or in the environment of a large tertiary

113

care center with its intensive neonate facilities. Viability arrives much later in Appalachia.

It is the purpose of this chapter to explore one other than the usual sources of value that will hopefully shed light on this crucial social and moral issue.

Just as in all other situations involving logic, one's presuppositions heavily condition the conclusions one reaches regarding the morality of artificially induced abortion (I say "artificially induced" because nobody blames the body for doing most of its own abortions spontaneously). Chief of these presuppositions is one having to do with the definition of "humanness," as in the question, "When does human life begin?"

One could as easily ask the question at the other end of life's journey. "When does human life end?" Our considerable agreement on the answer to this latter question is reflected in our fairly precise and generally accepted definitions of death, for example as in "brain death." We are nowhere near achieving such consensus on the question of when human life begins.

Behind these questions of "when?" there hovers over the abortion issue an even more fundamental question concerning the "what?" What do we mean by human? "What is man?" the Bible asks.

In the history of man's thinking about such matters several options present themselves that constitute the underlying presuppositions of the present controversy. One of these has been around for awhile and remains a live option for man today—even for some at this conference. It passes under the label dualism and may take one of two forms: one, dualism of soul and body, the other, a dualism of life and matter called vitalism. These dualities have in common a belief in independent entities (called, on the one hand, spirit or soul; on the other, life) which categorically differ from and exist apart from a material body. The body is conceived of as nothing more than material substance until either soul or life is infused into it. According to a dualism of either stripe, man becomes human at the moment of this infusion and his body reverts again to its material, objective status as an inanimate "thing" at the separation of the soul or spirit.

Dualism is often associated with the writings of Plato, who had much to say about man's condition in death in his *Phaedo*. For example, he responded to Crito's question, "But how shall we bury you?" with his, "Any way you like if I don't slip through your fingers." The position has always been suggested by dream states and mystical experiences. It is currently being supported by appeals to near-death visions.

The implications of dualistic thinking for abortion are obvious. On this ground

114

humanness begins at the moment a human soul is infused, believed to be at the moment of conception. Since it is a human soul that is infused, the embryo/fetus presents human claims from the very beginning, and willful destruction of the embryo/fetus constitutes the crime of murder. The position is often absolute and non-negotiable.

A second option, materialistic reduction, leads to exactly the opposite conclusion. I once heard a physician refer to pregnancy as the commonest tumor in the female uterus, and a colleague state that abortion is thus a medical rather than a moral issue. Both were in effect actually denying "human" value to the developing embryo/fetus. It was a "thing." The consequences of that denial are too obvious to require comment. The Germans have a word for it, "Verdinglichung," thingification, the ultimate human insult.

Seventh-day Adventists have generally held a third option, at least by implication, since the very beginning. I shall call it wholistic. This view incorporates something of both of the other options while also denying them in important particulars. Neither an immortal soul nor an entity called life, possessing independent existence apart from the body, nor the materialistic reduction do justice to what we mean when we refer to human. Man is a multidimensional unity, to use Paul Tillich's famous phrase. By "human" we indicate a "self" in which there is integration and interplay between the psychological, the mental, the physical, the chemical, the social, the circumstantial, the environmental, and all the other dimensions that make up this complex, aware, interaction of qualities we call human.

According to wholistic thinking, none of these dimensions possess human reality apart from that interaction, except, perhaps, symbolically. We think of grandmother's corpse as still "belonging" to and thus symbolizing grandma even though we also speak of her as having "departed." We place *her* in the grave, not merely a complex collection of materials such as calcium, carbon, proteins, and the like. Also, we do not simply discard an infant who is born without the possibility of ever developing a "mind," although care centers often incinerate (or procure for investigative purposes) dead embryos and early fetuses which are delivered out of time.

"Symbolic humans" accrue their symbolic value with association and with the passage of time. The embryo/fetus takes on increasing symbolic human meaning as it matures. Expectant mothers come to carry babies not fetuses (or uterine tumors). It is more difficult to speak of "the commonest tumor" when it exhibits a heartbeat and independent motion. Accrual of symbolic value is part of the reason for the present controversy over anencephalics as possible organ transplant donors. If they could provide donor hearts while still early embryos, possibly no one would object overmuch.

Taking the Bible seriously, Adventists have believed that no human "self" exists apart from a body. The body is also conceived of as impersonal matter (except symbolically) when totally deprived of its own mind and its interaction with the minds of others. This is all implicit in the Hebraic (biblical) understanding of man, including that of the New Testament with its emphasis on the resurrection of the body (e.g., our resurrected Lord left Joseph's new tomb empty).

The self may have *potential* for existence in situations of temporary suspension of consciousness such as in natural sleep, anesthesia, and limited coma, but selfhood can only be truly posited in such cases on the basis of anticipation of the restoration of those wholistic human interactions. We speak of the-not-yet self or the-now-dead self only in terms of whether there are such expectations.

This manner of thinking has obvious relevance to the ending of life. When the self has been irrevocably lost through aging, accident, or disease, care providers are no longer under obligation to continue extraordinary treatment measures.

It also has significance for the issue at hand. A not-yet self, embryo or fetus, who through defect or injury can never become a self, need not be accorded the same intensity of care that would be rendered an individual with self-potential, particularly if in doing so we deprived others who might benefit from our limited resources. An anencephalic embryo/fetus, for example, clearly does not have the same claim upon those resources as does one with self-potential, if for no other reason than it cannot benefit from the care in any way that has human meaning. It cannot even become a self, by definition.

Selfhood may, in some other situations, be a relative quality ranging from almost total diminution of the self on the one hand to virtually full expression on the other. Selecting between selves and non-selves or between higher or lower at this relative level could, of course, prove extremely difficulty. By "non-self" I do not refer to the merely diminished self, but to that loss below which even the minimal qualities of humanness referred to earlier are obviously irrevocably and forever absent.

The judgment of "non-self," because it is a human judgment and because the criteria may be extremely subtle, may always have to be undertaken with at least a modicum of humility, leaving significant room for a measure of doubt. It may also mostly have to be made with material "markers" such as those provided by vital signs and the indicators of "brain death." Moreover, since selfhood, by definition, always involves other selves, it should be a consensus call. It is inappropriate to treat as a non-self what is perceived to be a self by someone else. To override such a perception is to invite moral insensitivity and confusion.

Having explored the *what* and the *when*, let us now examine one of the main sources of the value of the embryo/fetus. Chief among these I consider to be what Albert Schweitzer refers to as a generalized "reverence for life." Although for Schweitzer this principle may reflect some influence of Eastern religion on his thought, I consider the notion to be so crucial for Christian ethical thinking that I wish to develop it at some length. From a biblical perspective the abortion issue may be largely a reverence-for-life issue, reverence for life being a special instance of reverence for the Creator of all things including life.

The conception and birth of a baby is a miracle of creation. Renowned pianist Artur Rubinstein was the seventh child born into his family. When his mother became pregnant with him her sister demanded that she seek an abortion, remonstrating that her family couldn't afford to feed the children she already had. Rubinstein's mother refused. "And so you see," Rubinstein recounted later, "I am a miracle." It is a miracle that represents one of the clearest expressions of *imago dei*, the image of God in man—the ability to create. When God wanted a thousand angels He created a thousand angels. But when He wanted a family of human beings He created just two and let them share in the creation. Reverence for life includes reverence for this shared gift.

Allow the famed missionary doctor, philosopher, theologian, and musician, Albert Schweitzer to express what he considers to be *the* fundamental ethical principle:

> The elemental fact, present in our consciousness every moment of our existence, is: I am life that wills to live, in the midst of life that wills to live. The mysterious fact of my will to live is that I feel a mandate to behave with sympathetic concern toward all the wills to live which exist side by side with my own. The essence of Goodness is: Preserve life, promote life, help life to achieve its highest destiny. The essence of Evil is: destroy life, harm life, hamper the development of life.

> The fundamental principle of ethics, then, is reverence for life....

> In the main, reverence for life dictates the same sort of behavior as the ethical principle of love. But reverence for life contains within itself the rationale of the commandment to love, and it calls for compassion for all creature life.

> Only the ethics of reverence for life is complete. It is so in every respect. The ethics that deals only with the conduct of man toward his fellow men

can be exceedingly profound and vital. But it remains incomplete. Thus it was inevitable that man's intellect should ultimately have reached the point of being offended by the heartless treatment of other living creatures....By ethical conduct toward all creatures, we enter into a spiritual relationship with the universe....

To the truly ethical man, all life is sacred, including forms of life that from the human point of view may seem lower than ours. He makes distinctions only from case to case, and under the pressure of necessity, when he is forced to decide which life he will sacrifice in order to preserve other lives. In thus deciding from case to case, he is aware that he is proceeding subjectively and arbitrarily, and that he is accountable for the lives thus sacrificed.

The man who is guided by the ethics of reverence for life stamps out life only from inescapable necessity, never from thoughtlessness. He seizes every occasion to feel the happiness of helping living things and shielding them from suffering and annihilation.

Whenever we harm any form of life, we must be clear about whether it was really necessary to do so. We must not go beyond the truly unavoidable harm, not even in seemingly insignificant matters. The farmer who mows down a thousand flowers in his meadow, in order to feed his cows, should be on guard, as he turns homeward, not to decapitate some flower by the roadside, just by way of thoughtlessly passing the time. For then he sins against life without being under the compulsion of necessity....[1]

Schweitzer's extension of the principle to all forms of life may seem overblown to some (hyperbole is a well-known genre of "prophets"). But scriptural support for Schweitzer's ethical principle is not lacking. Something of this is contained, for example, in the familiar statement of Jesus, "Are not five sparrows sold for two pennies? Yet not one of them is forgotten by God" (Luke 12:6). Matthew recalled the statement as, "two sparrows sold for a penny?" Combining these two versions makes an interesting point. "Buy four at two for a penny and you get one thrown in free." God doesn't even forget what we would call a free [worthless?] sparrow. It is not worthless to Him.

In terms of our present issue, God also places value on yet-unborn human lives, at least some of them, as in Isaiah 49:1, "Before I was born the Lord called me," and Jeremiah 1:5, "Before I formed you in the womb I knew you, before I set you apart; I appointed you as prophet to the nations" [NIV]. I do not know if it is permissible to generalize from these passages.

There is an interesting expression of Schweitzer's logic in an Old Testament progression. In the Genesis creation story, our first parents are depicted as being initially provided a diet that did not involve the taking of the life of the plants that provided it. In Genesis 1:29, their food, as over against that of many of the rest of the animals, was the fruit and the seeds of fruit and seed-bearing plants. After their fall and the denial of access to the tree of life, they were given "the plants of the field" themselves as food (Gen. 3:18). Then, finally, after the flood of Noah, when food sources were presumably minimal, man was permitted to eat his fellow animal creatures.

> The fear and dread of you will fall upon all the beasts of the earth and all the birds of the air, upon every creature that moves along the ground, and upon all the fish of the sea; they are given into your hands. Everything that lives and moves will be food for you. Just as I gave you the green plants, I now give you everything.[2]

Everything? Not quite. The distinction between "clean" and "unclean" that would be the basis for kosher Jewish dietary law is also drawn (see Gen. 7:2).

Perhaps even more importantly, that other kosher prohibition of the eating of the blood of slain animals was instituted.

> But you must not eat meat that has its lifeblood still in it. And for your lifeblood will I surely demand an accounting. I will demand an accounting from every animal. And from each man, too I will demand an accounting for the life of his fellow man. Whoever sheds the blood of man, by man shall his blood be shed; for in the image of God has God made man.[3]

Throughout Jewish history this pattern remained constant. It also carried over into the New Testament Christian church. In Acts 15:20 Gentile converts were to be required to honor the age-old command to refrain "from blood."

The significance of this restriction and its long survival is not all clear, but it surely had little to do with matters of health. There is no practical possibility of removing every trace of blood from the flesh of the slaughtered animal, even under the direction of the most kosher-rigid of rabbis. Rather, I suspect, the prohibition was a ritual, symbolic protection of Schweitzer's ethical principle. In Genesis 9:4, the blood "stands for" life. Given the truly enormous sacrifice of animal life in the Old Testament culture, it surely could be an important provision.

To my knowledge Albert Schweitzer does not directly apply his reverence-for-life principle to the abortion issue. He brushes the issue in a number of places by implication, however, and in so doing he provides clues to ways in which the main weakness of the principle may be overcome.

Schweitzer's statement of the principle is incomplete. As a generalized attitude, reverence for life is both profound and profoundly biblical—especially as it expresses an orientation of worship toward the Creator, Preserver, and Restorer of life. "I am the resurrection and the life," Christ proclaimed (John 11:25), and again, "I have come that they may have life and have it to the full" (John 10:10). But as a generalized attitude it lacks the specificity that ethical decision-making requires.

The truly hard bioethical choices often arise in circumstances of competing claims where, for example, instead of asking whether a person shall be allowed to die, the question is more likely to be *which one* shall live or die? Perhaps, in the present case, which shall die, the mother or her fetus? How does one resolve conflicts where the issue is not just life itself, as in reverence for all life, but *which life*, when someone has to go? The competition can also appear as a conflict over scarce resources.

Current technology is raising such questions in new and perplexing ways. Which fetuses shall be selected, for example, in the new selective reduction of multifetal pregnancies? In multifetal pregnancies each additional fetus increases the danger of fetal disaster. One author writes of a series of seven gravid patients who received selective reduction. One of these had nine fetuses, one sextuplets, two quintuplets, two quadruplets, and one triplets.[4]

Now, we know from experience that nine fetuses are not going to survive (unless they are rabbits, maybe). To do nothing is to lose them all. Shall we selectively kill six, five, or seven of them so that the remainder may have a chance for life? And which ones? Our lifeboat scenario remains alive and well. How would Schweitzer counsel us?

Schweitzer alerts us to the weakness of his ethic, although perhaps not intentionally, when he refers to the necessity of the truly ethical man's making "distinctions only from case to case...when he is forced to decide which life he will sacrifice in order to preserve other lives." And while doing this "he is aware that he is proceeding subjectively and arbitrarily [being] accountable for the lives thus sacrificed."

But making such "decisions" "subjectively and arbitrarily" does sound more like coin-flipping than it does like choosing. That may be the way one has to go with nine unknown fetuses, but we should be clear about it. "Which ones" is in this case primarily a medical, not an ethical, decision. The ethical decision is made when one decides to kill a certain number of fetuses in order to save the rest. The medical decision, "which ones," should be based on the optimum possibility for survival of the others, that is, what offers the best chance for their survival. Given the present state of "abortion on demand" in this country, it is unlikely that the ethical question, "shall we do it?" will prove over-burdensome for most obstetricians who are engaged in selective reduction.

What is required if a reverence-for-life ethic is to have practical utility is some way of positing *relative* life/value. There must be some way of deciding that some forms of life are higher or lower on a value scale when the situation is one of competition. Otherwise, if all of life is equivalent, flipping coins is all we have.

Schweitzer seems to imply that there is a life/value hierarchy when he speaks of "necessity." He does this even as he seems to reject such value distinctions:

> The ethics of reverence for life makes no distinction between higher and lower, more precious and less precious lives. It has good reason for this omission. For what are we doing, when we establish *hard and fast* [emphasis mine] gradations in value between living organisms, but judging them in relation to ourselves, by whether they seem to stand closer to us or farther from us. This is a wholly subjective standard. How can we know what importance other living organisms have in themselves and in terms of the universe?[5]

The reason for this statement, however, immediately follows:

> In making such distinctions, we are apt to decide that there are forms of life which are worthless and may be stamped without it mattering at all.[6]

Recall the statement that pregnancy is the commonest uterine tumor.

But Schweitzer leaves us dangling when he says on the same page, "He makes distinctions only from case to case, and under pressure of necessity, when he is forced to decide which life he will sacrifice in order to preserve other lives." To decide to sacrifice one life in order to preserve other lives involves a judgment about one life's value as over against another's, and that constitutes a hierarchy of value even if all the lives on the scale are precious.

Schweitzer is not addressing the abortion issue directly, of course, but the issue must surely be included in what he calls this "fundamental principle of ethics." Surely such an ethic must include some method for deciding which life shall be sacrificed "in order to preserve other lives." Does his contrasting "life" and "lives" suggest a criterion of numbers, the life-boat ethic? He does not say, but this can scarcely be the way to deal with a one-to-one conflict of mother and fetus.

Fortunately, that source-book for reverence for life and its Creator also provides a hierarchy of value. The Genesis creation of human beings was unique in sequence, manner, and meaning. Theirs was the ultimate creation, in them alone was the image of God imprinted, and to them was given the dominant role over the rest of creation. All of this suggests value priority. But it also aids us in deciding what constitutes humanness. Humanness is defined in terms of the qualities in which human beings differed from the remainder of creation, ultimacy, *imago dei* and dominion. It is a quality of life determined by the capacity for selfhood that makes the difference, not merely life itself.

If it should be impossible to recognize or distinguish this quality in the individual case, no selection that is ethically meaningful can be made. For example, when choosing which of the six, seven, five or so of those nine fetuses is to be preserved, "selection" is either a coin-flip call, or is based on such purely medical grounds as potentiality for viability and technical facility.

A choice between the mother and any one or even all of them might be a quite different matter, however. The selfhood quality of the mother and her unborn fetus is not actually equivalent, at least at that stage. The actual selfhood of the mother takes logical priority over the uncertain, potential selfhood of the fetus simply because of its higher level of certainty and because it involves so many interactions with other selves—and, incidentally, because the loss of the mother's life would place them both in jeopardy, at least early on.

As soon as we introduce quality-of-life considerations into the reverence-for-life equation, of course, in some ways we complicate things. To identify the quality of selfhood either actually or potentially will always be a judgment call, for which we may possess neither the perceptive ability nor adequate information. The call will always have to be made with a measure of the uneasiness of uncertainty. There is also the possibility that the self quality may be in jeopardy even though mere physiologic life is not, as in the case of serious threat to the mental health of the mother. Severe mental and emotional disturbance can seriously threaten the functioning self (this could be a basis for deciding that impregnation through the violence of rape or incest may be legitimately terminated).

Introducing this quality also helps in deciding what to do about seriously defective fetuses, especially those with severe central nervous system abnormalities. If the defect is so severe as to preclude the development of selfhood at any level, it would surely seem appropriate to assist the body in doing what it most often does spontaneously (spontaneous abortion often represents the body's own housekeeping work. Nature opposes prohibition-of-abortion-under-any-and-all-circumstances).

In summary, it seems to me that the ethic of reverence for life as proposed by Albert Schweitzer must be taken seriously. Surely there is none but can be impressed by the simple grandeur of the statement that "the essence of Goodness is: preserve life, promote life, help life to achieve its highest destiny. The essence of Evil is: destroy life, harm life, hamper the development of life."[7] As a simple statement of general attitude it is compelling, but it is incomplete. Decisions must be made, and what we require is some kind of method for applying that attitude to the ambiguous, conflicting, often confusing business of getting along in the world. I have suggested such a method based on a biblically oriented notion of the actual or potential "self" and its value.

As we contemplate the abortion issue, Schweitzer's admonition that we not act "thoughtlessly" surely is in order, as is his plaint, "When will all the killing that necessity imposes upon us be undertaken with sorrow?" Necessary killing even of a fetus must ever have pain and sadness as its companions so that, hopefully, it will never be done other than as an act of compelling necessity.

Naturalist Edwin Way Teale once wrote, "It is those who have compassion for all of life who will best safeguard the life of man. Those who become aroused only when man is endangered become aroused too late." May God grant that on this ground it isn't already too late. Surely no aspect of life is worthy of greater compassion than that life which lies at the very well-spring of human existence, that of the unborn child. Unfortunately, compassion alone is not enough. There must also be reason, judgment, and equity, and the courage to do what is necessary—for the sake of all of us.

Endnotes

[1] Albert Schweitzer, *The Teaching of Reverence for Life* (New York: Holt, Rinehart and Winston, 1965), 47 ff.

[2] Genesis 9:2-6 (NIV).

[3] *Ibid.*

[4] Joseph Shalev, M.D., et al., *The New England Journal of Medicine* 319, no. 14 (October 6, 1988):949.

[5] Schweitzer, 47.

[6] *Ibid.*

[7] *Ibid.*, 26.

9 A Compassionate and Christian "Quality of Life" Ethic

Richard Fredericks

The real question facing us is not what we should tell a woman in a crisis pregnancy to do, but what we should do for her. The real threat to happiness and self-worth for women in crisis pregnancies is not their developing children but isolation and fear caused by indifference and apathy, or hostility and rejection from those they should be able to turn to for love, forgiveness and emotional, physical and financial support.

Part I: Less Than Human?

In 1973 a 7-2 Supreme Court decision *(Roe v. Wade)* overturned the legislation of 48 states that prohibited or severely limited abortions except in life-threatening situations or rape. A simultaneous decision *(Doe v. Bolton)* made the "termination of the fetus" more simple by removing the need for medical review.[1]

In the United States today, one out of every four pregnancies ends in abortion. In fourteen metropolitan areas such as Washington D.C., Atlanta and Seattle, abortions outnumber live births.[2] Three abortions are done per minute, 4,200 abortions per day, 1.5 million per year—a total of more than 21 million since the Supreme Court legalized abortion in 1973. Since 1975 the "war on the unborn" has produced twice as many casualties each year as have all the major wars in U.S. history, from the Revolutionary War through Vietnam. Fewer than three percent of all abortions are for serious defects, rape, incest or danger to the mother.

The time spent in the mother's womb is now the most dangerous time in the entire human lifespan—speaking of the population as a whole. The probability of a premeditated fatal assault is never again as high. Simultaneously, abortion has made medical professionals, whose entire orientation was once toward preserving life, the nation's foremost terminators of life.[3]

125

Is this a gross violation of the sixth commandment? If 97 percent of all abortions are performed for matters of personal convenience, is this murder—the violent killing of innocent human life? The answer depends on how one views the "fetus."[4]

In the 1973 decision, the Supreme Court justices ruled that while the unborn are human, they are not persons. This understanding of the human fetus is rooted in the "quality of life" ethic. Stated in its most simplistic and essential terms, the "quality of life" ethic responds to modern social and economic problems by stating that some humans are

a) not true "persons," and

b) a great hindrance to a better lifestyle for individuals and society, thus

c) it is not wrong to kill them because it enhances (in an expeditious and cost-effective way) the quality of life for those who are true persons.

Basic to this ethic is the concept that not all human beings have either intrinsic value or equal value. Indeed, many *homo sapiens* should not be seen as persons at all. Rather, "personhood" is assigned according to various levels of physical and mental development. One must attain and then maintain these qualities in order to have a life worth living—or protecting.

In his widely used college textbook on ethics, Vincent Barry illustrates the dilemma well:

> What conditions should be used as the criteria of personhood? Can an entity [a human] be considered a person merely because it possesses certain biological properties? Or should other factors be introduced, such as consciousness, self-consciousness, rationality, and the capacities for communication and moral judgment? . . . For example, if we believe it is the capacity to think and reason that makes one human, we will likely associate the loss of personhood with the loss of rationality. If we consider consciousness as the defining characteristic, we will be more inclined to consider a person to have lost that status when a number of characteristics such as the capacities to remember, enjoy, worry, and will are gone. . . . This doesn't mean that a death decision necessarily follows when an entity is determined to be a nonperson. But it does mean that whatever is inherently objectionable about allowing or causing a person to die dissolves, because the entity is no longer a person.[5]

Recent developments demonstrate that this ethic has extended beyond the question of abortion. Passive euthanasia, allowing a "good death" for those deemed no longer fit to live, has become more acceptable[6]—and active euthanasia is increasingly practiced by members of the medical profession.[7] There already have been several cases in which newborns with some type of genetic deficiency were placed in a hospital nursery crib marked "Do Not Feed" and allowed to die of dehydration—a process that took six days in the case of Bloomington, Indiana's "Baby Doe" in April 1982.[8] This is a dramatic shift away from the Judeo-Christian view of human life as sacred which gave the preservation of innocent human life[9] priority over any socio-economic consideration.

An article that appeared in the journal *California Medicine* three years before *Roe v. Wade* legalized abortion-on-demand illustrates the need to repudiate the old ethic based upon the sanctity of life in order to be comfortable with abortion:

> The process of eroding the old ethic and substituting the new has already begun. It may be seen most clearly in changing attitudes toward human abortion. . . . Since the old ethic has not yet been fully displaced it has been necessary to separate the idea of abortion from the idea of killing, which continues to be socially abhorrent. The results have been a curious avoidance of the scientific fact, which everyone really knows, that human life begins at conception, and is continuous whether intra- or extra-uterine until death. . . . This schizophrenic subterfuge is necessary because while the new ethic is being accepted the old one has not been rejected.[10]

The crucial point is that we have moved from an objective (all innocent human life is protected by law) to a subjective (only those defined at this point in time as "persons" are legally protected) basis for decision-making. The door is open for the circle of "non-person humans" to expand.[11]

In 1857 the Supreme Court ruled in the *Dred Scott* case that the black race was less than human and the property of the owner. To free a slave would violate the Fifth Amendment by causing an undue financial hardship to those who were truly human (white slave owners). Listen to the precise reasoning of Chief Justice Roger B. Taney (himself a slave owner):

> They [blacks] have for more than a century been regarded as beings of an inferior order, and altogether unfit to associate with the white race, either in social or political relations; and so far inferior, that they had no rights which the white man was bound to respect; and that *the negro might justly and lawfully be reduced to slavery for his own benefit*. He was bought and sold, and treated as an ordinary article of merchandise and traffic, whenever *a profit* could be made by it (emphasis supplied).[12]

This also was a "pro-choice" decision, in this case the choice of the slave

127

owner that enabled one human to treat another as personal property to be kept or disposed of at will—especially if a profit could be made. Like the unborn children of the late 20th century, Black men, women and children in the 19th century were denied the rights and protection that come with personhood. The basis of that tragic decision was a narrow view of humanity that arbitrarily limited personhood to a particular skin color.[13]

This century contains a more direct analogy to America's increasing implementation of death-laws as solutions to social and economic problems. That analogy began in the Weimar German Republic (1919-33) and climaxed in the Nazi Third Reich (1933-45). Death as a solution gradually culminated in Hitler's "Final Solution" in which the Jews were declared nonpersons, an unacceptable burden and threat to society. The result was the Holocaust, the extermination [termination] of six million Jews.

In 1920 Felix Meiner published a small volume in Leipzig titled: *The Release of the Destruction of Life Devoid of Value* that paved the way for the physicians of Germany to become the directors of the Nazi killing program. In this volume German psychiatrist Alfred Hoche and lawyer Karl Binding declared the Hippocratic oath obsolete, denied that there is an absolute right to life, and decried the "wasted manpower, patience and capital investment" needed to "keep life not worth living alive." Hoche and Binding forcefully argued that the terminally ill, the unproductive, the feebleminded, and all "useless eaters" have the "right to the complete relief of an unbearable life" and should be "given a death with dignity."[14]

At the same time German schoolchildren were taught that "whatever is useful is right." Mathematical problems were given in which they were asked to figure the costs of supporting "useless" old people versus building housing for productive newlyweds. They were taught that the handicapped represented an obstacle to their economic prosperity. Killing the "useless" for financial reasons became acceptable moral reasoning. Before the first Jews entered the gas chambers, the "Charitable Transport Company for the Sick" carried 250,000 German citizens deemed "unfit to live" to places where they were given "good deaths." Among those no longer fit to live were World War I veterans who were amputees, the incontinent elderly, and Gypsies.[15]

At the Nuremberg War Crimes Trials, psychiatrist Dr. Leo Alexander demonstrated that the people who participated in and condoned the atrocities of those two decades were not demented monsters. They were very ordinary people who chose to remain silent rather than risk losing their own prosperity, popularity or positions. The majority of Christians in Germany *continued to attend church regularly* but remained silent. Silent![16]

Next to basic apathy ("I don't want to get involved" or "If the church is neutral so am I,")[17] the predominant response to the issue of abortion I have found among Adventists, especially clergy, is a denial that the scriptural principles have anything to say concerning this issue of abortion. If this is so, society and the church are left with a diminished view of humanity in which only those who are truly "persons"—as defined by society at any given moment—have a legal and moral right to life.

Part II: A Biblical Analysis of the "Quality of Life" Ethic

Two basic perspectives are necessary. First, Scripture has authority over human reason as the final arbitrator in all significant ethical and moral issues. And second, the principles and themes of Scripture are far from silent concerning abortion.[18] Rather, biblical theology and the morality that flows from it, in both the Old and New Testaments, stand in opposition to this type of solution to human problems. Biblical thought also opposes the philosophy of humanity and human happiness that supports such solutions.

Old Testament Themes

First consider three ways the *Old Testament* speaks to the issue:

1. *God is against murder.* "You shall not *murder*" (Hebrew: *ratsach*. Ex. 20:13). The sixth commandment may allow for some forms of capital punishment or self-defense. But the Hebrew term, and its context, consistently defines as murder, then forbids and unequivocally condemns, the taking of any innocent human life by violent means (Ex. 23:7). No exceptions are offered, no conditions (economic, emotional or otherwise) are given where taking an innocent life is acceptable to God. He repeatedly condemns (lit. declares a curse upon) any who take the life of an innocent human being in a futile attempt to atone for their own sins, as in Deuteronomy 24:16. Proverbs 6:16-17 states "six things which the Lord hates....hands that shed innocent blood."

More specifically, God views as especially heineous the sacrifice of children for the sins of the parents (see Jer. 7:30-34 and Mic. 6:7); and those who "ripped open the pregnant women [double murder] to enlarge their borders" (Amos 1:13). In Psalm 106, verses 35-40, God sends destructive judgments upon His people who have accepted the practices of the Canaanites, leading them to "shed innocent blood, even the blood of their sons and daughters." In Jeremiah 22, God directly links child sacrifice with greed, the desire for materialistic self-fulfillment (Jer. 22:3,13-17).

This link is confirmed by archeological evidences. Archeologists have discovered that the practice of child sacrifice in Carthage was motivated by economic reasons but with religious justification. Child sacrifice was more prevalent in wealthy homes than in poor ones. The wealthy disposed of their "unwanted" children in order to preserve their lifestyle and standard of living.[19] God declares this mindset both fatal and alien to His kingdom.

2. *God affirms the personhood of the unborn.* In both the Old and New Testaments the term used to describe a human being in the womb is *child*, the same term used to describe an infant after birth. There is nothing anywhere in Scripture to indicate God views the unborn child as only a potential life. Rather, all babies in the womb are spoken of as persons, as unique and distinct individuals with identity and worth, for whom God already has a destiny:

> "Before I formed you in the womb I knew you, and before you were born I consecrated you; I have appointed you a prophet to the nations" (Jer. 1:5).

> "Thus says the Lord, your Redeemer, and the One who formed you from the womb, I, the Lord am the Maker of all things"; "Thus says the Lord who made you and formed you from the womb, who will help you" (Isa. 44:2, 24, NASB).

> Thou didst form me in my mother's womb. . . Thine eyes have seen my unformed substance; and in Thy book they were all written, the days that were ordained for me when as yet there was not one of them (Ps. 139:13).[20]

3. *God is especially for the weak, the orphaned, the voiceless and the oppressed.* Those who are without a power base in society are the objects of His special regard; and are to be so treated by His people: "Vindicate the weak and fatherless, do justice to the afflicted and destitute. Rescue the weak and needy; deliver them out of the hand of the wicked" (Ps. 82:3-4). If the unborn are persons to God, they are the most defenseless of individuals. To be God's servant is to defend such as these in a selfish, brutal world.

New Testament Themes

It is the New Testament's record of God's redemptive acts through Jesus

Christ that most clearly rejects the assumptions undergirding the "quality of life" ethic and all its applications.

Fulfillment, on Jesus' terms, is discovered in the midst of a self-denying life lived for others, not through wealth, autonomy and the frantic pursuit of individual rights or self-fulfillment (Matt. 16:21-24). Christ redefined true fulfillment as valuing all others, especially children,[21] more than we value autonomy or personal comfort. This participation, even if it is in the "fellowship of suffering," (Phil. 3:12), with One who gave Himself on the cross for sinners, is the heart of Christianity. It declares all human life valuable. This agape lifestyle is illustrated in a number of New Testament themes:

1. *The gospel reveals a God who accepts and values each of us as persons, but not on the basis of what we have achieved—or ever will achieve.* Christ offered Himself in sacrificial love to those who were unworthy and incapable of earning such love by their attractiveness, achievements or assets. In other words, God does not accept or love us because we measure up; rather, God's love embraces us in our morally and spiritually defective state and declares us acceptable by grace. This is the antithesis of humans having relative status based on an acceptable level of assets or achievement.

> For while we were still helpless, at the right time Christ died for the ungodly (Rom. 5:6; see also Eph. 2:3-6; 1 Tim. 1:15).

> When the kindness of God our Savior and His love for mankind appeared, He saved us, not on the basis of deeds which we have done in righteousness, but according to His mercy... (Titus 3:4-5).

We must not miss this point. While the "quality of life" ethic is totally consistent with an evolutionary, atheistic "survival of the fittest" worldview, it is antithetical to the spirit of the Gospel. Since Eden, God has shown Himself to be redemptive through great personal self-sacrifice. He didn't respond to sin by ripping Adam and Eve to pieces, even though they were now morally deformed and would cause Him great suffering and inconvenience. Instead He opened a way back to the tree of life by giving Himself.[22]

Abortion promises redemption and peace through the blood of the unborn rather than the blood of Christ. His sacrifice becomes irrelevant. For many, it is a futile attempt to remove the consequences of sin by terminating the fetus, a solution which ignores their moral guilt, the need for repentance, and Christ's "atoning sacrifice for our sins, and not only for ours but also for the sins of the whole world" (1 John 2:2). False guilt (feeling bad about something which is not wrong) is unhealthy, but false innocence (feeling good about evil) is deadly.

Abortion also assaults the Gospel by breeding an attitude that permits people who are inconvenient or fail to measure up to be denied human value and life. This is the opposite of life lived as a response to God's grace. It conditions us to ask the question: "What can this person do for me?" rather than responding to our own unmerited acceptance from God with the question: "How can I offer such love to those who need it most?"

> This is how we know what love is: Jesus Christ laid down his life for us. And we ought to lay down our lives for our brothers (1 John 3:16, NIV).

> This is love: not that we love God, but that He loved us and sent His Son as an atoning sacrifice for our sins. Dear friends, since God so loved us, we also ought to love one another (1 John 4:10,11, NIV).

The enemies of early Christians were compelled to say, "behold how they love one another." In the book of Acts these first disciples were identified as "the people of the Way." They were a distinct community whose lifestyle was radically different from the society around them. Their values were different—above all, the value they put on human life. This became evident in their relationships, as the earliest non-biblical Christian moral code, the *Didache*, illustrates:

> Our oldest moral catechism prepared candidates for baptism by instructing them: 'You will not kill. You will not have sex with other people's spouses. You will not abuse young children. You will not have sex outside of marriage. You will not abort fetuses.'[23]

For these early Christians, the value of the unborn child was a logical extension of the Gospel. This put them at odds with the prevailing practice in Roman society where abortion was rampant. In every age, the way in which the Christian community deals with the weakest and most needy in its midst is an accurate reflection of how personally real the power of the Gospel is to its members.

2. *The Incarnation speaks strongly against abortion and the ethic that supports it.* Jesus Christ identified with all humanity—even the unborn. When the "Word became flesh" He began as an unborn child, a fetus. Part of the revelation of His "glory" (John 1:14) was to enter into the womb of an unmarried

but pregnant teenager. Was He at that moment "potential life" with only relative value?[24]

Remember, Jesus was born into poverty and hardship, destined for suffering. If we look at the nativity story in all its harsh reality, we wonder what advice we would have offered Mary today about her pregnancy. Birth in a filthy stable. Only rags available to dress the child. Jesus' identification with the poor and underprivileged rather than the successful, powerful or prosperous was so real He had literally "no place to lay his head." This is such a low "quality of life" by modern reasoning it would have been far better for Mary to terminate her pregnancy. Yet this life is the ultimate revelation of the "glory" of God (John 17:1-5).

3. *In the New Testament the "love of money" is not the key to happiness, but "the root of all the evils."* It is a mindset that causes "those who want to get rich" to "fall into temptation" and "wander away from the faith" (1 Tim. 6:5-11). Jesus emphatically declared that "no one can serve. . .God and money" (Matt. 6:24); that "life does not consist in the abundance of possessions," therefore His disciples must "guard against every form of greed" (Luke 12:16-21). When John, in Revelation, describes Babylon the great harlot in whom is found the blood of "all who have been slain on the earth" (18:24), he pictures her as that spirit in humanity that values gold and silver above human lives (18:11-13).

This is crucial. Most arguments for abortion or killing the defective appeal to economic self-interest. They warn that preserving and protecting such people threatens either present or potential financial prosperity. The biblical priority is radically different. Paul identifies greed as the sin of idolatry—the most fatal sin in the Old Testament (Col. 3:5; Eph. 5:5). More than any other topic Jesus talked about the danger of basing life's decisions and goals on money, and declared "it is hard for a rich man to enter the kingdom of heaven." "Turning His gaze upon His disciples, He said, 'Blessed are [even] you who are poor, for yours is the Kingdom of heaven.'" This meaning derived from discipleship is in direct opposition to the belief that a life of potential material hardship is a life not worth living.

The Epistle of James, while not directly referring to abortion, concerns itself with human injustice and the link between greed and violence against the innocent: "You lust and do not have; so you commit murder. . . . You have lived on the earth in luxury and self-indulgence. You have fattened yourselves through slaughter; and murdered the innocent who were not opposing you. Your gold and silver [money] will testify against you. . .in the last days" (James 4:2; 5:5-6:3).

133

Jesus said, "So therefore no one of you can be my disciple who does not give up all his own possessions" (Luke 14:33). Clearly the Christian's goal in life is discipleship to Christ, not self-centered autonomy or financial independence. Christ's call is to simplicity (not to poverty) in order to free up resources for kingdom work—the very work of helping the needy and protecting the weak. Happiness is found in the company of the committed whose purpose is to mirror Christ's unearned, undeserved love by identifying with those who need it most: the weak, the frail, the poor and the helpless:

> "For inasmuch as you have done it unto one of the least of these, My brethren, you have done it unto Me" (Matt. 25:40).

> The rest of the world goes about disposing of the very young and the very old, the very weak, the very vulnerable, and the very poor, calling that reality. But the church is called to adopt and embrace the little ones in the name of the Lord, who was once a little one.[25]

4. *Finally, the "quality of life" ethic is rooted in the greatest sin of all: man's desire to play God.* Trying to be autonomous—the creature living as if his finite reason were the highest authority and therefore taking the prerogatives of the Creator—this is the essence of sin. Paul speaks of "the lie" as "worshiping and serving the creature rather than the Creator" (Rom. 1:25, see context, verses 18-32).

The first lie the Bible records is Satan's assertion to Eve that she could "be as God" (Gen. 3:5). Isaiah identifies the one overpowering determination of the Satanic spirit as: "I will exalt myself. . .I will make myself like the Most High" (Isa. 14:4), and he described spiritual Babylon (the archetypal kingdom of human rebellion against God, cf. Dan. 4:30) in these words: "You sensual one, who dwells securely, who says in your heart, I am and there is no one besides me" (Isa. 47:8).[26]

In "quality of life" literature, two types of statements reflect the human desire for autonomy and omniscience. The first defends the "absolute rights" of men and women to total sexual freedom, and of each woman to do what she wants with "her own body" (meaning the unborn child). The second suggests that those who are born with physical, mental or emotional handicaps—or even into poverty—would be better off dead.

Do we have absolute rights to do what we want with our bodies? Is personal autonomy a "Christian right" to be defended by the church? "You are not your own; you have been bought with a price: therefore glorify God in your body"

(1 Cor. 6:20). The New Testament calls us to accept the Lordship of Jesus Christ. It never defends "personal autonomy" or defines freedom in terms of autonomy: "If anyone wishes to come after Me, let him deny himself, take up his cross daily, and follow Me" (Luke 9:23).

As to the second theme, by acting on the assumption that they know some unborn would be better off dead, others now play God. They act as if they are omniscient, speaking with certainty about the misery "unwanted" children will both cause and experience. Really? Who gave these prophets their crystal ball? Will this new child's life be a continual burden or a joyful praise to God? How can we know?[27] One famous Gospel singer in this century was the illegitimate daughter of a 16-year-old poor black girl who was raped.

In reality, over 90 percent of the teenagers who commit suicide come from rich families where they have successful, educated parents, no material hardships and no handicaps. Among adults it is the rich, the beautiful and the successful (by material standards) who commit suicide. Suicide among the poor is extremely rare and among the handicapped it is almost nonexistent![28]

The lives of most successful men and women are lives of endured hardships and obstacles overcome. Beethoven's family background included a deranged father, a syphilitic mother, a mentally retarded older brother and a sibling born blind. To argue for death as the best answer to life's problems lacks imagination and a sense of God's redemptive might. For an atheist this limitedness is understandable; for a Christian it is bankrupt.

In summary, God is actively involved with the unborn as persons of value. Therefore, since abortion is the taking of such an innocent human life, it becomes, Biblically, not only an act of murder, but an assault on the purpose of Christ's life, His Gospel and His call to discipleship.

Part III: A Call to Commitment and Compassion

Should the Seventh-day Adventist Church take a stand against the practice of abortion? Yes, for many reasons. The most common argument against this step is a very legitimate desire to protect personal freedom of choice. But for us as a Christian community the crucial question is not whether or not God has given this freedom to His people. He certainly has. Rather, for us the question is whether our choices are just and moral.

Individuals are free to practice adultery or cruelty, but such choices are neither moral nor Christlike. Neither is the choice to kill an unborn child in an attempt to solve a present crisis. Our choices must be in line with God's will for our lives.

Another roadblock to a biblically consistent Adventist position is a curious denial of ethical accountability because of eschatological speculations. What *could* happen is causing us to deny what *is* happening. Prominent speakers within our church have said that those on the side of the sanctity of life are the vanguard of the "religious right" that would bring in legislation limiting our religious freedom. They conclude that we must avoid being identified with these Christians in their struggle against abortion and infanticide. This is curious. Sad. Speculations about a future death decree should not make us actively participate in a present one. Surely, for the unborn of America, this is already a "time of trouble such as has never been."

Others have said it is a "Catholic issue." Is protecting innocent life the private domain of the Catholic Church? Proverbs 24:11-12 and a host of other warnings from God (in the minor prophets especially) call us to defend the weak, voiceless and oppressed. Of Josiah God said:

> "He pled the cause of the afflicted and the needy; then it was well. Is not that what it means to know Me?" declares the Lord. "But your eyes [apostate Israel] and heart are intent only upon your own dishonest gain, and on the shedding of innocent blood" (Jer. 22:16; cf. Jer. 5:26-29).

Often those on both sides of this debate have seen themselves as the defenders of compassion, either compassion for the unborn child or the woman in crisis. Surely this is a divine impulse and it must be our common ground, our point of agreement as a church. A response which is truly and consistently compassionate to everyone involved in a crisis pregnancy must be our constant goal.

This would require consensus on two points. First, there is a need to admit the increasingly obvious medical and psychological reality that abortion has a second victim: the woman. Abortion not only destroys a child, but damages and sometimes destroys the very person it is suggested it will help. Because of this, compassion for the woman (as well as the child) dictates alternative answers.

The second point of consensus must be our individual commitment to offering sacrificial and redemptive support to these women. Are we really motivated by compassion rather than expediency and self-interest? Then we must realize that all truly compassionate people are individually involved people. "And God is able to make all grace abound to you, that always having all sufficiency in everything, you will have an abundance for doing every good deed" (2 Cor. 9:8). By God's grace we have the resources to meet the medical, physical, financial and relational needs of every woman in crisis within our sphere of influence.

Believing that God's resources are adequate for the situations He gives us, we can preserve and affirm life for everyone involved.

Does abortion really solve the immediate emotional crisis? I have counseled with six students and one close friend following their abortions. The story in each case was sickeningly similar. Career plans, money, self-esteem, boyfriend's affection: abortion promised to keep all intact. They were told the fetus was their hindrance to a happy life. The counselor at the clinic promised a quick escape back to freedom once the unwanted "blob of tissue" was removed quickly and painlessly (for only $500, thank you).

In each case, the abortion only deepened the crisis and hastened already deteriorating relationships and self-worth. Two girls who had abortions to stay in school ended up leaving. Another who had it against her will because of extreme pressure by her boyfriend and parents now refuses to have any contact with either, and suffers from severe depression. Another girl, who worked in the women's residence hall, following a suction abortion, vomited uncontrollably every time she turned on a vacuum sweeper. Another suffered from recurring nightmares of a baby girl crying and found herself illogically hoping, each time she saw a little girl from the back, that it would be the child she had aborted. Still another of my students wrote this letter before we talked:

> I am writing to explain the many times I was absent to your class in the month of March. I can't really say the exact reason why I did not come because it is very, very personal. It is so personal, that my parents or friends do not even know what I have gone and am still going through. A reason, I can mention, for not coming is that sometimes I was just too depressed to be around people, and my problem too complicated to concentrate on anything else. Sometimes all I wanted to do was stay in bed. Things got so bad that I felt there was no hope anymore—I now know what it feels like to cry for help within the depths of your soul—when you feel like you are in hell.

Pam Koerbel cites a study of the emotional states of forty-six randomly selected post-abortion women responding to a questionnaire. In this study, 87 percent of the women reported an increase in feelings of guilt, 78 percent an increase in a sense of grief, 76 percent had increased depression and remorse, 67 percent experienced an increase in anger and more than 60 percent struggled with a sense of shame and bitterness about their abortion decision.[29] Recently I have had two single young ladies come to me for help. Both are pregnant and determined to keep their babies as a means of compensating for the terrible regret and loss of self-respect they felt from an earlier abortion. Compassionate?

A woman does have the "legal right" and the personal freedom to take the life of her child. But as Christians we must recognize she does not have God's grace or approval for such an action. Killing the fetus is a violation of God's commandment; it is sin and is therefore futile for healing a damaged life. Doing so will not solve an emotional and moral crisis, but will only horribly deepen it. As Dr. John Wilke stated: "It is easier to scrape the baby out of a woman's womb than to scrape the memory of that baby out of her conscience."

Talk is cheap. Our task as individuals and as a community is to provide the support women need to be givers—not takers—of life. To encourage women in crisis pregnancies to give their unborn child life we must stand by them and help meet their needs. The real question is not, "What should we tell a woman in crisis to do?" but rather, "What should we, as Christ's disciples, do for her when she reaches out for help?" We need to love, not just with "word or tongue, but in deed and truth" (1 John 3:18).

A young woman named Joan has been referred to in several articles in Adventist publications.[30] After disassociating herself from the church and her parents following high school, Joan became involved sexually with a married man. Later she ended the relationship and found a renewed relationship with Christ. She returned to college with her parents' help, intent on studying for dentistry, only to realize six weeks later that she was pregnant.

She sought counsel. She did not want to contact the man or tell her parents. The author states: "She had considered continuing the pregnancy and putting the baby up for adoption, but she saw no way to find a place to live, support herself, or explain her actions to her family and friends." Her options, he says, seemed to be suicide, abortion or dropping out of school and disappearing, and then concludes her story with these words:

> The conclusion to Joan's story will not help—her story has no fairy tale ending. After much indecision, Joan finally elected to leave school and confront her parents with her problem. She also decided to continue the pregnancy and relinquish the infant for adoption. But when the baby was born, she changed her mind and chose to keep it. She felt so little acceptance by her parents and her church that she sought public assistance and now lives alone with her child. She has not returned to college and has no hope of doing so at this time. She, her child, and all whose lives touch theirs will continue to need a special measure of God's forgiving and redeeming love.

What is the tragedy in this story? Is it Joan's courageous decision to give her child life? Not at all. This story illustrates the failure, on the part of the affluent Adventist college community to whom she turned, to be authentic and sacrificial Christians. Listen again to the options listed by Joan's counselor: abortion, suicide or "disappearing." Why were he and his community unable to come up with a fourth? Where were the heart and hands of this church?

Joan should have found, not platitudes or "non-judgmental feedback," but the continued assurance of God's forgiveness and help (in the context of her own recent recommitment to Him) followed by a tangible, practical outpouring of financial, medical and emotional support. All those resources were available, and the reason God had given them was for just such a purpose. The tragic failure here belongs to those who allowed Joan to face the consequences of a brave decision alone.

William Willimon, a professor of Christian Ministry at Duke University, gives a practical example of what it really means to be Christ's agents to someone in crisis:

> One Monday morning I was attending a minister's morning coffee hour. We got into a discussion about abortion. A bunch of older clergy were against it, a bunch of younger clergy for it. One of those who was against it was asked, "Now wait a minute. You're not going to tell me that you think some 15 or 16-year-old is capable of bearing a child, are you?"
>
> "Well," the fellow replied, backing off a little bit, "there are some circumstances when a abortion might be OK."
>
> Sitting there stirring his coffee was a pastor of one of the largest black United Methodist churches in Greenville. He said, "What's wrong with a 16-year-old giving birth? She can get pregnant, can't she?"
>
> Then we said, "Joe, you can't believe a 16-year-old could care for a child."
>
> He replied, "No, I don't believe that. I don't believe a 26-year old can care for a child. Or a 36-year old. Pick any age. One person can't raise a child."
>
> So I said, "Look, Joe, the statistics show that by the year 1990, half of all American children will be raised in single-parent households."
>
> "So?" he replied. "They can't do it."
>
> We asked, "What do you do when you have a 16-year-old get pregnant in your church?"

He explained, "Well, it happened last week. We baptized the baby last Sunday, and I said how glad we were to have this new member in this church. Then I called down an elderly couple in the church, and I said, 'Now we're going to baptize this baby, and bring it into the family. What I want you all to do is to raise this baby, and while you're doing that raise the momma with it because the momma right now needs it.' This couple is in their 60s, and they've raised about 20 kids. They know what they're doing. And I said, 'If you need any of us, let us know. We're here. It's our child too.' That's what we do at my church."[31]

As Adventists, our challenge is to adopt actively the worldview of Scripture and to find a better alternative than death in the face of economic and emotional problems. Armed with a commitment to life, and confident in the resources of our Creator, we are called to demonstrate Christ's alternative within a decaying society:

"A new commandment I give to you, that you should love one another, even as I have loved you" (John 13:34). "For the Son of Man came not to be served, but to serve and to give Himself as a ransom for many" (Mark 10:45).

Endnotes

[1]See *Doe v. Bolton*, 410 U.S. 179, 192 (1973). These decisions came too late to terminate Jane Doe's pregnancy, and as of 1990, her child (whom she gave up for adoption) is an eighteen-year-old teenager.

[2]See Curt Young, *The Least of These* (Chicago: Moody Press, 1984), 30.

[3]The Hippocratic Oath, which appeared for centuries on physicians' diplomas, calls on the doctor to never cross the line and become executioner upon penalty of divine curse, specifically stating: "I will neither give a deadly drug to anybody if asked for it, nor will I make a suggestion to this effect. Similarly I will not give a woman an abortive aid. In purity and holiness I will guard my life and art."

[4]With 3 million couples longing for a child to adopt, the phrase "unwanted child" is, in the truest sense, a misnomer.

[5]Vincent Barry, *Applying Ethics: A Text with Readings*, 2nd ed. (Belmont, CA: Wadsworth Publishing Co., 1982), 189-190.

[6]In March, 1986, the American Medical Association's Council on Ethical and Judicial Affairs ruled that it is "not unethical" to allow patients to die who are in persistent vegetative states by withholding all food and water even when death is not imminent.

[7]"The Doctor Decided on Death," *Time* (February 15, 1988).

[8]During those six days ten couples came forward and offered to adopt the child.

[9]The term "innocent" is used for accuracy to qualify this statement. I believe arguments for capital punishment and "just war" can be derived from Scripture, but no such argument can be derived favoring the killing of an innocent human to enhance the quality of life of another human.

[10]*California Medicine* 113, no. 3 (September 1970):67-68.

[11]In the *Roe v. Wade* decision, the Supreme Court justices did not support their reasoning with scientific evidence, but rested it on a particular value judgment about humanity.

[12]*Dred Scott v. Sandford*, 60 U.S. 393 at 404-407.

[13]For a detailed and documented treatment of the *Dred Scott* decision, see Young, 1-20.

[14]Gary Bergle, "The Never Again Is Happening Now," *People of Destiny* (September/October 1984):12; quoting from Karl Binding and Alfred Hoche, *The Release of the Destruction of Life Devoid of Value*, English Reprint (Santa Ana, CA: Robert L. Sassone, 1975), 76. For a far more complete treatment of the involvement and mindset of the medical profession in Hitler's extermination program see: Robert Jay Lifton, *The Nazi Doctors: Medical Killing and the Psychology of Genocide* (New York: Basic Books, 1986).

[15]John Powell, *Abortion, The Silent Holocaust* (Allen, TX: Argus Communications, 1981), 30-39; see also Gary Bergle, 1.

[16]Language propaganda was used in Germany. Jews became "bacteria." The vans that carried people to their deaths were dubbed the "Charitable Transport Society." Killing centers were called "medical experimentation centers." This language propaganda has analogies to America's abortion industry as well.

[17]There are, however, numerous organizations at the grass-roots level for women suffering from what is medically termed: "post-abortion syndrome" (PAS).

[18]I have not seen a "pro-choice" ethic that is even remotely derived from a biblical base. While the Bible may be referred to as a starting point, the thought forms and language which undergird a defense of abortion are (and I believe, must be) consistently relativistic, humanistic and hedonistic.

[19]Lawrence E. Stage and Samuel R. Wolff, "Child Sacrifice at Carthage: Religious Rite or Population Control?" *Biblical Archeological Review* (January/February 1984):31-49.

[20]Some religious scholars, seeking to avoid the twin facts that, scripturally, an unborn baby is a human child and killing any innocent human is murder, have used a curious rationalization. They argue that since no Bible text specifically states "aborting an unborn child is murder" it therefore is not murder in Scripture. This extreme bit of proof-text logic has even appeared in scholarly articles. One could argue with equal validity it is all right to murder a six-year-old or a 36-year-old, for there is not a single text that states "Thou shall not murder a six-year-old child."

[21]See especially Mark 10:13-16 and Matthew 18:1-6. Jesus did not say that unless children become as adults they cannot enter the kingdom, but the opposite.

[22]Many have argued for abortion as the lesser of two evils, and suggested as an ethical analogy the lies told by those hiding Jews from the Nazis; or by those helping runaway slaves escape to freedom in the North. It is an illegitimate comparison: in both these illustrations those involved risked and at times gave their own lives (personal sacrifice) to save the lives of two groups of humans who had been legally declared non-humans. Abortion is exactly the

opposite; it devalues to a sub-human level and terminates another human to preserve one's own lifestyle.

[23]William Willimon, "A Crisis of Identity: The Struggle of Mainline Protestant Churches," *Sojourners* 15, no. 5 (May 1986):28.

[24]In this context it is valuable to notice how Luke, a physician, documents the conception of John the Baptist. An angel tells Zechariah that his son will be "filled with the Holy Spirit while yet in his mother's womb" (Luke 1:15, see also vs. 41-44, NASB).

[25]Willimon, 28.

[26]Emil Brunner writes: "All human sin has an element of weakness; it is mingled with anxiety for one's life, a fear of losing something by obedience to God." Emil Brunner, *Man in Revolt* (Philadelphia: Westminster Press, 1939), 131. Ellen G. White, in describing the voice of Satan to the soul, writes: "I can give you riches, pleasures, honor, and happiness. Hearken to my counsel. Do not allow yourselves to be carried away with whimsical notions of honesty or self-sacrifice. . . . Thus multitudes are deceived. They consent to live for the service of self, and Satan is satisfied." *Desire of Ages* (Mountain View, CA: Pacific Press, 1948), 130.

[27]"We will never know how many Helen Kellers and Beethovens are destroyed each year in America's abortion mills, or how many Anne Sullivans are left without the challenge that makes an Anne Sullivan. We climb a mountain because it is there and calls us. We solve a problem because it is there and challenges us. How terrible if someone leveled all the mountains and removed all the problems. How little opportunity would be left for human beings to become both really human and really Godlike." George Tribou, quoted in John Powell, 129.

[28]In a recent letter (9/1/88) one of the editorial team of the *Adventist Review* stated "that to take a pro-life position is to say that death is the worst possible fate. This is not so." He then backs up this assertion by quoting Jesus, in reference to Judas: "It would have been better for this man if he had not been born." This thinking is tragic at two levels. First, he apparently argues, in advance of the fact, that many lives are hopeless. This is odd for a man who professes faith in the redeeming and transforming power of God. Secondly, he twists Scripture from a spiritual to a materialistic context and implies Jesus is referring to material or emotional hardship rather than persistent and final rebellion when He acknowledges the horror of Judas' fatal choice.

[29]Pam Koerbel, *Abortion's Second Victim* (Wheaton, IL: Victor Books, 1986), 140-141.

[30]See *Ministry* (May 1988):12, 16.

[31]Willimon, 27.

10 Control of the Body— Control of the Mind:

Autobiographical and Sociological Determinants of a Personal Abortion Ethic in Seventh-day Adventism

Michael Pearson

Introduction

On Friday, May 6, 1988, David Alton's bill to amend abortion law in Britain failed to gain its second reading in the Palace of Westminster, and thus became so much more legislative detritus. His bill was designed solely to reduce the time period in which a woman could have an abortion from 28 weeks to 18 weeks. It was a simple, and many would say, reasonable and worthy aim, which might attract support even from some in the pro-choice lobby. And yet it was not so simple. All attempts to reform the 1967 abortion law have failed, and those opposed to abortion have concluded that, rather than mount a frontal attack on the act, they will attempt to erode its provisions at various points by bringing in a series of less ambitious bills. By this means it is hoped ultimately to reverse the presumption in favor of a woman's right to abort a fetus which exists in Britain, and of course in many other countries.

Alton and his supporters were angered not so much by the failure of the bill itself as by the manner of its failure. The bill's opponents used parliamentary procedure to—if I may use the expression—abort the bill. It was a classic case of filibustering.

The feature of the situation on which I wish to focus is that the matter, which had become a prominent issue in the media and was of considerable public concern, was resolved on procedural rather than ethical grounds. While opponents of the legislation had publicly defended their corner on ethical grounds before the parliamentary debate, ultimately they were able to put up a smokescreen between themselves and the painful question of how we are to relate to unwanted fetuses. They distanced themselves from the agonizing complexities of the issue.

I wish to argue that all of us, not least in a forum like this, face the temptation to do something similar. All our highly intricate moral, theological and medical argumentation may be little more than plausible rationalization of wishes, emotions and attitudes which are very deep-seated, respectable clothing for our prejudices, possibly sometimes even self-vindications. I am not saying that our exchange of ideas is not very necessary and valuable; of course it is, but we must try to discover what really generates the momentum for our opinions. That requires a high level of honesty within ourselves and among ourselves. We have to acknowledge that our minds are adept at creating the most plausible justifications for views that we *want* to adopt on a more-than-cerebral basis.

Anyone who proposes such a view of the matter should perhaps be prepared to submit his/her own views to scrutiny, and so I want to analyze first the autobiographical underpinning of my own position on abortion. Afterwards I want to provide a brief study of the sociological influences at work in the confessional family of which I am a part, for certain features of the ethos of the Seventh-day Adventist Church may predispose me to adopt a particular view.

Autobiographical Determinants

1. If you wish to attach a label to me, it would have to be the "pro-choice" label. Such labels are often unhelpful, and oversimplify all kinds of complexities, but I believe there are circumstances in which it is legitimate to abort the fetus—to do so is to choose the best of the options available. Though I have become more conservative in my views of late, I still find the pro-life case less than compelling.

I hold this view against a background of experience which is clearly deficient in important respects. Not being a member of the medical profession, I have never been present on an occasion when a fetus was being aborted; I have never seen the contents of the womb in the dish; I have never had to consign the contents of the womb to the garbage can. I have never confronted at the level of my own family the guilt and the remorse of a woman who has had an abortion, nor have I shared in any intimate way the relief of a woman who has chosen abortion as a way of extricating herself from difficulties which seem to her otherwise insurmountable. These and other important deficiencies in my experience clearly influence my judgment on the ethics of abortion.

2. The first rather obvious but important biographical detail about me is that

I am male. I have never experienced, and could never experience, the process of bonding with a child growing within. It seems to me that an adequate Adventist response to the question of abortion can never be formulated until Adventist women have articulated their views on the subject. Conclusions formed in a male-dominated forum like this must remain partial.

Like many males, I am attracted to solutions to problems which are tidy and simple, but fail to see the emotional implications of a particular course of action. Thus in a crisis I am likely to consider abortion as a serious option. Many males are, of course, strongly opposed to termination. But that is also, in a sense, a tidy solution, for it minimizes the need for agonizing and the quest for self-knowledge. I suspect, however, that they are mostly opposed to other people's abortions. And in saying this I am not accusing them of hypocrisy. When confronted with a life crisis ourselves, we have a tendency to modify our ideals, temporarily at least, as M. Potts, Peter Diggory and John Peel have shown. In their book *Abortion*, they show that Roman Catholic nurses who are opposed to abortion in principle are included to resort to it themselves when in personal difficulty at no less than an average rate. Subsequently, they often re-affirm their anti-abortion stance.[1]

3. Furthermore, I am politically "liberal," inclined to "live and let live." Thus I am prone to favor legislation which provides a range of possible options for personal behavior. I therefore favor abortion law which is relatively permissive, though I greatly dislike the way in which many people use the freedom which the law confers. I think that there is more to be lost than gained by a return to the days before abortion law reform. It would be mistaken to think that tightening up the law would necessarily reduce the number of abortions.

4. At this point, the autobiographical detail becomes a little more precise. I acknowledge that I have been particularly influenced by the experience of counseling a student who had had an abortion. The relationship which eventuated in the pregnancy was not a serious one; the father had had some history of drug abuse. There was a history of antagonism within the young woman's family, a history which, one suspects, had driven her to seek affection elsewhere. Without much prospect of support, she had opted for an abortion, and by and large felt relief afterwards though she still had to deal with feelings of guilt. It seemed to me to be a case where the law permitted her to choose the lesser of evils.

I find that conviction disturbed but not dislodged by the case of a delightful and intelligent student whom I am currently teaching. She gives a most moving testimony to the courage of her mother who rejected urgent medical advice to abort her on the grounds that she (the mother) had a serious heart condition.

5. I confess also to being influenced by the experience of a friend who

145

discovered that her contraceptive coil had somehow become embedded in a fetus that she discovered she was bearing. She was told that the fetus, if it survived, was likely to be seriously malformed. In the distressing circumstances, it seemed to me that she and her husband were justified in electing to abort the fetus.

6. I am keenly aware also of a distressing experience I had once in an Adventist church. During Sabbath School I sat behind a young but haggard-looking couple who carried on their laps a child who moaned throughout the proceedings and whose body periodically jerked violently and uncontrollably. I later discovered that the couple had been warned at a fairly early stage by their doctors that their child would be severely mentally handicapped. I also learned that their pastor had advised them that abortion was a sinful act which God could not condone. Casual observer that I was, I felt that the pastor himself bore a heavy responsibility in the matter. My instinct was that it would have been better had the child never been born.

7. All of these experiences were poignant and formative in their own way, but they were sufficiently distant from me that I could to some extent throw them off. But now I have to come the closest to home. There has been one experience of my life which has brought me the closest to the abortion dilemma. Immediately after the birth of our second child, my wife experienced an alarming deterioration in her physical and mental health. It was due in part to a hormone deficiency; the symptoms also resembled those of post-natal depression somewhat. The strands of the illness were very difficult to unravel. It subsequently became clear to me that I bore some responsibility in the matter by being uncomprehending and rather unsympathetic to the plight of an imaginative and intelligent woman suddenly thrust into the unfamiliar and tiring role of being responsible 24 hours a day for two lively and demanding children. With the benefit of hindsight, I can acknowledge the courage and faith of my wife. We entered into a long, dark tunnel from which it took us some eighteen months to emerge. It was not unrelieved darkness; it was a roller-coaster experience, but with many more downs than ups. It was perhaps the most painful experience of my life, but paradoxically, probably the most fruitful as well. As the darkness deepened, I found myself asking, and yet hardly daring to ask, questions about what was to be done if my wife became pregnant now. I felt that with two children under the age of three, we would have faced a desperate situation. I asked myself at a deep level the question: Would you consider an abortion under such circumstances? The answer came back "yes." I am glad to say that the dilemma never actually confronted us, but the prospect of it was sufficient to drive me to seek a permanent contraceptive solution.

I was obliged in that time to confront myself in a way that I had never had to before, and that moment of self-awareness has led me not to wish to preclude anyone from electing for abortion in circumstances which they perceive to be as threatening as mine then seemed. I would be lacking in integrity to deny anyone a right which I might then have wanted to claim for myself.

I believe that if the pro-life case is to be compelling, it must be articulated from the other end of the long, dark tunnel. A clinical statement of principles, theological or philosophical, is simply not sufficient, though it is necessary.

That is the end of my autobiographical sketch. My judgments are based, I confess, on fragmentary evidence, but then life is such that we rarely have the luxury of possessing all the relevant information before we make our decisions. I suspect that all of us have had particular experiences which have influenced our opinion in one direction or another. You may have had experiences similar to mine which have convinced you that abortion must be retained as a legal option. The painful experience of witnessing the wanton destruction of fetal life may have convinced you otherwise. It seems to me essential that we acknowledge, at least within ourselves, and to each other, the force of such powerful emotional, intuitive and volitional factors as we try to face the dilemma honestly. As we do so, we must bear in mind that in this forum, attitudes will be confirmed or modified, attitudes that will figure prominently in the minds of people who will seek advice from us in their moment of distress. We owe it to them to be open enough to have the dearest of our preconceptions challenged, so that we can offer them our wisest counsel.

Sociological Determinants

I now want to pass from the realm of the autobiographical to that of the sociological. I want to argue that just as there are *personal* factors which predispose us, without determining us, to accept a particular position on abortion, so too there are *sociological* factors within our own particular religious communion that similarly have an impact on us and of which we may be less than fully conscious— determinants in the biography of Adventism, if you will.

1. I have sought to demonstrate elsewhere[2] that Adventists as a group are occupationally ambitious, and as a consequence place a high priority upon attaining a good education. Accordingly, Adventists are disproportionately highly represented in the professions and in tertiary education. An unplanned pregnancy clearly might seriously disrupt the plans of those young Adventists with high

147

educational and occupational aspirations.

Similarly, an Adventist couple perhaps in their thirties or forties, wishing to provide a denominational education for their growing children, might find that goal jeopardized by an unplanned pregnancy. Again an unmarried Adventist woman might opt for abortion if she felt it to be in the best interests of children who might be legitimately conceived later in her life. Appeal to the principle of good sterwardship has in its time covered a multitude of sins and might be employed here.

2. There is considerable evidence to show that those who use birth-control methods efficiently are more disposed to resort to abortion in the case of contraceptive failure than those who do not. Further evidence exists to show that there is a positive correlation between the use of the pill and sterilization, and favorable attitudes to abortion. One suspects also that an uncritical use of the IUD, which some would regard as an abortifacient, might exist together with a willingness to terminate a pregnancy in the case of a family crisis.

3. Kristin Luker's profile of the typical pro-choice activist was that she was forty-four, married to a professional, herself had a college degree, was employed outside the home, had two children, and had a family income of $50,000.[3] It fits the Adventist woman better perhaps than the profile of the pro-life activist, who was married with three or more children, had only a high-school education, was not employed outside the home, and had a family income of only $30,000. One wonders whether the number of children that these activists, on both sides, had, derives from some previously held ideal, or whether the ideal derives from the size of their family and is in some measure a self-vindication.

4. All the above suggests that purely according to the criterion of socio-economic status, Adventist women are certainly potential candidates for abortion in case of an unwanted pregnancy.

5. The nature of the relationship between religious affiliation and readiness to seek abortion is a matter of some debate. Daniel Callahan has argued that the more devout and informed a woman is, the more likely she is to reject the abortion option.[4] Norman Ryder and Charles Westoff similarly have discerned a correlation between the frequency of a woman's church attendance and her refusal to opt for abortion.[5] Potts et al., on the other hand, assert that women seek abortion regardless of their own religious convictions or the official position of their church. Religious affiliation tends simply to create problems of conscience rather than to discourage abortion-seeking behavior.[6]

6. There is evidence to suggest that fundamentalist groups are generally much more likely than are liberals to reject abortion except on the strictest of therapeutic

grounds.[7] Yet Adventists are somewhat difficult to locate on the liberal-fundamentalist continuum, as R. Theobald has rightly observed.[8]

We must ask whether there is anything in the particular nature of Adventism which, having been absorbed over many years by an Adventist woman (or man) by a process of osmosis, will incline her to choose a particular option.

7. Bernard Häring, the eminent Catholic moral theologian, has observed that in the United States, legality has often been taken to confer moral rightness on a particular piece of behavior.[9] Adventists, for various reasons, are generally careful to perform their civic responsibilities and maintain solidarity with surrounding society. It is therefore distinctly possible that the legalization of abortion has led some members to admit the moral legitimacy of this procedure.

8. Potts et al., have noted a correlation between the propensity to take risks and the willingness to terminate a pregnancy.[10] While Adventists not uncommonly take risks, or "acts in faith" as they would see it, it is doubtful whether this tendency would extend to the moral side of life. Rather, an Adventist woman is more likely to be somewhat fatalistic—having been reared on notions of "doors" being "opened" and "closed" by God—and accept an unanticipated pregnancy as being an act of providence, even in some cases a punishment.

9. The fact that Adventists distinguish themselves in everyday life from other people by Sabbath observance is significant here. Respect for the Decalogue may incline a woman against an abortion; the prohibition against killing is only a couple of lines down from the call for Sabbath observance.

10. The Adventist preoccupation with the maintenance of good physical health as a religious duty might incline a woman to pursue the natural, if onerous, path of an unwanted pregnancy rather than undergo an unnatural procedure with possible unforeseen complications.

11. The fact that this meeting is taking place at all is an acknowledgment that the church has not in the past aligned its theology with its institutional practice. The church has not demanded of its scholars that they produce a coherent response to the question. In this respect, we are like other Protestant organizations. The Roman Catholics have a much better record for doing moral theology. We have tended to adopt a pragmatic approach to such problems. Observers both inside and outside the church have noted that pragmatism is a characteristic feature of Adventist life, which is not entirely a bad thing.[11] It was this pragmatic approach which allowed Adventist physicians to respond to the needs of the Vietnamese boat women who were raped by marauding Thai fishermen and became pregnant in the most distressing circumstances. A pragmatic approach allows for flexibility of response, but may produce uncertainty, inconsistency or even loss of integrity.

We have been remiss in omitting to do adequate serious work on abortion (and many other subjects) and communicating it at the popular level. How do women actually perceive the church's attitudes on abortion? They probably see confusion. They see that their church really has too often preferred to talk about wedding rings, coffee-drinking, theater-going, and the like, rather than discuss weightier matters of an ethical or socio-political nature. They could perhaps be forgiven for thinking that the church regards such an issue as of only relatively minor importance. If they see the church as concerning itself at all with the problem, they again face a confusing prospect. On the one hand, articles which appear in Adventist periodicals like *Review, Ministry*, and *Insight* adopt generally an anti-abortion posture. On the other hand, they may be aware that at the institutional level the church has provided its hospitals with a policy which inclines towards being liberal.

What perceptions might Adventist women (and men) have of the denomination's theology which might bear on the abortion issue?

12. An important area of investigation, and one that has received far too little attention in Adventist circles, is the matter of attitudes towards immortality. In Catholic theology, a soul is infused into the embryo at the very moment of conception, and it, as an inheritor of original sin, must not be allowed to perish without baptism. The matter is clear-cut. There is a soul to save as soon as the sperm fertilizes the egg. The situation in Adventist theology is far less clear. At death, a person "goes down into the grave there to lie unconscious until the resurrection day."[12] Adventists do not believe that there exists a separate entity called a soul; rather in the gestation period, man "becomes a soul."[13]

Adventists have tended to explicate their doctrine of conditional immortality from the point of view of the one who dies. He or she "sleeps," unconscious of the years which intervene between death and resurrection. He or she awakens then as if it were the next moment of their lives, rather as someone who awakens from sleep may express surprise at the fact that he or she has been asleep. From the point of view of the bereaved, however, Adventist doctrine may offer less immediate comfort than traditional Christian doctrine. The loved one dies, the body decays, there is no soul which endures. Where is the loved one? What is this identity that will be reconstituted at the second advent? It seems that there is a kind of genotype, a unique formula, which exists in the mind of God—but nothing else. I would suggest that the idea that a woman bears in her body a genotype which is going to pass into a genotype again—rather than immortal soul—via the circular route of life, is in itself sufficient somewhat to diminish respect for the fetus.

But more than that, countless millions of genotypes existing after their death in the mind of God will be called into life at the second advent only then to face the extinction of judgment—the second death. I fear that this comes uncomfortably close to being a model of abortion on a cosmic scale. In the center of Adventist theology then, we have a story of countless millions of lives, having been reactivated or reconstituted, being jettisoned, even if for the best of reasons, or "therapeutic grounds." Such a mechanism may predispose some Adventists to regard human potential in a less serious way than would those who believe quite unequivocally that at conception there exists an entity which is of eternal significance. You may think that my explication of the second death as an abortion procedure writ large is far-fetched, even perhaps irreverent, and of course I would not want to suggest that any Adventists who consider abortion to be a valid option are necessarily aware of such a view at the conscious level. But I think that we would be unwise to exclude the possibility that the Adventist view of immortality affects our perceptions of the abortion decision, for it seems to contain within it the principle of the expendability of human life.

13. On the other hand, Adventist doctrine might in some ways encourage an anti-abortion stance. A common argument in favor of abortion is that through the evolutionary process the body has developed a mechanism for expelling the abnormal fetus from the womb spontaneously. Induced abortion becomes then only an extension of that process. As creationists, Adventists are unlikely to find that kind of explanation convincing. Furthermore, belief in an imminent advent might lead some to ignore the justification for abortion on the grounds of a spiralling world population. Moreover, some members would undoubtedly regard wide-spread abortion as evidence of the evils attending the climactic last days of human history. Again the notion of a detailed scrutiny of individual behavior—the investigative judgment—will only enhance this effect.

14. Again let me say that I am not suggesting that any such considerations would operate at the conscious level. Nor am I suggesting that there is any way of knowing how these considerations will weigh in any individual case. I am contending that years of living in a spiritual and theological ambience of this type will affect at a deep level an individual's response to a deep personal crisis.

15. With the twin authorities that Adventists normally consult—the Bible and Ellen G. White's writings—apparently silent, or at best less than unequivocal, on the matter, Adventists have had to consult their own consciences. At this point traditional Adventist hermeneutics may let down rank-and-file members seeking to come to a sanctified decision. Not finding a "thus said the Lord" on the matter, they may assume that the decision is a purely private and subjective

one. Unfortunately, we have not encouraged our members to cast their nets widely in the sea of biblical wisdom to find their answers, and in this we have been remiss.

16. Let me, in conclusion, restate the point I am making. Significant autobiographical determinants of our personal abortion ethic underlie the rationalizations for that ethic which we are prone to offer in public debate. Furthermore, that ethic is forged in a particular socio-cultural context. Our experience of life in the Seventh-day Adventist Church is an extremely important part of that matrix. I am not at all arguing that our attitudes are determined, in the formal philosophical sense of that term, by autobiographical and sociological influences. I am saying that the more we are aware of those influences at work, and are able to articulate them, the more we are likely to reach mature and sanctified decisions.

It goes without saying, I hope, that none of us, no matter how well-informed we may be on the subject of abortion ethics, has the right to tell a woman or a couple that a particular course of action is right or wrong in a given situation. To do so would be to usurp the role of God's good Spirit in guiding them to a free and wise decision. We can only help to fill in details on the map; we cannot tell them which route to take.

It does seem to me, however, that if we wish to encourage, as we might well do, the formation of a more conservative pro-life presumption in the church, then there is a considerable amount of consciousness-raising to do. If we think it morally desirable that one of our sisters should go through with an unwanted pregnancy rather than seek an abortion, then we the church have to be prepared to offer the emotional, financial and social support that would make carrying the baby to term seem a possible option. To the extent that we withhold that support, remain content to be judgmental, and fail to generate an ambience of concern, we bear some measure of responsibility for those abortions which do take place in our midst. That is a view which will not find a ready acceptance in our ranks; rugged individualists that we are, we are suspicious of the idea of corporate guilt. But until such time as we are prepared to carry one another's burdens more effectively than we now do, we dare not cast the first stone.

Endnotes

[1]M. Potts, Peter Diggory, and John Peel, *Abortion* (Cambridge: Cambridge University Press, 1977), 119.

[2]Michael Pearson, *Millennial Dreams and Moral Dilemmas: Seventh-day Adventism and Contemporary Ethics* (New York: Cambridge University Press, 1990).

[3]Kristin Luker, *Abortion and the Politics of Motherhood* (Berkeley, CA: University of California Press, 1984).

[4]Daniel Callahan, *Abortion: Law, Choice and Morality* (New York: MacMilliam, 1970), 298.

[5]Norman Ryder and Charles Westoff, *Reproduction in the United States* (Princeton, NJ: Princeton University Press, 1971), 279.

[6]*Abortion*, 119.

[7]Ibid., 363.

[8]R. Theobald, "Seventh-day Adventists and the Millennium," in Michael Hill ed., *A Sociological Yearbook of Religion in Britain* 7 (London: SCM Press, 1968), 126.

[9]"A Theological Evaluation," in J.T. Noonan, ed., *Morality of Abortion: Legal and Historical Perspectives* (Cambridge, MA: Harvard University Press, 1970), 142-43.

[10]*Abortion*, 536-38.

[11]B. Wilson, "American Religious Sects in Europe," in C Bigsby, ed., *Supercultures: American Popular Culture and Europe* (Bowling Green, OH: Bowling Green University Popular Press, 1975), 114; D. McAdams, "The 1978 Annual Council," *Spectrum* 9, no. 4, 372.

[12]Francis D. Nichol, *Answers to Objections: An Examination of the Major Objections Raised Against the Teachings of Seventh-day Adventists* (Washington, DC: Review and Herald Publishing Association, 1952), 372.

[13]Ibid., 511-19.

11 The "Hard Cases" of Abortion

Teresa Beem

Baby Jessica fell into an old well. The world was alerted and we glued ourselves to the television, praying, crying, and hoping that the little girl would soon be rescued. The hours turned into days and our prayers grew fervent. Was she still alive? Was she starving to death? A great shout of joy could be heard around the world when finally, after almost 60 hours, she was pulled, tattered and bruised, from her blackened tomb. Jessica was alive, thank God!

We learned through the desperate struggle of many volunteers, by the heartfelt prayers of millions of people, just how precious this one child's life was. One small child, just able to walk—and literally every stone was turned to save her.

As I was caught up in the true-life drama of Jessica, a pang of irony gripped my stomach. Baby Jessica's story has some similarity to the subject we are discussing: a small child, encapsuled in darkness, unable to be seen, many people speculating as to whether she was alive. More important than the similarities, though, are the differences. Jessica had the world on her side. Many volunteers helped to save her. There was no doubt in anyone's mind that Jessica must be saved at all cost. She was no more human, no more valuable, no more vulnerable, no more a member of God's family than an unborn child. So where are the rescuers of those children when their mothers wish to kill them by abortion? Where are the cries of millions around the world for them? Yes, there are those brave souls who call themselves pro-lifers, that selflessly work to rescue the unborn child, and I hope I can be counted among them; but there are far too few.

I am a pro-lifer. I believe that upon conception a unique individual, a gift of God, has entered the human family. No one but God created that life, and no one has the right to take that life but God. When we destroy one of our fellow men we destroy a part of His creation. I don't believe in bombing abortion mills or terrorizing the people who run them or go to them. I do, however, believe

155

that we as American citizens should actively pursue the reinstatement of the unborn child's right to live.

Every twenty seconds in the United States a child's life is destroyed by an abortionist;[1] almost 20 million since the Supreme Court decision in 1973. I hold that the Supreme Court decisions of *Roe v. Wade* and *Doe v. Balton* legalized abortion in the United States for any reason at any time during a woman's nine months of pregnancy.[2] More than 95 percent of those are done for social or emotional reasons.[3] Most Americans will agree that this useless genocide should be halted.[4] What about the other abortions? Why are they performed? Are they "necessary"? These abortions are performed for reasons of rape, incest, mental or physical handicap of child, and endangerment of life or health of the mother.[5]

The purpose of this chapter is to present some reasons for looking at some of the "hard cases" that are used to legitimize abortion with a different perspective.

Rape and Abortion

One cold January evening, sixteen-year-old Kay ran through an underpass on her way home. She was grabbed in the darkness and raped. She told no one. Soon she began experiencing horrible nightmares and paranoia. For four months she calmed herself by rationalizing that her missed periods and queasiness were due to the trauma of the rape. Soon it became physically evident, and her fears were confimed: Kay was pregnant.[6]

This is an exceptional story. Becoming pregnant after a rape is extremely rare. The FBI estimates that half a million rapes occur annually in the United States. Less than one percent of rapes end in a pregnancy.[7] There are many possible reasons for such a low incidence of pregnancy:

1. The woman may be using birth control.
2. The rape occurred during the non-fertile or "safe" time of the menstrual cycle.
3. The woman may not be able to conceive due to natural or deliberate sterilization.
4. She may be too young or too old to conceive.
5. Ovulation may be disrupted because of the extreme trauma of rape.
6. No intercourse took place, or sperm deposited elsewhere.
7. Fifty-eight percent of rapists are sexually dysfunctional at the time of the rape.[8]

Yet there are instances, like Kay's, when a woman does become pregnant. Should she be able to obtain an abortion, legally or morally, because the child was conceived after rape?

In 1973, the Supreme Court heard the story of a Dallas woman who said she'd been gang raped and become pregnant. I believe the high court's ruling on this case opened up the possibility for a woman to kill her child for any reason.[9] But fortunately, the ruling was too late for the baby of the Dallas woman; the mother had already given birth and adopted her into a loving family. It might be interesting to hear that baby's opinion on this topic.

Kay gave her child up for adoption also. She has this to say:

> I can live with the fact that I have been raped, but I could not live in peace if I had killed my child. I do not agree with those who advocate abortion for rape or incest. One violent, cruel act doesn't justify another. Our laws do not condemn the rapist to death, so it is insane that we would issue a death sentence for an innocent baby. Robin (the child conceived by rape) is no different and no less valuable than any other human being. In fact, I have often imagined Robin and my other daughter (born through marriage) standing together before a gathering of all the pro-abortion people. I would ask the crowd to decide which one should live: Does one deserve to die because of the way she was conceived, because of the sin of her father?

The Bible has something similar to say in Deuteronomy 24:16 (NKJ): "Fathers shall not be put to death for their children, nor shall children be put to death for their fathers, a person shall be put to death for his own sin."

Kay chose life for her child. This is not unusual. About half of the women who become pregnant by rape carry their children full term. Only one of 25,000 annual abortions is performed on a woman pregnant from rape.[10] Less than 100 abortions occur each year in the United States because of rape or incest.[11]

So there *are* women, although few, who obtain abortions because of rape. Jackie was one of them. She was sexually assaulted at knife-point in Hollywood. She also became pregnant. She was told by her family and friends that abortion was the only answer. They offered no solutions. Jackie recalls:

> I believed them when they said my nightmare would be over and I could get on with my life after the abortion as if nothing had ever happened. I felt an emptiness that nothing could fill, and quickly discovered that the aftermath of abortion continued a long time after the memory of the rape had dimmed. For the next three years I experienced horrible depression and nightmares. I would dream of

giving birth, but they would take my baby away from me. I would hear crying and I would search, but I could not find her anywhere. I would just hear her cries echoing in the distance.

When a woman has an abortion, she may experience post-abortion syndrome or psychological trauma. This pain can be doubly devastating when combined with the after-effects of rape. If a woman willingly engages in sex and becomes pregnant, her post-abortion symptoms can be any one or several of the following:

1. Depression, suicidal thoughts, suicide
2. Nightmares and/or flashbacks of the abortion
3. Preoccupation with becoming pregnant again or having babies
4. Anxiety about fertility and childbearing issues
5. Interruption of bonding with present and/or future babies
6. Survival guilt
7. Alcohol or substance abuse
8. Brief reaction psychosis
9. Anniversary syndrome[12]

The rape victim, although unwillingly pregnant, will probably experience some of these symptoms combined with the emotional remembrance of the rape. Could carrying this child be any worse? Most believe it would be more scarring. Yet one expert says that the "victim's problems stem more from the trauma of the rape than from the pregnancy itself."[13] The author of *Psychological Aspects of Abortion* writes that for a woman pregnant from rape "the factor making it most difficult to continue her pregnancy is how her loved ones treated her."[14] Another experienced counselor wrote, "Abortion does not un-rape a woman."[15] The director of Suiciders Anonymous of Cincinnati reports that "the pregnant rape victim's chief complaint is not that she is unwillingly pregnant, as bad as the experience is. . . . We found this experience [the rape] is forgotten by remembering the abortion, because it is what *they* did."[16]

Our first story, about Kay, reveals that her feelings began to change as her pregnancy continued. "Surprisingly, the nightmare diminished as I felt the baby move. This new life brought the first glimmer of healing from the rape."

Jackie, who chose abortion, wrote a letter to her "daughter," whom she named Jennifer, asking her forgiveness for aborting her. Here are some excerpts from that letter:

Dear Jennifer,

I knew the moment you were conceived, although I tried hard to ignore it. Since you were the result of rape, I felt so lonely and confused. In the beginning I wanted only to destroy you. . . . For years afterwards your cries echoed in endless dreams until finally healing took place. Then I named you, and allowed myself to grieve over your death. I also was a victim as a result of making my decision on a few scraps of misinformation. . . . Now I press on to help women who have made the mistake of abortion, and to also help others not make the mistake I made. The healing can only come through the powerful love of Jesus.

Until we meet again, My Jennifer, I Love You.

Should a woman have a legal right to abortion? Especially a rape victim? So far I have used women who, because of personal experience, say no. Can we use their testimony to decide for other women? We might be able to find many more testimonies of women who chose abortion because of rape and felt they did the right thing. As Adventists, however, we must look at the question in a much broader sense. We obey laws, yes, but we answer to a much higher power when we make our choices. We make decisions not only from personal and other people's experiences, not only by what we feel at the time, but by what God's Word says. We should base our actions upon the laws in the Bible. There we find God's commandment not to kill (Deut. 5:17, Ex. 20:13). We learn that we are not put on this earth to find our own happiness, nor to manipulate people and things to solve our own problems. We are here to follow Jesus' example and show love and compassion to our fellow humans.

We are all given trials, just as Job in the Bible. We are held up by Satan to the entire universe, and our works and reactions to those trials either glorify God or mock Him. We show our commitment to God by humble, unselfish submission to His commands. He turns our sorrow into joy; He takes what seems like tragedy and turns it into triumph.

It seems all too clear to me that making abortion illegal, except in cases of rape or incest, invalidates the whole argument of illegal abortion. Let me explain. The reason we should not kill pre-born people is that they are people and have the right to be protected. Biologists, geneticists, fetologists—to name a few professionals—have proven that human life begins at conception.[17] We have allowed the killing of that unborn child because society feels sorry for the young woman. We give her the fairly new concept of the "right-to-control-her-own-body" because we can see she is emotionally unready to be a mother, or so she convinces us. If we allow the rape victim access to abortion for emotional reasons, we must allow all women the same. Either all unborn children have the same rights or they do not. We cannot pick and choose those who are "really human" by the way in which they are conceived.

Another problem with allowing rape victims access to abortion is that there are several types of rapes.

1. Statutory rape involves a girl, 15 years old or younger, who willingly has intercourse with a man of legal age.

2. Date rape occurs when a woman on a date is forced into sex.

3. Marital rape takes place when a man forces his wife into sex.

4. Assault rape is the most commonly thought of when we speak of rape. This is when an unknown, possibly armed, man surprises a woman and sexually assaults her. It is often accompanied by beatings and threats on the woman's life.

Although all are degrading and forced (with the exception of statutory rape), could all be used to gain legal abortions if abortion-on-demand was done away with? Marital and date rape would be almost impossible to prove. If the law only considered assault rape, women would begin staging rapes to get abortions and perhaps innocent men would be put in jail. Rape can be proven only if the woman immediately reports it to the police and gets medical attention. If she does this, she can receive hormonal therapy to prevent pregnancy. This makes the abortion-because-of-rape argument invalid.

An anonymous caller to a radio talk show told her story:

> I am the product of rape. An intruder forced his way into my parents' house, tied up my father, and, with him watching, raped my mother. I was conceived that night. Everyone advised an abortion.... My father, however, said, "Even though not mine, that is a child and I will not allow it to be killed." I do not know how many times that, as I lay secure in the loving arms of my husband, I have thanked God for my wonderful Christian father.[18]

Kathy, at 16, was raped when the man from whom she had accepted a date drove her to the lake instead of taking her home, as she had requested. She screamed and screamed. Somehow she knew she would become pregnant. She did. Kathy's story occurred many years ago, before the legalization of abortion, so she tried to kill her child herself. She drank ant poison, jumped off tall haystacks, and punched her stomach. Kathy recalls:

> Patrick is now 22, and I thank God abortion was illegal when he was conceived. If it had been available, I do not know for certain what I would have chosen, but I am glad I did not have the option. I pray for the day when it will again be outlawed. I guess both Patrick and I are classic examples of God's mercy and grace and what He can do in the case of rape.... Every life is of immeasurable value and importance, no matter what the circumstance of their conception. God gives each person something unique to contribute, and when even one life is lost, we all lose something.

What about the women who choose abortion? Surely we cannot say they made a mistake, can we? I would never presume to judge anyone's decision in a case such as this, but I will say that she will never know what that child could have meant to her, or an adoptive family or society. Romans 8:28 says, "All things work together for good to those who love the Lord...."

Even if conceived outside the sacred marital bed, there is no such thing as "wrongful life." If a child conceived of rape is "wrongful life," is God no longer Master of the Universe, the giver of life? If He remains so, then surely none of His creation is expendable.

If Christianity demands that we forgive the father, we must also forgive the child. We often forget that the child is still a part of the mother. The baby may be half the rapist's, but it is still the mother's flesh and blood. Can we justify killing all of the child to rid it of its "ugly" half? Maybe we should take the Bible literally when it says He will not give us more than we can bear.

I do not mean to sound legalistic or less than compassionate towards a woman who has gone through something as horrible as rape. I, being a woman, have lived in dread of being raped. I, along with probably every woman in America, check the back seat of my car before I get in. I also feel somewhat panicked when I must enter a dark, empty house alone at night. Yet I question the kind of compassion used by society when persons automatically opt for an abortion if a woman becomes pregnant following a rape. No matter how well-meaning our judgment seems, abortion probably isn't the best answer for the woman. It never is for the child.

Kathy's son, Patrick, a happily married, handsome young man, tells us, "As a child of rape, I have a unique outlook on abortion. If abortions had been legal when I was conceived, I would not be alive. I would have never had the chance to love and give of myself to others. I have had wonderful opportunities to share my testimony, too. Whenever someone says, 'What about rape?' I have the perfect answer!"[19]

AIDS and Abortion

I have often heard people who seem to be grasping for straws in search of a legitimate reason for abortion ask, "What about a woman who has AIDS and becomes pregnant? Shouldn't she abort that child? It is going to die anyway." I always retort, "If we are going to kill someone because that person has AIDS, why not start with the mother! Let's begin killing the transmitters rather than the innocent receivers!"

We shouldn't kill persons because they are terminally ill. I know some feel it would be better to abort a preborn child rather than to allow it to be born and suffer (an odd thought: killing someone for his or her own good!). Shouldn't the mother have the right to make that decision?

Let us clear this up. When we speak of a woman's "right to choose" we are speaking of her right to choose to kill her child. If we give her that right before birth, why not extend the right to the time immediately following birth? Maybe even to three days after birth? Why not declare a baby legally alive a few days after his or her birth? Then we can give the parents a real choice! Since only after birth can we test that baby for AIDS or some other grave handicap, since only then can we know for sure the baby is the "right" sex or has blonde hair, since only after birth can the parents really know if they wish to handle the responsibility of the newborn, shouldn't we give them the "right to choose" then? The Nobel Prize Laureate and scientist who cracked the genetic code, James Watson, suggested these very ideals in his article "Children of the Laboratory."[20] The same mentality and arguments we use to allow abortion slide easily into allowing infanticide.

We are all dying. From the moment of conception, we all learn to live with the fact that time will eventually bring death. Some people die sooner than expected; some lucky few defy time and see their great, great grandchildren. We can never accurately predict when anyone's life will end. That is, as it should be, in God's hands. We cannot justify killing an unborn child who has AIDS or anyone with a terminal illness because doctors believe their lifespans are short. We must not kill people because they will soon die.

Because they want to spare the family emotional and financial burdens some justify abortions of unborn AIDS victims. Yet, we find that these same people exhibit a different philosophy when we speak of a relative of theirs who has cancer, or needs a triple bypass or kidney transplant, or has AIDS as an adult. They would spend hundreds of thousands of dollars to provide a few extra years, no matter what the quality of life for those adults. Certainly we should extend the same chance to the preborn child who may need extensive medical treatment. No one's life should be measured monetarily. No parents should be encouraged to abort a child for financial reasons. C. Everett Koop, in an address to a group of medical professionals said, "It is really not up to the medical profession to attempt to alleviate all of the injustice of the world that we might see in our practice in the form of suffering and despair. We can always make the effort to alleviate the pain of individual patients and provide maximum support for the individual family. If we cannot cure, we can care, and I do not mean to ever use the words 'care' and 'kill' as being synonymous."[21]

We are not placed on the earth to seek our own gain. We are here to glorify God by our giving to others. Jesus said in Matthew 25:40, "Whatsoever ye have done to the least of these, my brethren, ye have done it unto me." We are all God's children, bought by Christ's blood, made in His image. Because of sin we are all deformed, diseased, and handicapped compared to His original creation. God has not destroyed us because of it. As degenerate, sinful humans, we are awfully pompous to think we should decide which among us is of less importance and worth. This is a classic example of the "pot calling the kettle black." 1 Samuel 2:6 (NIV) says, "The Lord brings death and makes alive; He brings down the grave and raises up." If God chooses, let Him destroy the mentally retarded, the dying, the severely handicapped, the diseased, the insane...the proud, the liars, the adulterers. Sin has reached us all. Yet we all have a purpose in God's plan. Isaiah 45:9-11 (NIV) says, "Woe to him who quarrels with his maker, to him who is but a potsherd among the potsherds on the ground. Does the clay say to the potter, 'What are you making?' Does your word say, 'He has no hands'? Woe to him who says to his father, 'What have you begotten' or to his mother, 'What have you brought to birth?' This is what the Lord says, the Holy One of Israel, and its maker: concerning things to come, do you question me about my children or give me orders about the work of my hands?"

Romans 9:20-21 (NIV) also expands this thought: "On the contrary, who are you, O Man, who answers back to God? The thing molded will not say to the molder, 'Why did you make me like this?' will it?"

According to a professor of population ethics at the Harvard School of Public Health, "The moral question for us is not whether the suffering and dying are persons, but whether we are the kinds of persons who will care for them without doubting their worth."[22]

The sick and the dying teach valuable lessons to those who care for them. They learn compassion, faith and innumerable lessons that could be learned no other way. People in life-and-death situations actually minister to those who serve them. If we rid society of the sick and dying by killing them, we will be losing an opportunity for maturation and growth.

Malcolm Muggeridge, the writer and humorist, spoke of aborting babies with severe disabilities. I think we can use his wise words to speak about the unborn AIDS victim:

> No more sick or misshapen bodies, no more disturbed or twisted minds, nor more hereditary idiots or mongoloid children. Babies not up to scratch would be destroyed, before or after birth, as would also the old beyond repair. With developing skills of modern medicine the human race could be pruned and carefully tended until only the perfect blooms—the beauty queens, the MENSA I.Q.'s, the athletes—remained. Then at last with rigid population control to prevent the good work from being ruined by excessive numbers, affliction would be ended, and death itself abolished, and men become not just like gods, but in their perfect mortality, very God.
>
> Against this vision of life without tears in a fleshy paradise, stands the Christian vision of mankind as a family whose loving father is God. Here the symbol is not the perfected body, the pruned vine, the weeded garden, but a stricken body nailed to a cross, signifying affliction, not as the enemy of life, but as its greatest enhancement and teacher. In an army preparing for battle, the unfit are indeed discarded, but in a Christian family, the handicapped are particularly cherished and give special joy to those who cherish them. [23]

The Life of the Mother and Abortion

In 1985, Dr. Joseph MacDougall told the story of one of his patients, a twenty-three-year-old mother with a one-year-old child. She was hospitalized, suffering from tuberculosis, and was near death. One day Eleanor (the patient) asked if she could please go home for Christmas if she was still alive then. The doctor promised her that she could only because he knew she would not make it till then. It seemed so little to do to make her happy. Yet, on Christmas Eve Eleanor still hung on to life. True to his promise, the doctor allowed her to go home. When she returned her condition was worse and soon she was down to 80 pounds. New complications developed; she became nauseous and vomited continually. As ridiculous as it seemed the doctor gave her a pregnancy test and, to everyone's astonishment, it was positive. The doctor said, "On the very outer frontier of life itself, she now bore a second life within her. When I told her, she smiled and sort of blushed." Legally, medically, they strongly advised an abortion, yet Eleanor and her husband said no. The doctors didn't push because they knew her body would reject the baby anyway. They began to feed her intravenously, and although they kept insisting she was dying, Eleanor refused to die and kept her child. The doctor stated, "Then an incredible thing began to happen. In late June of 1948, we noted some improvement. . . . She began to eat and to gain weight. An x-ray showed that the growth of the TB cavity had stopped. The diaphragm was pushing up against the diseased lung to make room for the child she bore. Nature was doing exactly what we had failed to do: it was pressing the sides of that deadly hole together."

Eleanor gave birth to a normal, healthy baby. In a few months she was so much better they allowed her to go home. The baby whom everyone said would hasten her death actually saved her life.[24] A miracle, I know. Yet we can never predict when God will intervene with a miracle.

When doctors have done everything possible, and when a woman's life is endangered by a pregnancy, the doctor must advise what he or she thinks is best. Then it must rest with the mother; only she can make the decision of abortion. She can also go to the Bible for some principles to guide her. There we find the story of a little lost lamb (Luke 15:3-6). The shepherd had a flock of sheep that he tended. But when the smallest, frailest, most vulnerable was in trouble, the shepherd left his flock to rescue him. He was even willing to put his life in danger to save the lost one (John 10:11).

A mother is like the shepherd. She knows when one of her children needs her. She sometimes puts her other children on temporary "hold" to tend to the one most in need. We might apply this parable to the woman facing a therapeutic abortion. For a minute, imagine a terrifying scene. One of your children, your youngest, a toddler, breaks free of your hand and runs into the street as a truck speeds dangerously towards him. You, the mother or father, are standing at the curb holding onto your two older children. What would you do? Would you consider the consequences to your own life and weigh the responsibilities to your other children and allow the child to be run over by the truck? Would you sacrifice one child because of your responsibilities to another? No, I would guess that you would fling yourself into the street without the slightest hesitation, regardless of personal injury or death, to save your little child.

I know abortion isn't quite like that. It is a premeditated, calculated decision about a child you have never seen, a child to whom you may not be as emotionally bonded as you are to the ones you can see. But I have based my entire argument on the fact that the unborn *is* a child. Snuggled warmly inside the protective womb where no one can see him or her develop, the unborn child *is* a living human being. Even though a mother has not held the baby in her arms or wiped its runny nose, or heard its first cry, she kills one of her children if she has an abortion.

I do not mean to sound cold or hard. I can understand why a woman might choose an abortion under such rare and sad circumstances. I have two small children myself and I cannot imagine not being there for them. I cannot imagine giving up being their mother to give life to another child, leaving them, heaven forbid, to the responsibility of others. Yet, I will tell you this, I would find it close to impossible to kill any of my children to save my own life.

After the birth of my older brother, the doctor told my mother not to have any more children. She had literally ripped herself apart carrying my brother, and to have any more children would be foolish and dangerous to her life. Either the Lord has looked after my foolish mother or the doctor was wrong, because my mother gave birth to me a year later. Then she had another child, and another, and another, and another. Six children proudly and figuratively stand next to my young, vibrant mother, proving that abortion is not always the answer even when the doctors say it is the only answer.

The Bible says there is no greater love than that a man should lay down his life for friends.[25] Do not misunderstand me, the Bible does not coerce or demand this of anyone. And I am not suggesting that we should convince a woman to carry her child to term if it would mean losing her life. Neither should we pass legislation making therapeutic abortion illegal. Therapeutic abortions should remain legal. When I say therapeutic, I mean those abortions that are required to save the lives of the mothers.[26] Studies suggest that such cases account for less than one percent of all abortions. But let us remember the woman with tuberculosis. If we automatically choose abortion when we face a life-and-death decision, we rule out God's possible intervention with a miracle. We should not pass laws that would require a woman to die because she is pregnant; however, abortion is not the automatic answer for the Christian. If I am ever faced with this decision, I hope that I have the faith and relationship with Christ that I will be open to the leadings of the Holy Spirit. Dr. MacDougall concludes his story of Eleanor by saying, "It [a miracle] happened, I am convinced, because there is a power, a wisdom, a balance, a mystery beyond man's comprehension—and man should recognize and accept it."[27]

Conclusion

Pro-lifers are often given the stigma of being uncompassionate, unrealistic fetus lovers, who are against the woman in a personal crisis. That is why I chose to discuss so many stories about real people in real crises instead of citing cold statistics. I have let the people who have endured and overcome rare tragic circumstances speak to you about their views on abortion and why they feel it is wrong. I have also expressed my opinion along with a few experts. Yet, I have spoken of the hard cases, the cases in which you might disagree with my conclusions and still remain on the conservative pro-life side. I only hope that my remarks have opened your minds and hearts to new ideas for even the seemingly open-and-shut cases.

My dream is that you and I together can join in the effort to uplift the humans of God's creation. I pray that our society may see the wonders of God's hand even in the tiniest of human beings. Since the beginning of man's existence, when God breathed into Adam's nostrils and ignited the spark of mankind, the gift of human life, the image of God, has been passed down; first, through Adam to Eve and then to the first child at conception. Thus the chain of life has continued till now and will continue into the future. We are all a part of that chain and have a kindredship to our fellowman. We must protect and preserve the life and dignity of each human because we are Americans, but more importantly because we are Christians. And because we are Christians we must do it with love and compassion.

> Deliver those who are drawn towards death, and hold back those who stumble to the slaughter. If you say, 'Surely we did not know this, Does not He who weighs the heart consider it? He who keeps your soul, does He not know it? And will He not render to each man according to his deeds?'
>
> Proverbs 24:11 (NKJV)

Endnotes

[1]Melody Green, "Baby Choice" video (Lindale, TX: Americans Against Abortion, 1987).

[2]Dave Andrusko, ed., *A Passion for Justice* (Washington, DC: National Right-to-Life Committee, 1988), 20. John Willke and Mrs. John Willke, *Abortion Questions and Answers* (Cincinnati: Hayes Publishing Company, Inc., 1985), 21.

[3]Gary Bergel, *Abortion in America* (Intercessors for America, 1985), 6, 148.

[4]Senator Orrin G. Hatch, *The Value of Life* (Washington, DC: National Committee for a Human Life Amendment, Inc., 1984), 14.

[5]Willke and Willke, 148.

[6]All three stories of raped pregnant women come from a reprinted pamphlet "Raped and Pregnant—Three Women Tell Their Stories," (Lindale, TX: Last Days Ministries, 1986).

[7]Beverly Wilding Harrison, *Our Right to Choose* (Boston: Beacon Press, 1983). Basile J. Uddo, "On Rape, Incest and the Right-to-Life," *The Human Life Review* X, no. 3 (Summer 1984):58. "What the Public Really Thinks About Abortion," *Concerned Women for America* (Washington, D.C.):147.

[8]A. Helligers, U.S.C.C. Lecture at Abortion Conference, Washington, D.C., (October, 1967). A. Nicholas Groth and Ann Wolbert Burgess, "Sexual Dysfunction During Rape," *New England Journal of Medicine* 297 (October 6, 1977):764-766. *Sexual Medicine Today* (January 1978) p. 16 states "sexually dysfunctional." This term refers to impotence, premature ejaculation, or retarded ejaculation.

[9]President Ronald Reagan, *Abortion and the Conscience of the Nation* (Nashville, TN: Thomas Nelson Publishers, 1984), 15. Willke and Willke, 20-21.

[10]*Concerned Women For America*, 147.

[11]Harrison, 147.

[12]Teri Reisser and Paul C. Reisser, "Help for the Post-Abortal Women," Booklet #146 (Pomona, CA: *Focus on the Family*), 7-16. Patty McKinney, Terry Selby, Jill Lessard, and Karen Sullivan Ables, "How to Survive Your Abortion," (Taylor, AZ: The Precious Feet People):7-8.

[13]Mahkorn and Dolan, "Sexual Assault and Pregnancy," *New Perspectives on Human Abortion* (Washington, D.C.: University Publishers of America, 1981), 182-199.

[14]Mahkorn, "Pregnancy and Sexual Assault," *Psychological Aspects of Abortion* (Washington, D.C.: University Publishers of America, 1979), 53-72.

[15]Curt Young, *The Least of These* (Chicago: Moody Press, 1983), 208.

[16]M. Uchtman, Director Suiciders Anonymous, Report to City Council (September 1, 1981).

[17]Robert A. Wallace, Jack L. King, and Gerald P. Sanders, *Biology: The Science of Life* (Glenview, IL: Scott, Forseman and Co., 1981), 867-870. Gerald J. Tortora, Ronald L. Evans, and Nicholas P. Anagnostokas, *Principles of Human Physiology* (New York: Harper and Row Publishers, 1982), 383-384. Report, Subcommittee on Separation of Powers to Senate Judiciary Committee S-158 97th Congress (1st session, 1981): 7-10. John Willke and Mrs. John Willke, *Handbook on Abortion* (Cincinnati: Hayes Publishing Co., 1979), Chapter 3. Willke and Willke, *Questions and Answers*, 42.

[18]Willke and Willke, *Questions and Answers,* 151.

[19]"Raped and Pregnant—Three Women Tell Their Story."

[20]J. Watson, "Children From the Laboratory," *American Medical Association Prism* (May 1973):2.

[21]Reagan, 61.

[22]Ibid., 60.

[23]Ibid., 80-82.

[24]Dr. Joseph MacDougall, "When All Else Failed." Taken from portions of a 1985 Birthright Convention Banquet speech in Toronto, Ontario (Lindale, TX: Last Days Ministries).

[25]1 John 3:16-18 (NASB); John 15:13.

[26]Study from Alan Guttmacher Institute, research arm of Planned Parenthood (July 1988). "Family Planning Perspectives." Study group of 1,900 women in 38 abortion facilities during period of November 1987 through March 1988. Study reveals 4% of women stated health reasons as one of contributing factors for abortion. None were believed to be of life-threatening proportions.

[27]MacDougall.

Part IV

Church and Society

12 Adventist Guidelines on Abortion

James W. Walters

Introduction

Seventh-day Adventism is in many ways a paradoxical faith which defies stereotyping. This is good news for those of a philosophical bent. It is unwelcome news for those who desire easy answers.

On matters of individual freedom, we Adventists have sided with the likes of William O. Douglas, one of the most liberal U.S. Supreme Court justices within the century, who, e.g., consistently ruled in favor of allowing free (often obscene) speech. Interestingly, being champions of freedom has forced our church to strongly oppose Bible-believing Senator Jesse Helms and even popular President Ronald Reagan in their contention for prayer in schools.

On the exclusivity of Jesus Christ, Adventism is not one of the garden-variety evangelical denominations. An Adventist is not "a New Testament Christian" in the way a Southeasterner whom I canvassed in my college days for religious books claimed for herself. Even if we can rid ourselves completely of legalism—anathema to all good Christians—we are doctrinally and temperamentally committed to the revelation of God through the *entirety* of the Scriptures.

On biblical interpretation, Adventists are on record as favoring a most progressive position within conservative Christianity, where a view of biblical inerrancy is common. Ellen G. White has persuasively written that the Bible is a divine-human product, with the writers serving as God's human "penmen"—not his pens. However, just to further the paradox of Adventism, on the literalness of Genesis 1 and 2, Adventism is decidedly traditional in spite of its commitment to education and science, while a number of theologically conservative thinkers are more open to the insights of theistic evolution (e.g., Bernard Ramm).

All this suggests that Adventism is not wholly predictable, and its position on abortion is no exception. Given the denomination's generally conservative

173

theology and its extensive health commitment, one would guess that the denomination would be strongly pro-life; yet it is not. The most official pronouncement on the subject holds that abortions in Adventist hospitals are acceptable for such common reasons as maternal health, fetal handicap, rape or incest, an early teen pregnancy and, most significantly, "When for some reason the requirements of functional human life demand the sacrifice of the lesser potential human value."[1]

Whereas the socio-political positions of the religious right are predictable, analogous positions of our denomination vary considerably. The lack of consistency is a problem from the point of view of systematic theology, but it is a sign of potential vitality. Adventism is not a flat, one-dimensional creation; it is complex, dynamic and inviting of discussion and inquiry. This quality will remain so long as the Bible is taken seriously by the church—not as a shibboleth, but as a historical revelation of God's relationship with people. The Bible is a multifaceted work which contains much diversity which overlays its fundamental message of divine grace.

Guidelines

At this time in the denomination's history there are two good reasons for a reexamination of abortion policy. First, there appears to be a growing disparity between the church's announced policy and the general membership's intuitive sense of rightness on abortion. On the one hand, the church's pro-choice policy is being largely followed by denominational medical centers and physicians, but on the other hand, a large number of members uncritically reflect an anti-abortion position. A right-leaning membership should be no surprise, given the many new adherents in the Third World coming from Roman Catholic backgrounds and the percentage in America probably influenced more by a conservative national ethos on the topic than by historic Adventist dogma.

A second reason for the church to take a serious appraisal of abortion is that such an undertaking is long overdue. Given the denomination's stake in health-care delivery—a billion-dollar-a-year ministry—the lack of a well-reasoned, historically Adventist statement on abortion is unfortunate.

Given the nature of the church, indicated in part below, there is no need for a new, 28th "fundamental belief" or even creation of a policy detailing the truth about abortion. Rather, I suggest the need for a set of guidelines which thoughtfully apply historic Adventist beliefs to the abortion issue. Abortion, finally, is not an issue decided in isolation from undergirding beliefs about life and death—

and such beliefs go to the heart of our Adventist faith. So rather than the denomination simply making a pro-life or pro-choice ultimatum, a more theologically sound approach would be to provide the membership with help in thinking through the religious issues at stake.[2] Here are the contours a set of distinctively Adventist guidelines might take:

1. Religious Liberty

Religious liberty—or more fundamentally, respect for freedom of conscience— is intrinsic to Seventh-day Adventism. Adventist forebearers were cast out of their churches in the 1840s because of adherence to an advent truth which most mainline believers rejected. This experience was traumatic and resulted in suspicion of all coercion—even a suspected coercion which comes with necessary organization. Millerite leader George Storrs warned fellow Adventists not to form a new church: "No church can be organized by man's invention but what it becomes Babylon the moment it is organized."[3] Most important for our purposes, a healthy respect for liberty of individual conscience developed. For historic Adventism, a person's conscience is inviolable.

The new denomination viewed respect for freedom of conscience as a cornerstone—and also saw personal freedom as a founding principle of the United States government. Adventist founder-prophetess Ellen G. White approvingly saw providence at work in this new world of freedom: "The fundamental principle of Roger Williams' colony was 'that every man should have liberty to worship God according to the light of his own conscience.'"[4] This insight was to become a pillar of the American experience for which Adventism has high praise. Ellen G. White and subsequent Adventist leaders praise the U.S. Constitution as a guarantor of religious liberty as an inalienable right.

Curiously, however, the popular Adventist mind does not logically associate a strong belief in religious freedom with the cloth from which it is cut—namely, an ideologically neutral state. Many Adventists, appropriately, hold ideals similar to the religious right in terms of personal lifestyle. Nevertheless, an Adventist who continues to adhere to the centrality of liberty of conscience will markedly differ from a Rev. Jerry Falwell in terms of national goals. The religious right is committed to a Christian America; historic Adventism stands for a religiously *neutral* America.

The editors of *Liberty* have long understood the interlinking of religious freedom and state neutrality. Their parlance is "church-state separation." Take, for example, a couple of representative articles from a decade ago when rightist religion was on the rise in America. In her essay, "Must One Be Christian to Be a First-Rate American?" free-lance writer Margaret Hill presents a cogently argued "No." Supreme Court Justice William O. Douglas, a champion of separation of church and state, authored a piece, "A Justice's Case for Free Speech." Subsequently *Liberty* editorialized that although it did not agree with all Douglas's positions, it admired his principled advocacy of separation of church and state. However, it is this very stance that some Christians see as unacceptably liberal since it allows religion, irreligion and anti-religion freedom to advocate competing ideas and follow opposing life-styles. In a word, religious freedom is inseparable from civil liberty. Ellen G. White recognized this in applauding the American republic's "foundation principles—civil and religious liberty."[5]

The Supreme Court of the land, whose essential task is to interpret the Constitution and its amendments, has ruled in *Roe v. Wade* that a woman's constitutional right to privacy finally grants her the option of choosing an abortion within certain confines. The Court deliberately chose to avoid ruling on the difficult philosophical question—finally, a religious issue—of "when life begins." It recognized the different convictions on this matter throughout our pluralistic society, and opted for upholding a pregnant woman's freedom of choice especially during the first trimester.

If we Adventists grant that citizens of equivalent moral standing may disagree on just when an embryo-fetus possesses a constitutional right to life, to desire that the Court opt for, say, bestowing that right on the conceptus is religiously coercive, and hence an illogical *Adventist* position.

2. Human Life

The centrality of Biblical authority in Adventism commits us to take seriously the high view of human life taught in Scripture:

> And God blessed them, and God said to them, "Be fruitful and multiply, and fill the earth and subdue it; and have dominion over the fish of the sea and over the birds of the air and over every living thing that moves upon the earth" (Gen. 1:28).

> When I look at thy heavens, the work of thy fingers, the moon and the stars which thou hast established; what is man that thou are mindful of him, and the son of man that thou dost care for him? Yet thou hast made him little less than God, and dost crown him with glory and honor. Thou has given him dominion over the works of thy hands; thou hast put all things under his feet... (Ps. 8:3-6).

176

For God so loved the world that he gave his only Son, that whoever believes in him should not perish but have eternal life (John 3:16).

Human life is like no other part of God's creation. Truly, the apex of human powers is godlike. Only humans are empowered by God to take charge of life by continuing in the Creator's stead—the domestication of creation, the establishment of civilization, the development of the arts and sciences. Only humans can actively and knowingly participate in the moral universe, conceptually know right from wrong, and worship the Transcendent. Distinctly human life has no comparison throughout the known material universe; it is uniquely precious.

Human life emerges from the wisp of a swimming sperm reaching its destination; life departs with the whisper of breath. It begins with a single egg, then divides by geometric progression until a multi-billion-celled organism of unfathomable complexity is developed. One thing is agreed: human life begins at conception and there are no clear lines dividing one stage from the next. Life is process from beginning to end. If all goes well, 280 days after fertilization, a single-celled human entity has become a bouncy baby boy or girl.

In light of our knowledge of the seamless development of human life, the outrage of Christians at those who participate in and foster many of the million-and-a-half annual abortions in our country is understandable. Human life, *per se*, is precious and deserves protection.

Many pro-choice advocates disagree: the human life of the fetus is only *potentially* valuable life. That is, because the early fetus has not yet realized its potential, it does not have the attendant rights. They are wrong. In a sense a person who is sleeping for the night is merely a "potential" person for some eight hours, yet to take the sleeping person's life is equally heinous in the law's eyes as a murder at noonday. The fetus is equally human life; it just will take more weeks and months to "wake up." From the human life perspective, the issue is not one of timing; it is one of substance—human substance.

3. Image of God

In the Genesis creation story God made the heavens and earth, and then created the myriads of species of flora and fauna. Finally, on the sixth day only man and mammels were made; the apex of the week's activity. Only on the final day did God say, "Let us make man in our image." The idea of persons being created in the divine image has long captivated the Adventist imagination. Pivotal in the discussion has been the classic statement by Ellen G. White: "Every

177

human being, created in the image of God, is endowed with a power akin to that of the Creator—individuality, power to think and to do.[6]

What does it mean to be created in God's image? The immediate impression is usually that of some sort of physical resemblance, but a moment's thought undercuts any idea that the Infinite is confined to mundane bodily existence. Mrs. White is right: the essence of our elevated being is directly and inseparably related to our rational faculties and intelligent action—"the power to think and to do."

That which gives most humans a unique claim to existence beyond that of other creatures is our ability, or at least our potential ability, to experience life in dimensions unknown to other creatures. In our society today those humans who do not have this potential capacity or who have irretrievably lost it, do not share an equal claim. For example, an anencephalic infant is routinely given only comfort care—no life-extending modalities are given, including antibiotics. At the other end of life, a patient reliably determined to be in a permanent coma may ethically have all artificial life support withdrawn—including nutrition and hydration, according to a recent ruling of the American Medical Association. Granted, anencephalics and permanently comatose patients are extreme cases of human life, but standard or permissible moral treatment of these lives suggests that *human* life, *per se,* does not produce a special claim to existence.

Does this line of reasoning apply to abortion? Yes. From the image-of-God perspective, the question is not simply whether the subject is genetically human: the issue is the state of the human subject. For example, a conceptus may be perfectly normal and have great potential, but because it is so far removed from realization of that potential most Christians do not see—and never did see—its claim to life as equal to that of, say, a mature fetus. St. Thomas Aquinas, for example, held that abortion was permissible before "ensoulment"—at 40 days of gestation for a male fetus, 80 days for a female. Although contemporary Christians are not so certain about ensoulment and its initiation, we share Aquinas' intuition that an embryo has a lesser claim to life. For example, some three-quarters of all products of human conception are spontaneously aborted. Yet we hear of no one bemoaning this loss of human life and beginning a crusade to raise funds for science to remedy this "massacre." Further, most Christians are not opposed to a woman's use of an IUD, although the device clearly aborts a usually healthy, week-old human life.

Image-of-God thinking suggests that abortion is permissible if the fetus has not yet achieved a reasonable development toward becoming a being with the "power to think and to do."

4. Wholism

Too often the discussion of abortion becomes fixated on one element: the physical life of the fetus. The physical element of life is central, but finally it is only one dimension of a wholistic view of human life. Significantly, Holy Writ records that the boy Jesus "increased in wisdom and in stature and in favor with God and man" (Luke 2:52).

A cornerstone of Adventist thinking is the unity of life—spiritual, physical, mental and social. It is no happenstance that our relatively small Adventist denomination operates a large parochial school system and manages a world-wide system of hospitals and clinics. Ellen G. White's denominationally influential book *Education* takes a broad view of its subject, defining education as "the harmonious development of the physical, the mental, and the spiritual powers." In keeping with her own counsel, Ellen G. White's ministry to her church was broad. In addition to writing thousands of pages of spiritual counsel, encouragement and admonition, she wrote five books on health and temperance and three on education. The physical, mental, spiritual and social elements of life are anything but disparate elements in her philosophy of life. Typical of statements which contend for the inseparability of life's physical and spiritual elements is, "health should be as faithfully guarded as the character."[7]

Abortion, of course, destroys the physical life of the fetus, but spiritual, mental, and social aspects of significant others' lives are deeply involved as well. Yes, abortion is the taking of human life; however, it is not the taking of self-conscious life. (Few physicians would agree with the premise of the pro-life movement's widely-distributed video "The Silent Scream," that a 12-week fetus knowingly screams as the obstetrician's instrument moves into the womb.) But fully self-conscious lives are very much affected by abortion, and from the point of view of wholism this is relevant. For instance, the pregnant woman's mental well-being, the survival of a couple's weak marriage, or the family's economic health may be an issue in a particular case. What are good reasons in one case may be mere excuses in another. But who is to decide? Most morally sensitive citizens agree that rape and incest are compelling reasons for allowance of an abortion. The majority believe that whatever reasons a woman may have in the first trimester are sufficient to warrant her seeking an abortion. But is this stance proper? From the point of view of wholism, there is a qualified yes.

The point of Adventist wholism is not to indicate all the legitimate elements of a calculus on an abortion, but to contend that a multifaceted consideration should be encouraged. This is done in many abortions, but with others it is not. What is needed is a mechanism to encourage a woman's reflection on important moral aspects of abortion before a decision is made. The current Supreme Court has struck down attempts by municipalities and states to implement educational measures for women seeking an abortion. Interestingly, the state of California has mandated that a man seeking a vasectomy read an informative booklet on the subject and wait a minimum of 72 hours before the operation.[8] If the seriousness of this procedure is sufficient to warrant such educative material and reflective time, isn't at least a modest attempt to persuade a woman to seriously consider a variety of factors in a contemplated abortion justified? The Adventist doctrine of wholism suggests as much.

5. Progressive Truth

Adventism began with the conviction that truth is progressive. Adventist pioneers saw the beliefs of the majority of Christians in upstate New York of the 1840s as well-intentioned, but finally inadequate. God had "new light" for his children! The conviction of *progressive* truth is a fundamental belief of historic Adventism. Not surprisingly, we find Ellen G. White extolling the importance of progressive truth, "the great principle so nobly advocated by (John) Robinson and Roger Williams."[9]

In Adventism the notion of progressive truth is inseparable from personal choice—the right, even obligation, of the individual believer to decide matters of truth for him or herself. The call to "come out of Babylon" was made to individuals, not organizations. The emphasis on individual grappling with issues and personal responsibility for deciding matters of conscience did not yield with the formative years of the denomination. A half century later Ellen G. White is writing in the general church paper that "We must study the truth for ourselves. No living man should be relied upon to think for us. No matter who it is, or in what position he may be placed, we are not to look upon any man as a perfect criterion for us." In the same article the author urges that even fundamental beliefs bear scrutiny: "If the pillars of our faith will not stand the test of investigation, it is time that we knew it. There must be no spirit of pharisaism cherished among us."[10]

A basic implication from the notion of progressive truth for the abortion issue is an openness to investigation. The premises of any belief may profitably be investigated, with the distinct possibility of progress which may confirm—or contradict—earlier insights. According to Ellen G. White the idea of open investigation holds for even the church's most sacred beliefs. This openness is even more appropriate for an issue such as abortion, which is a relatively new topic of church discussion and on which no official dogma has been set.

As another guideline of this essay states, the Bible does not take note of abortion at all, and in the passage which is of closest relevance (Ex. 21:22-24), fetal life is not given equal status with mature human life. Further, Ellen G. White never comments on the practice of abortion. Indeed, the Adventist church has not seen this issue as of sufficient ecclesiastical importance deserving an official pronouncement for the membership.

The Adventist belief in "progressive truth," however, could lead to quite different responses to the abortion question. On the one hand, we could reason that progressive revelation of God's will on abortion is leading us to declare the "present truth" that the million-and-a-half abortions each year in this country are nothing short of mass murder. Accordingly, the church institutes a ban on abortion for all church members and medical institutions. On the other hand, we could find that further examination of the issues involved in the millenia-old practice of abortion only confirm the tradition of leaving the matter up to individual discretion.

6. Do Not Kill

"Thou shalt not kill." This is the classic statement on killing in the Bible. Understandably, many Christians take this dictum as a clear ban on the practice of abortion.

The case for taking the sixth commandment of the decalogue as banning abortion begins with the intuitive simplicity of the issue: the commandment bans killing; abortion is the taking of life; therefore, abortion is in direct violation of a fundamental biblical principle.

The case against a direct application of the sixth commandment to abortion rests on an understanding of the commandment and how it was applied in Bible times. Legitimated killings are well recognized: the killing of animals for food (Gen. 9:3), holy war (Deut. 13:10), and criminal punishment (Ex. 21:29). The commandment did not apply to suicide; in the suicides recorded in the Bible, none is condemned in terms of the type of death (e.g. 1 Sam. 31:4,5; 2 Sam. 17:23).

Abortion itself is not mentioned at all in the Bible. However, there is a biblical passage which is widely recognized as relevant, namely Exodus 21:22-25. The crucial verses are:

181

If men strive, and hurt a woman with child, so that her fruit depart from her, and yet no mischief follow: he shall be surely punished, according as the woman's husband will lay upon him; and he shall pay as the judges determine. And if any mischief follow, then thou shalt give life for life (22,23; KJV).

Although there are some scholars who hold that the possible interpretation of "her fruit depart from her" means a premature delivery (see the evangelical scholars' NIV translation), most contemporary scholars have translated the relevant Hebrew to mean "miscarriage" (e.g., see NEB and RSV).

Assuming the validity of the "miscarriage" translation in light of scholarly consensus, the meaning of the passage is quite straightforward: the two men fighting harm a pregnant woman who is presumably attempting to separate them. If the woman is unharmed but only suffers a miscarriage, a fine shall be levied by the husband and authorized by the judge. If the woman is harmed, *lex talionis*, requiring infliction of like harm (up to life for life), is invoked.

Although the passage is not beyond dispute, the most obvious conclusion is that fetal and mature human life are valued differently. Merely a fine was deemed appropriate for loss of fetal life, whereas loss of the woman's life required the taking of the perpetrator's life as well.

7. Second Advent

The "Advent hope" could be used in our denomination as an excuse for social inaction. After all, so the reasoning could go, if Christ is to come and set the world aright, why bother ourselves with social action? But such reasoning—at least in an explicit form—is not widespread in Adventism. Further, is it not a part of our tradition to work as though the Advent were a thousand years distant but live as though it were tomorrow? As the diverse writings of Ellen G. White show, and as denominational involvement in health, welfare and religious liberty testify, this church is committed to making a difference now.

In light of how Adventists have understood their hope for a better world, belief in the Second Advent does not offer a simple answer to the abortion question. A pregnant woman cannot be simply told to not worry about her aborted fetus, for she will soon see her little one in heaven. Such well may be the case; however, it may not be. But the doctrine of the Second Advent operates at a more profound level of human existence than such an answer may suggest.

Fundamentally, the Advent hope is a belief that human life is not merely some cosmic flotsam passing through the universe toward oblivion. Rather, hope in the Advent is a belief that, beyond the competence of science and the scope of knowledge, there is a loving God who will finally, in the last day, set wrongs right and usher in an era of eternal peace. The ideal principles of this world will be the real principles of that world. Thus, Jesus taught us to pray, "Thy kingdom come, thy will be done, on earth as it is in heaven." Belief in the world to come empowers the believer to implement the eternal principles even now.

This logic has relevance for abortion: We need to apply basic Adventist insights to this human problem facing church and society. However, even after this is done, given the fallen nature of this world, there may still be the rending dilemma of choosing between the *lesser* of two evils—an abortion or a major life-disrupting birth. An Adventist will often choose the latter. If the former is chosen for good reason after careful thinking and prayer, the Advent hope for a better world is a comfort.

Ellen G. White envisions two possibilities for the status of humans who never entered the realm of moral and religious accountability. She does not comment on the status of fetuses, but comments on the future state of some slaves and certain babies.

In a provocative observation on grossly mistreated slaves in 19th-century America, Ellen G. White writes: "God cannot take to heaven the slave who has been kept in ignorance and degradation, knowing nothing of God or the Bible, fearing nothing but his master's lash, and holding a lower position than the brutes. But He does the best thing for him that a compassionate God can do. He permits him to be as if he had not been. . . ."[11]

Ellen G. White wrote to one mother who inquired about her deceased "little one's being saved." She replied: "Christ's words are your answer: 'Suffer little children to come unto me, and forbid them not: for of such is the kingdom of God.' The Lord has often instructed me that the many little ones are to be laid away before the time of trouble. We shall see our children. We shall meet them and know them in the heavenly courts."[12]

Conclusion

An Adventist view of life is rich in offering of perspectives from which to view an issue such as abortion. That the richness presents choices, perhaps confusing choices, is no reason for despair. It merely suggests that abortion decisions, like more common decisions, require good principled judgment.

Let me draw an analogy. Consider an Adventist family's decision regarding a Sabbath afternoon activity. At least three biblical guidelines which illumine

Sabbath observance are:
1) Take a physical rest from a week of strenuous work,
2) Celebrate the natural, created world, and
3) Help those who are deprived of life's fullness.

Should Joe and Mary get some rest while their 10-year-old twins are over at friend's for a Sabbath afternoon Bible game? Or, should the family take this opportunity to hike up Icehouse Canyon in the nearby mountains? Or should they visit Joey, a shy schoolmate who just joined at mid-term but has missed the last three days because of illness?

The three guidelines indicated are all relevant and important. Identification of those guidelines is helpful, for it sets out the boundaries of the playing field within which the choice is made. (Different guidelines, of course, would mean another ballpark—even a different game!) All right, here in the analogy, our guidelines put us in the middle of the Sabbath afternoon decision-field; so what do we do? We decide which guideline "fits." That's not necessarily easy. We first have to give close attention to *context* of the decision: the energy level of mom and dad, the personalities of the twins, the supposed loneliness of Joey, the time since the last nature outing, the supervision of the twins at the friend's home at which a Bible game would be played, etc. The guidelines of physical rest, nature celebration and service to others are to be weighed in light of the concrete context in which the decision is called for.

The same common-sense application of doctrinal guidelines applies to deciding abortion questions. No single guideline wins out every time in each circumstance. That does not mean that the guideline which may not be determinative the second time is a bad one. It is good and was considered; it just didn't fit in the different context as well as did another equally good guideline. The context of the decision is important in determining which of several doctrinally sound guidelines is most weighty for the decision at hand.

The reader may contend that the manner in which Sabbatarians decide an after-church activity is of relatively minor consequence. I grant this. But my point is a procedural one. The common-sense procedure of consulting doctrinal guidelines—which may in a given context indicate contradictory actions—is applicable to abortion cases. For instance, because a pregnant girl is 12 years old, we may decide that an abortion found out only at the 19th week is appropriate, whereas normally such a late abortion would be impermissible.

The stakes in abortion decision-making, of course, are higher than those in deciding how to spend one's Sabbath afternoon. However, the need of the church is identical—neither proscription nor "anything goes." A helpful response by our church at this time in our history would be a set of theological guidelines, delineated in well thought-out, handy form, which can inform the conscientious layperson, professional, and administrator.

Endnotes

[1]"Interruption of Pregnancy (Recommendations to SDA Medical Institutions)," Issued by the General Conference officers, August 10, 1971.

[2]On a pragmatic note, any prohibition of abortion has a high probability of falling on near-deaf ears in a denomination which has long upheld the sanctity of individual choice. A recent survey suggests that even the hierarchial Roman Catholic Church, which, of course, is strongly anti-abortion, is not being heeded by its membership: in this country the abortion rate of Catholic women is reported to be 30 percent higher than among Protestant women. See "High Catholic Abortion Rate Reported," *Los Angeles Times* (October 7, 1988):Part 1, 32.

[3]See R.W. Schwartz, *Light Bearers to the Remnant* (Mountain View, CA: Pacific Press Publishing Association, 1979), 47.

[4]*The Great Controversy*, (Mountain View, CA: Pacific Press Publishing Association, 1911), 295.

[5]See Margaret Hill, "Must One Be Christian to Be a First-Rate American?" *Liberty* 75 (September/October 1980):8-10. William O. Douglas, "A Justice's Case for Free Speech," *Liberty* 72 (July/August 1977):16-17. Reprinted from *The Quill* (September 1976). (I used this religious liberty argument earlier in a piece, "Adventism, Religious Liberty and the Election," *Courier*, a Loma Linda University Student Newspaper [October, 1988].)

[6]*Education* (Mountain View, CA: Pacific Press Publishing Association, 1952), 17.

[7]*Education*, 195.

[8]See "Understanding Vasectomy," Booklet B, 3rd ed. (February, 1983), Office of Family Planning, California Department of Health Services, Sacramento, California; California State Register 81, No. 16 (March 1, 1986), Title 22, 70707.4, "Certification of Informed Consent for Sterilization."

[9]*The Great Controversy*, 297.

[10]*The Advent Review and Sabbath Herald* (June 18, 1889).

[11]*Early Writings* (Washington, DC: Review and Herald Publishing Association, 1945), 276 (emphasis added).

[12]*Selected Messages*, Vol. 2 (Washington, DC: Review and Herald Publishing Association, 1958), 259.

13 Abortion and the "Corporate Conscience" of the Church

Diane Forsyth

Introduction

Hundreds of thousands of children are conceived every year by people who are either unable or unwilling to care for them.[1] How should the church respond with ethical integrity to this societal condition?

In a letter dated November 14, 1988, Neal C. Wilson, President of the General Conference of Seventh-day Adventists, wrote that "We are perplexed and unsure at times whether the church should try to be a conscience for individual members or even whether the church ought to have a corporate conscience in some of these areas." Abortion was one of the areas to which he referred.[2]

In taking or avoiding official actions, the church does speak from a "corporate conscience" of some sort. The question is, what sort of conscience? Having a "corporate conscience" is something to fear if it suggests uniformity or the sacrifice of individual integrity. It is something to celebrate if it is a matter of corporate integrity. Having a "corporate conscience" is also something to celebrate if it is continually developing, as people of integrity come together for the good of the community and the individuals in it.

The corporate church is responsible for being ethical in its printed or spoken communication about abortion. The pastors, chaplains, teachers, and other representatives of the church who communicate with individuals facing abortion are responsible for being ethical. How should they do that? What should inform the conscience of the church? What should constitute an ethical response from the church regarding abortion?

In this chapter I will offer an ethical guideline, and then, with the use of some case studies, discuss some implications and applications of that guideline.

187

The Ethical Guideline

The Christian church is the body and representative of Jesus Christ.[3] The nature and tasks of the church center in Jesus. As Christ's body, the church follows the impulses and directions of Christ the head, and can be true to its nature and task only when it truly represents Christ. *Jesus Christ is the ethical guideline for the church.*[4]

The church is ethical when it learns how Christ initiates and responds, and then initiates and responds that way. Understanding how Christ initiates and responds is like exploring a many faceted jewel. Each of those facets becomes an ethical subguideline. Here are six of those subguidelines that should inform the conscience of the church as it responds to abortion:

1. Accurately assess people and situations.[5]
2. Protect and defend the weak and vulnerable.[6]
3. Confront offenders.[7]
4. Respond compassionately to the needs of people.[8]
5. Proclaim the good news, calling for repentance.[9]
6. Make a difference (contribute to transformation).[10]

Some Cases

With these ethical responses in mind, consider some case studies and observations about the abortion experience. Please keep in mind that while the case studies used in this chapter represent the experience of many people, this representation is not complete. *All* women who face abortion are not like these women. These stories are representative, but not exhaustively so.

As you read these experiences, please do not try to decide what they should have done. Instead, ask "How could the church and its representatives respond to this situation in good conscience, applying the 'Jesus ethic?'"

> Shelby Winters, eighteen, cannot stop crying. Her face, under a tangle of blond curls, is red and swollen, and she is surrounded by a pile of damp Kleenexes. In her blue jeans and football T-shirt, she hardly looks old enough to be able to conceive at all, but she is scheduled for an abortion the next morning. Married for a year to a farmer and living with his family in Indiana, she is being forced by financial and in-law troubles to abort her first child.
>
> We got married last year and went to live on his family's farm. His mother doesn't care for me at all. As soon as she found out I was pregnant, she wanted

me out of the house. My husband had to quit technical school to get a job so he can pay for us to live somewhere. The job he got only pays $2.25 an hour, which isn't enough to get a house on and is certainly not enough for a baby.

My mother-in-law says a baby would hold us together, and she is waiting for the day when we'll break up. . . .

My brother-in-law says if I don't get the abortion I'll be so stupid he won't even want to look at me. He told his wife if she gets pregnant, she should get out of the house.

My husband doesn't demand that I get the abortion, and says that if I really can't go through with it, he'll find some way.

I can't go to my father for help. My father thought I was pregnant when we got married. He said he'd pay for an abortion until I told him I wasn't pregnant. He wanted me to wait until I had a career or married somebody rich. He can't believe I'm married to a farmer. . . . If I ever went to my father for help now, he'd make me spend my whole life paying him back. My mom lives in Albany, New York, somewhere, but I don't know how to get hold of her.

I think abortion is best for both my husband and me. . . .

The problem is deep down I want to keep the baby. I realize it's not the smart thing to do. The abortion will give us more of a chance to get something. But I think about the baby all the time, about my little girl. That's what I had always hoped it would be if I would have had it. If it had been born, what would she have looked like? I just guess I feel bad that when my next one comes along that I would have had another one that I loved. . . .

I come in tomorrow. I'm going to go through with it. I hope I feel better than I do today. I love the baby. I love my husband. I just think it would be better for him if I have the abortion. I'll get over it. I'm sure there'll be a lot of times when I'll think about it, but we got so many problems now. So many. I know I can have another baby someday. But it's this one I love now. I just love her so much. . . . But my mother-in-law says we got to be off the farm in two weeks—if I keep on having my baby.[11]

What should the church and its representatives do, in order to respond in good conscience to Shelby Winters?[12] Consider how often and how "naturally" people respond to a story like Shelby's by saying things like, "She should . . .," "He should . . .," "That wasn't necessary because . . .," "What a tragedy, it could have been prevented by . . .," "How stupid, if only . . . ." Recommendations and judgments flow freely before people and situations are accurately assessed. But it is the responsibility of the church, corporately and individually, to assess accurately first.

We must recognize and respond to all the destruction in the case, not just part of it. Jesus gave life, abundant life.[13] That life conquered *all* manner of destruction. The church and its representatives must also be committed to lifegiving that conquers *all* manner of destruction. Abuse, for example, is part of destruction. Jesus said,

> You have heard that it was said to the people long ago, "Do not murder, and anyone who murders will be subject to judgment." But I tell you that anyone who is angry with his brother will be subject to judgment. Again, anyone who says to his brother, "Raca," is answerable to the Sanhedrin. But anyone who says, "You fool!" will be in danger of the fire of hell.[14]

A footnote in the RSV indicates that "Raca" is an obscure term of abuse. The NIV footnote indicates it is an Aramaic term of contempt. It becomes clear that Jesus is saying that murder includes angry, abusive behavior. Murder also includes destroying another person's sense of worth, i.e., "You fool!"

What becomes of a person who has been treated murderously, but who comes out of it maimed instead of dead? What is our responsibility, as rule givers and care givers, to that person? One or both of those who have conceived a life have often been treated murderously. As a result, they may become unable or unwilling to care for a child.

In addition, for people like Shelby, the feeling of abandonment becomes Calvary-like. See her turn in every direction—to mother-in-law, brother-in-law, husband, father, mother—all without help. Hear her say, "My mom lives somewhere, but I don't know how to get hold of her." It's an echo of "My God, my God, why have you forsaken me?"[15]

Hear the abandonment in the following story told about life and death in an abortion hospital. However painful, practice hearing, *really hearing* as Jesus did:

> Once I watched a woman take leave from her enterprising husband, who has managed to deliver her onto the D & C floor. It is a strictly forbidden practice. She is fair and blond, he is red-haired and ruddy.
>
> "Okay," he says, "you'll be okay. But now I must go."
>
> "Go?" she asks. "Go? Where will you go?"
>
> "Don't start again," he says. "Don't, just don't."
>
> "I won't do it," the woman says, in a dead monotone. Whatever strength she might at other times possess, it is not discernible now. She looks like one about to die.
>
> "But you will," he answers, "you must." He, too, speaks in a monotone, but his atonality is of determination and not of defeat. "Don't go crazy on me, Laurie," he says. "We have been through this eighty-four times. You got pregnant and I am sorry. It does not change the situation."

'What situation? Tell me what is the situation? I love you. We are about to have a child. What situation, Steve?" She is weeping, and I judge the rising note of hysteria in her voice as dangerous.

"Laurie, please. Please. Don't make me go through it again. Let me go."

"I don't know what the situation is. I don't know why I am here."

Suddenly he is very angry. His hands are on her shoulders, and he is shaking her back and forth. "Because-I-am-through," he shouts. His speech is broken into syllables, in rhythm with his enraged assault on her. "Be-cause-I-do-not-want-you, or-this-mar-riage-or-this-child. Be-cause-I-want-out. Out. Out."

He is brutal beyond belief. Yet there is no way to ignore his desperation. . . . (At this point a nurse intervenes telling him he must leave.)

The elevator arrives, and the man enters it. "Goodbye, Laurie," he says. "Goodbye," she shouts as the doors clang shut. "I hope I die."[16]

Commenting on the destructive forces in the lives of pregnant women, one therapist with whom I talked told this story:

A bright, capable, married woman in her late twenties (I'll call her Donna) came for counsel about abortion. Donna grew up with a father who was physically abusive of her mother and her younger sister. Donna tried to protect her mother and sister by trying to control her father. When she saw the signs of her father's anger, she would try to distract him. She would try to explain her sister's behavior, She would try, but of course, she couldn't control him.

When he would begin beating her sister or her mother, or both, Donna would move through the house closing doors behind her until she got to the room where the piano was. While her mother and sister were being beaten, she would sit and play the piano, feeling guilty because she couldn't stop her father.

When Donna came for counseling, control was extremely important to her. She was trying to keep everything in control.

She had married a man who had periods of extreme anger. At these times he was physically abusive to their dog.

When she became pregnant, she was frightened of what she or her husband might do to the baby. She might not know what to do if she didn't maintain control. When she had broken out of control in the past she had been physically abusive to herself by overeating and by pulling her hair out, leaving visible bald spots. She was afraid that during one of these times, she might hurt someone else—their baby. And she certainly couldn't trust her husband during his periods of extreme anger.

"Donna, don't you see what a tragic contradiction it would be to destroy the infant you are afraid of hurting?" If you find yourself saying that, as you listen to Donna's story, then you are probably letting advice and decision-making get in the way of "knowing what is in" Donna. That is something the church and its representatives fall into easily. But Jesus accurately assessed the person and situation first. Jesus completely saw and compassionately responded to the wounded sufferer. He knew the pain and destruction that person suffered.

Erika Ney was 42 and single when she became pregnant for the first time and decided to have an abortion. Hearing her story at the abortion hospital, Magda Denes said, "The loneliness of Erika Ney creeps into my bones. Has she decided well, I wonder. Will she not regret tomorrow losing this last chance to have someone of her own to love?"[17] Jesus completely saw and compassionately responded to all the loneliness and pain a person experienced.

> Tragedy sharpens human features and unnaturally enlarges the eyes. The faces here are topographical testimonies to critical times and accumulated sorrows. Each is a map to serially sustained and survived savageries. . . .
>
> And what of these histories? What of these forsaken, neglected, lonesome lives. . . .
>
> Will, God's or otherwise, appears an obsolete notion. The most frequent gesture is a shrug. The most prevalent phrase is "I don't know."[18]

Jesus was completely aware of the wounded person's suffering. He was equally aware of each person's destructiveness and rebellion. Those who have been destroyed so often become the destroyer. Those who suffer so often rebel.

I read the stories of Vanessa Truth and Karen Tuthill and felt angry with their rebellion. I felt punitive toward them. About Karen I wrote in my notes: "Her suffering seems *so just*." I thought of those who wrote imprecatory Psalms. I knew why.

I don't believe Jesus felt about people like I felt when I read Vanessa and Karen's stories. But I do believe the Church and its representatives often respond with punitive anger.

> Vanessa Truth, a New York photographer and actress, has run the gamut of abortion emotion. Now thirty-six, Vanessa had her first abortion three years ago; it was very positive and made her feel in control of her life. Her second abortion depressed her, as she felt there was a spirit somewhere trying to express itself through her. Her third abortion a year ago, which she didn't tell the man about, meant little to her.
>
> Several years before her first abortion Vanessa had her "love-child, a wanted child, a child that was lusted after." When the love-child was six, Vanessa and her husband divorced and Vanessa, at twenty-eight, started living with someone

who was eighteen. She describes that relationship as "very strange" and "fantastic." After he left, she had the abortion that left her feeling "just incredible." She said, "I have never felt so in control of my destiny or my life. I could really make that decision. It felt fantastic. I never had a bad moment." She described that pregnancy as "a nuisance" and "very inconvenient; utterly inconvenient."

Just before her third abortion, Karen Tuthill discussed her first two abortions with Linda Bird Francke. She was twenty-three at the time of her third abortion. A few years before she had moved from Hartford, Connecticut, to New York. She felt "sort of unattractive" and had an inferiority complex. The first night in New York a waiter at the restaurant asked her to go out. She was excited because he chose her. She said, "I went and I did it." In the year that followed, she "went through every waiter in that restaurant." She said, "My roommate and I kept a scoreboard, and boy, we've been busy. It got so we couldn't remember the names and the faces. It finally tallied up to fifty different guys for me. It was fun."

I settled down for a bit after that first year, but I sure wasn't a Polly Pureheart. And I got negligent about the pill because I didn't have any particular boyfriend. Then I suddenly went through a hot streak and discovered I had something growing inside me. I have no idea who the father was."[19]

Karen went to Eastern Women's Center for the abortion. They told her that with the local anesthetic it wouldn't be terribly painful. But it was. She was screaming and the doctor was getting worried. "Hang on," he kept saying, "It'll be over in a minute." She kept screaming back, "You said there'd be no severe pain and you lied!"

Just before her third abortion, Karen said, "Maybe I should go to a psychiatrist, but I really don't have the money or the interest. Truth is hard to take, and I just don't know if I'm ready for it."[20]

I read, and I was angry at Karen. In my mind, I said vindictive things to her like, "You deserved to suffer severe pain." I read about Karen and Vanessa and others, and I was angry. Angry that they repeat illicit sexual relationships—and abortion—again and again.

I don't think I'm alone in my anger. It sounds to me as though whole segments of the Christian church are prone to that kind of response. In sermons and articles, and in the personal counseling of its representatives, the church "takes positions" and legislates and punishes and isolates. The church makes the woman stand before Jesus, condemned and contemptible in their sight. But Jesus says to the church, "If any one of you is without sin, let him be the first to throw a stone at her." To the woman He says, "Woman, where are they? Has no one condemned you? . . . Then neither do I condemn you. Go now and leave your life of sin."[21]

Remembering that Jesus assessed the whole person, the whole story, accurately, I look again at Karen, promiscuous Karen. I hear her say, "When I was thirteen, I was raped by a guy in Rhode Island."[22] Karen is not alone. She has a multitude of promiscuous sisters, and mothers, and daughters. One in every six of these sisters and mothers and daughters who live in the United States has been incestuously abused.[23]

> This common female experience has been taking its toll on the lives of girls and women, no doubt for centuries. For the most part, neither society nor the perpetrators has yet been held accountable for the occurrence and continuation of this secret trauma. This book has been written with the hope that it may contribute to breaking the vicious incest cycle of betrayal, secrecy, unaccountability, repetition, and damaged lives.[24]
>
> When asked to specify how their experiences of incestuous abuse had affected their lives, many victims spontaneously mentioned negative feelings about men, sex, or themselves. But few women made a direct connection between their childhood victimization and later life experiences such as *adolescent pregnancy*. . . . Such experiences, however, were far more common among women who had been incestuously abused than among those who had not.[25]

The secrecy and unaccountability that typically accompany incest are, if anything, more pronounced in the Church, especially fundamentalist churches. The deans in women's dormitories at Adventist colleges could, but they can't, tell the stories of a shocking number of young women at Adventist colleges who are the victims of incest.

What do other teenage and adult women need, those who are experiencing varying degrees of suffering, rebellion, shame and guilt? Mary Studer Shea writes:

> Everyone is trying to do the pregnant woman a favor, and none of us needs such friends. I am always intrigued by the tales of various acts of charity being foisted upon the poor by well-meaning do-gooders, and the resultant shock and dismay when the poor turn and spit in their benefactors' eyes with great contempt and walk off with the goodies. I have seen patronizing, ignorant, morally superior Birthright people, and, believe me, I'd never turn to them for help or send them a friend of mine.[26]

What did Jesus do in response to suffering and rebellion? What would Jesus do? Therefore, what are we, His body and representatives, to do? This is an old question which often produces simplistic and even stupid answers. Yet answering it with wisdom and insight is the way to a good conscience for the Church.

Six Ethical Guidelines

At the beginning of this chapter I offered six responses that were typical of Jesus, responses that are particularly appropriate in the discussion of abortion. I would like to look at each of these again now that we have glimpsed real experiences.

Each of the six responses in the "Jesus ethic" involves the way we view either the wounded sufferer or the destructive rebel—or both. The ability to recognize each and respond to them, particularly when they are combined in one person (as they usually are) is crucial to our understanding and application of the "Jesus ethic."

The "Jesus ethic" has been around so long that some might think it is redundant to offer it now. But two responses to the "Jesus ethic" have rendered it less effective than if it were unknown. One is the assumption that "everyone knows that." That leads to the other assumption. Those who try to really know and live the "Jesus ethic" discover how challenging it is. Some of them say it doesn't work, isn't relevant, isn't practical—anything to avoid it. So, although the "Jesus ethic" is in one sense extremely familiar, it is often not well known or practiced.

Now, for the brave and the strong, let us have another look at the six responses in the "Jesus ethic."

1. *Accurately Assess People and Situations—First*

Whatever convicts us and stirs our sympathy or anger is likely to receive a disproportionate amount of our attention and energy. In order to accurately assess like Jesus did, we do not need to be less convicted, sympathetic or angry. But we do need to be alert to the ways that our convictions, sympathy and anger may distort the picture and prevent us from seeing and responding to persons and experiences the way Jesus did. Simply being human and therefore unable to respond in every direction at once may also prevent us from seeing and responding to whole persons and situations!

We need a theology of children, beginning with the unborn. It would, of course, be preeminently foolish to try to analyze and synthesize the wonder of children into a section in a systematic theology! Yet we still need a theology of children. We ponder other majesties and mysteries in systematic theology. We could make a place there for children too. Among many other things, we need to believe what is really true about the value of children. They are not just premature adults who will become smart, valuable and productive someday when they grow up. Character development and education of children has always been stressed among

Adventists, and this is good. But it is too bad that this seems to give parents and children the idea that what's *really* important is the fully developed character, the fully educated young adult. It's time to claim the wonder and value of children—as they are, beginning with the unborn. They don't have to grow up, get educated or be accomplished before they are *really* important.

What contributes to child abuse? What social and religious trends and teachings feed it? How does the subordination of women, and the further subordination of children, subtly but powerfully contribute to the minimizing and demeaning of children? It's a short step from there to abuse when abusive people parent children. There are also some things I'd like to hear about men and abortion, some things I suspect are true, that could help the whole picture to emerge.[27] These things have to do with what we call irresponsibility and abandonment. We often do to others the very thing that hurts or frightens us the most. Here is one evidence of this kind of behavior:

> There is growing evidence that a significant number of the perpetrators of incestuous abuse were themselves sexually abused as children. For example, Nicholas Groth (1979) reports that 46 percent of the sexual offenders who showed a persistent and exclusive preference for children reported being sexually victimized as children.[28]

It seems strangely contradictory that men who prize authority, control and power would relinquish it so readily and flee from the birth of a child. Yet this isn't as surprising when we realize that we humans do to others the very things we fear the most, in this case relinquishing responsibility for the unborn. What are we to do with the irresponsibility that hurts and angers us so much? The story of Jesus tells me that He would respond in a healing manner to the fear that produces irresponsibility.

What must abandonment be as it is feared or experienced by men? I suspect it is a great horror, or they wouldn't so frequently abandon the women who carry their children. Is it possible that men suffer more from abandonment, or the fear of it, than women do? Might they feel profoundly left out of the birth experience?

No matter how much we try, we won't see the whole picture. We won't even see one whole person in the picture. But seeing the whole is still the goal. The church is here to respond to the whole picture, and the whole persons in the picture, like Jesus did.

As the church and its representatives increase their capacity to accurately assess, it will become clear that each person is a wounded offender. Each suffers and each rebels. None is innocent. Each sins. As we try to see the *whole* picture, and *whole* person, we end up seeing more brokenness than wholeness. This switch from wholeness to brokenness disappoints us; yet it serves a good purpose. It contributes to our humility, and to our ability to identify with the weak and vulnerable.

2. *Protect and Defend the Weak and Vulnerable*

Several years ago I read one of Gerald Winslow's articles about abortion, in which he discussed protecting the weak and vulnerable. I want to apply this point to the ethics of the church. After citing Deuteronomy 10:17-19, Winslow continues:

> And special care is prescribed for those who are most in need. As Bennett has stated: "God's love for all persons implies a strategic concentration on the victims of society, on the weak, the exploited, the neglected". . . the weak and vulnerable require special attention.[29]

Both pro-life and pro-choice people could cherish this statement. The unborn child is extremely weak and vulnerable and certainly requires special attention. Voices from the other side would say, "Women, especially poor and ethnic minority women, are exploited and made vulnerable beyond belief and certainly require special attention." But I didn't include this statement to defend or oppose abortion. I included it to help illuminate one dimension of the conscience of the church.

Jesus *was* poor. That, combined with what He taught and preached, and who He healed, gave special attention to the weak, exploited and vulnerable. What the church and its representatives preach, teach, and print about abortion must also give special attention to the weak, the exploited and the vulnerable, *all of them*, including frightened men who are made vulnerable by conceiving a child. We are not fit to "come on strong" with convictions until we are truly aware of and sensitive to the weakness, vulnerability, and potential exploitation that comes with being *completely dependent* as the unborn infant is, and as are the procreative and sinful humans who conceive the child.

3. *Confront Offenders*

This is not a guideline for how pro-life and pro-choice people are to treat each other! We are talking about the conscience of the church and its representatives, and how they are to respond to the abortion dilemma and those caught in it. The nature and task of the church both center in Jesus. His reasons for and ways of confronting offenders must be the reasons and ways of the church also. With Jesus' kind of courage and with His kind of nondefensive power, the church and its representatives must respond to the offenders—after they figure out who those offenders are and what their offense is.

"Do you want us to call fire down from heaven to destroy them?"[30] That was how James and John suggested confronting offenders. At times that is exactly what I want too. For example, when I read that:

> American teenagers seem to have inherited the worst of all possible worlds regarding their exposure to messages about sex: Movies, music, radio and TV tell them that sex is romantic, exciting, titillating; premarital sex and cohabitation are visible ways of life among adults they see and hear about. . . . Yet, at the same time, young people get the message good girls should say no. Almost nothing that they see or hear about sex informs them about contraception or the importance of avoiding pregnancy. For example, they are more likely to hear about abortions than about contraception on the daily TV soap opera. Such messages lead to an ambivalence about sex that stifles communication and exposes young people to increased risk of pregnancy, out-of-wedlock births, and abortions.[31]

If there were any hope that fire from heaven would clean up the sexual insanity of our society, inoculate every living person with respect for long-term love commitments, and scare the wits out of all who dare to imagine that it doesn't matter who you have sex with or when—then I would want fire from heaven *now*. People who've gone crazy sexually deserve to be shaken up. If the church and its representatives could call down fire from heaven, then they might get the attention of sinners and command a little respect. Fire—now—on all the sexually crazy people. Let's get to the root of this abortion problem, and let's do it now, Lord. "But Jesus turned and rebuked them, and they went to another village."

Yet Jesus did confront offenders. How did He do it? What can we learn from Him? This is closely related to Jesus' use of power and calls for our careful and ongoing attention. It is essential for the church and its representatives to have the courage and wisdom to confront offenders like Jesus did. We must confront destructive rebels, remembering that they are often the same people who suffer life's most cruel blows. Each person is to some degree suffering and in need of comfort and simultaneously rebelling and in need of correction.

4. *Respond Compassionately to the Needs of People*

That brings us back to compassion. Is there anything more misrepresented or more neglected? What does it mean to you? A warm fuzzy? An indulgent parent to spoil you? The willingness to overlook injustice? God help us.

Compassion calls for the frightening willingness to leave our convictions unexpressed long enough to find out—to really know and taste and be sickened by—what is happening to people, including the destructive ones.

Compassion gives us the courage to stay around when we would rather flee from apathy for fear its ugly, terrifying nothingness will consume us too.

Compassion, the real thing, is grueling. Hear Magda Denes' exhausted compassion:

> I need a vacation from this place (the abortion hospital). I am seeing too much. Too many dilemmas, paradoxes, absurdities, . . . too many undistinguished dramas, everyday tragedies, gray martyrdoms come to my attention.
>
> There are too many Jeanettes. Too many others. Faces blur, voices merge. Not two the same, and all alike.
>
> Humanity, I love you in small doses and from a distance. Because from up close your maggot-eaten, vulture-picked wounds stink to the high empty heavens.[32]

Compassion is the bravest, toughest work of all. It is our work. There is no way to really be the body and representatives of Jesus Christ and not be compassionate.

Faith can be exhausted by compassion; it can also begin compassion. The most powerful sentence by Abraham Joshua Heschel is: "Faith is the beginning of compassion, of compassion for God. It is when bursting with God's sights that we are touched by the awareness that beyond all absurdity there is meaning, truth and love."[33]

5. *Proclaim the Good News and Call for Repentance*

The good, and sometimes unbelievable, news is: The high heavens are not empty. We *can* burst with God's sights and be moved by the awareness that beyond all absurdity there is meaning, truth and love. We must have the audacity to tell the shruggy-shouldered, apathetic sinners there is good news—the high heavens are not empty; we are not forsaken and abandoned.

In addition to telling them the good news, we must also call them to repentance. In order to be able to repent, sinners need to know what they are guilty of, and what they are not guilty of. Guilt like Aletha felt because she couldn't, somehow, keep her angry father from beating her mother and sister—feeling guilty like that is abundant in the lives of many women who seek abortions. They need enormous and patient help to discover and become really convinced that they are not guilty because they couldn't control their father's anger. By the grace of God the guilt that isn't guilt can be cleared away, so sinners can see genuine guilt. Genuine guilt must have a place to find repentance and forgiveness, or it becomes a grinding monster. But guilt that leads to repentance and forgiveness is created by the Spirit. We can't do it. In fact, we make matters worse by trying to make people feel guilty. It's our part to watch with people for the work of the Spirit. Then when the Spirit gives them genuine guilt, we can tell them the good news that there is something they can do with their guilt; they can repent and receive forgiveness.

6. *Make a Difference and Contribute to Transformation*

I am really sick of sweet, accepting church showers for unwed mothers. I am sick of abortions; sicker yet of repeat abortions. I'm sick of teenage mothers looking daggers at their straggly children in the grocery cart at the supermarket. The poor, bedraggled, petulant child finally makes the wrong move one too many times, and child-mother yanks and slaps her toddler—again—destroying another piece of the child's being. I'm sick of it all. I want it to be different.

Jesus makes a difference. How?

How does Jesus make a difference in the lives of teenage or adult men and women who destroy the children they conceive?

Both suffering and rebellion desensitize and consume the victim or offender until only an empty and indifferent shell remains. Observing the teenagers and adults at the abortion hospital, Magda Denes wrote, "I am caught by the horror of helplessness and apathy that lies at the core of most of these lives."[34] Michael Bracken, a research associate in the Department of Epidemiology at Yale University says,

> There is a great concern among clinic personnel who see young girls coming in to abort that though their decision is probably the right decision, the process they've gone through to reach it is very sort of shruggy-shoulders, and they're not really learning from the experience. The decision-making has not been a period of growth for them. They've not learned anything from it. This is especially true among repeat abortions.[35]

How do we, in the name of Jesus, go about making a difference? By doing charitable deeds? By moral indignation? How?

> With all the emphasis on the abortion, we seem to have forgotten this happens to real suffering women, not just to aborted babies. The issue violates the intrinsic

unity between mother and in-utero child. The abortionists concentrate on the woman; the pro-lifers on the child. And both are wrong. The abortionists have depersonalized the process by calling the baby fetal tissue, and the pro-lifers have done just as badly by making the woman merely a recipient or host womb to be as conveniently unburdened as the abortionists want to do, only they want to do it a mere nine months later down the road.

I can simply hear no more right thinking on either side of the abortion issue. I find both sides, and particularly those of the pro-life stance, to be stalwart, morally indignant, singularly without compassion, and therefore, totally uncompelling as persuasive forces to change any behavior whatsoever.[36]

Then how? How is behavior changed? How do we make a difference? Like Jesus did. He healed people. He forgave people. He set people free. All those things made a difference. The people *were* healed, forgiven and set free. Jesus didn't just tell them to believe in being healed, forgiven and set free.

The church can do the same even when its healing, forgiving, freeing efforts are not effective as quickly or as dramatically as Jesus' were. We can set our course in that direction. We can cooperate with God to bring healing, forgiveness, and freedom.

An Invitation

In conclusion, I invite, rather urge, the church to consider its own ethical integrity in response to abortion before it does more to formulate guidelines for the ethical integrity of others. It does not "go without saying" that our church and its representatives are committed to the "Jesus ethic." We need to be intentional, concrete and specific about committing ourselves to ethical integrity. One concrete move in that direction would be to prepare ethical guidelines for those who administer the guidelines before preparing guidelines for others to follow.

The church and its representatives need a good conscience because that's the only way to be who we are and do what we've been asked to do. And without a good conscience our response to abortion will offend and add insult to injury.

As Christ's body, the church follows His impulses. As Christ's representatives the church does what He asks. Jesus Christ is *the* ethical guideline for the church. Six of the responses of Jesus inform the conscience of the church in response to abortion. These are: 1) accurately assess people and situations, 2) protect and defend the weak and vulnerable, 3) confront offenders, 4) respond compassionately to the needs of people, 5) proclaim the good news, calling for repentance, and 6) make a difference.

We won't do it all at once. In fact, we'll never do it all adequately. But we can set our course in that direction. The church and its representatives can claim the wonderful unblemished response of Jesus to human need as our gift and our goal.

Endnotes

[1]The Alan Guttmacher Institute in New York and Washington, D.C. reports 1,100,000 abortions are performed annually in the United States. Linda Bird Francke, *The Ambivalence of Abortion* (New York: Random House, 1978), 16.

[2]Neal C. Wilson, Washington, D.C., to David Larson, Loma Linda, CA, November 14, 1988.

[3]1 Cor. 12:27, Matt. 16:19, Eph. 3:10-11 (NIV throughout unless otherwise noted).

[4]John 14:6.

[5]Luke 14:28-30, John 2:25.

[6]Mark 10:14-16.

[7]Matt. 23, Mark 11:15-17.

[8]Matt. 9:36.

[9]Mark 1:14-15.

[10]Jesus made the difference that people needed when they were, by choice or not, captive to forces that destroyed them physically, emotionally, spiritually, or mentally. He healed, forgave, cast out demons, set people free. Matt. 4:23; 8:28-33; 9:2; Luke 4:16-19.

[11]Francke, 94-95.

[12]John 2:25.

[13]John 10:10, Rom. 5:17.

[14]Matt. 5:21-22.

[15]Matt. 27:46.

[16]Magda Denes, *In Necessity and Sorrow, Life and Death in an Abortion Hospital* (New York: Basic Books, Inc., 1976), 176-178.

[17]Denes, 190.

[18]Denes, 91, 199.

[19]Francke, 51.

[20]Karen's story is recorded in Francke, 58-63.

[21]John 8:3-11.

[22]Francke, 59.

[23]"Our study suggests that a minimum of one in every six women in this country has been incestuously abused. Yet most victims suffer this often devastating experience in silence. Some keep the secret all of their lives. Hence my title." Diana E. H. Russell, *The Secret Trauma, Incest in the Lives of Girls and Women* (New York: Basic Books, Inc., 1986), 16. This 426-page book includes 89 tables summarizing research findings.

[24]Russell, 16.

[25]Russell, 200-201 (italics mine).

[26]Mary Studer Shea, "Cry With the Mother," *Theology Today* 41, no. 3 (October 1984): 326.

[27]See, for instance, Arthur B. Shostak and Gary McLouth with Lynn Seng, *Men and Abortion, Lessons, Losses, and Love* (New York: Praeger Publishers, 1984).

[28]Russell, 83.

[29]Gerald Winslow, "Adventists and Abortion: A Principled Approach," Spectrum 12, no. 2: (December 1981):14.

[30]Luke 9:54.

[31]"Abortion: Why Don't We All Get Smart?" *Christianity and Crisis* 45 (April 1985):123-125.

[32]Denes, 163.

[33]Don Postema, *Space for God: The Study and Practice of Prayer and Spirituality* (Grand Rapids: Bible Way, 1983), 142.

[34]Denes, 126.

[35]Francke, 31.

[36]Shea, 325.

14 Communicating Grace: The Church's Role in the Abortion Controversy

Sara Kärkkäinen Terian

Introduction

Abortion in a church that operates medical facilities presents a test case of the relationship between the church and the world around it. Existing within a secular society, the church must constantly address itself to the question of what its role is and should be within such a society. Members of churches must participate in secular life; in today's world, the church is not an all-encompassing institution. In matters involving moral and ethical dilemmas, however, Christians properly look to their church for guidance. This implies that the church has something to offer which is above and beyond conventional wisdom or the usual practice of the society. There is a dialectical relationship between the church and the world; the church is to be "in" but not "of" the world. It is influenced by the world—in desirable and undesirable ways—but sees its mission as "salt," or effective presence, in the world. In the case of abortion, the question is whether the church should follow the lawful practice of the secular society and perform elective abortions at its medical facilities, and what its message to the world should be regarding this controversial issue. The first question is of greater importance than the second because whatever the church preaches, its practice speaks louder.

Religion, Sociologically Speaking

The extent to which ethics, human freedom, and such issues are considered by a religious body partially places that religious body on the sect-church continuum. As Ernst Troeltsch has noted, a church is by definition "a compromise with the world," sharing its generally accepted values.[1] This means a degree of secularization, and the fact that the Adventist church operates medical establishments at all shows a certain degree of secularization.[2] But it is through such establishments that the church can be of service to the world, and Adventists are rightly proud of this "right arm" of their church. A sect withdraws from the world to avoid secularization; consequently, it is less able to serve.

Another classification of religious groups in their relationship to the society at large is evident in Max Weber's ideal types of priest and prophet, priest representing an established church and prophet a movement. The prophetic view of religion is more critical and shares with Marxism the goal of changing the world. The fact that this goal is in the center of Adventist theology hardly needs documentation. Adventism defines itself as a prophetic movement. In the Adventist interpretation, prophecy is generally restricted to eschatological concerns and preparing people for that event. While foreseeing the future is the most commonly known role of the prophet, the prophetic idea includes more. In the Old Testament tradition, a prophetic voice is a voice of conscience; pre-exilic prophets made repeated calls for social justice.[3] Prophets also communicated both condemnation and pardon.[4] In the New Testament, a prophet is one who reminds people of what the Lord has said.[5] Thus Jesus' concern for people and his forgiving grace are in the center of the prophetic mission. Following the prophetic model, it could be said that the church's mission in the world is to communicate God's grace and to inspire people to extend such grace to one another. The goal is to change the world, but to change it from within, whereas Marxism seeks to change it externally.

Church and State

It is necessary to keep in mind that our focus here is on denominational policy: whether the church should or should not provide abortions. This question comes before the question of whether abortions should be allowed at all in society, a topic not explicitly discussed in this chapter. In the United States, the separation of church and state is an attempt to separate the religious from the practical and political spheres of life, i.e., to provide certain division of labor as well as freedom of conscience. To many conservative Christians in America—including Adventists—this separation is a very precious, sacred tradition that they would definitely want to preserve. The separation is more formal than actual, however, in that each influences and uses the other for its own purposes.[6] It thus entails both privileges and obligations for both partners. For comparatively small, conservative denominations, the separation primarily means religious freedom, that is, freedom to worship according to their conscience and freedom from obligations that would compromise their conscience, such as bearing arms. But in granting this freedom, the state expects something in return. Religious denominations are seen as the major vehicle for value education and the propagation of moral consciousness in the American people—an "obligation" that evangelical Christians view as a privilege and a mission.

Furthermore, religious denominations are expected to extend the same freedom to others as they expect for themselves; in other words, they are to "live and let live." This arrangement is an acknowledgment of the non-exclusiveness of the "truth" held by any one religious group; it is an accommodation to the cultural and religous pluralism of this country. One function of the state is to coordinate the various groups into one society. In this coordination, some matters—such as the provision of equal rights—are proper for the state to handle, whereas other matters that do not endanger the rights of other people are left to the individuals' conscience and to the religious groups to which they belong. Thus, in spite of the push from the Moral Majority, the state in a pluralistic society such as the United States must by necessity be non-sectarian, even though a certain consensus on the most important values is implied.[7] The dictum that one must not impose one's own values on others is valid only to the extent that those values differ too greatly from the dominant values.

The government itself, however, inadvertently influences the values and lifestyles of its citizens. It does not, of course, dictate values or lifestyles and does not get involved unless some citizens' lifestyles threaten "strongly held national values."[8] But by its legislation the state exerts quiet influence so that in actuality most people are less "free" than they think themselves to be. Abortion legislation provides an example. A historical study of abortion trends in Britain, Canada, and the United States shows that legalization of abortion increased its frequency by more than six times (up to 30 times in the U.S.).[9] On the other hand, the negative effects of governmental restriction of abortions are pointed out by many other studies.[10] Either way, it is evident that legislation affects behavior.

While abortion can hardly be reduced to a lifestyle issue, research has shown that "the abortion issue is symbolic of conflicting styles of life."[11] According to Staggenborg, those who in principle oppose abortion subscribe to a "modern" lifestyle which holds the family as a "precious emotional unit." In this lifestyle, a woman's identity is very much tied to reproduction and the rearing of children, and anything that threatens the family is evil.[12] Those who support the option of abortion, on the other hand, subscribe to a "post-modern" lifestyle in which there is instability in the family, women have greater autonomy, divorce is more common, and peer-group values are important.[13]

It appears that this "post-modern" lifestyle is fairly prevalent among Adventists as well, leading many Adventist women to consider abortion as a viable option in case of unwanted pregnancy. Another incentive has come from the legalization of the practice by both church and state. As Michael Pearson notes, "it is conceivable . . . that legalization of abortion has shaped Adventist perceptions of its morality."[14] Interestingly, this "legalization" first came from the church: the permissive "Abortion Guidelines for Adventist Medical Institutions" was first issued in 1970 and again, slightly revised and further liberalized, in 1971.[15] The Supreme Court ruling took place in 1973. Thus Adventists have had double legitimation to guide them in formulating their personal philosophy on the issue. This is an instance in which the Adventist Church followed the liberal strand in American society.[16]

One reason for such a ready acceptance of a liberal practice in a conservative church could be that, since Adventists want special privileges in matters of Sabbath observance and military service, in most other matters there is a tendency to bend over backwards to show that Adventists are not that conservative after all. This is with the hope of being counted among the mainstream of Christianity, with a few conservative, unique features to provide identity. Some speakers have also suggested that supporting the pro-life religious right will contribute to limiting the religious freedom enjoyed in this country, and have thus justified taking a non-conservative stance.[17]

In the matter of abortion, it appears that political pressure has pushed both the liberal churches and the state to endorse a policy that remains a matter of heated controversy in both circles, with vocal advocates on each side and a relatively silent and uncommitted majority in the middle.[18] Thus the policy does not entirely reflect commonly accepted values in this society.

The Adventist Tension

There appears to be some confusion in the Adventist Church as to the role it should assume in today's society, and how its medical work should fit into that role. Is it a prophetic movement with a mission to the world, with the medical work as a tool in evangelism? Or is it merely a social organization with the dual function of providing religious services to its members and medical services to the world, operating in the context of liberal societal values? Historically, Adventism has seen itself as a prophetic movement—the medical work was subordinated and could be spiritualized in the perfectionist context of early Adventist theology. While the theology has been transformed from perfectionism to righteousness by faith, the medical organization has grown into a major industry that no longer fits theologically. As Malcolm Bull notes, "the medical work is implicitly in conflict with the specifically religious aspects of the Adventist tradition."[19] The question of abortion crystallizes this conflict.

It is in the concept of service that the religious and the medical sectors unite. The Adventist Church appears to lack a consistent theology of service which includes an ethic formulated not so much on apologetics as on a true examination of the most fundamental principles on which the church's doctrine and practice are based. Bioethics need to be based on appropriate metaethics. Utilitarian ethics may fit a secular state that tries to coordinate and administer life in a pluralistic society, but such ethics would not be proper for a conservative church that still acknowledges its prophetic mission. As was mentioned above, the state looks to the church for help in tightening the moral fiber of society. If the church has not formulated its own philosophy, it is ill-equipped to take a stand on the diverse issues with which society struggles.[20]

Humanness of the Fetus

In the abortion debate, respect for persons has been discussed in the context of assessing the humanness of the fetus.[21] Although that is not the major point of this paper, a note on it will be illustrative. As is well known, the major problem in this debate is the difficulty of ascertaining the point at which the fetus becomes a human being.

Some facts of embryology can perhaps help solve this problem. Most embryos—some scientists say at least 60 percent—fail to implant themselves in the lining of the uterus and are lost without anyone knowing they were there.[22] This takes place within the first few weeks after fertilization. As the embryo is transformed into a fetus,[23] the first thing that develops is the brain. Brain activity and conscious sensation develop gradually, but are present within the first one to two months. Memory also develops early: "well before the end of the first trimester, the baby produces vasopresin, a hormone that aids memory function."[24] Although some have rejected the brain-life idea as a criterion,[25] it must be remembered that in the euthanasia debate brain death is a widely accepted point at which life-supporting machinery can be turned off, and this is not seen as inducing death.[26] Thus, "if the death of the brain is the end of a human, is its birth not his beginning?"[27] For one who accepts this viewpoint, IUDs and "day after" pills present no ethical problem but are, rather, blessings that prevent other ethical problems, such as overpopulation and forced pregnancy in rape victims.

A point has been made that whereas the fetus is a type of human life, it is not a "person." Joseph Fletcher has even constructed a list of the qualities of personhood which have to do with the faculty of reason, some sense of the past and the future, and a capacity for interpersonal relationships.[28] Thus, in light of Maclagan's exposition, a fetus and a small child would only be concerned with the pleasure-pain principle, not the realization of values. They are still to be respected, however, not only because of our emotional bonds with them—especially with the small child—but also because of the value of their potential personhood. The reverse side is the other end of life in which personhood may be little more than memories, if even those, yet such a human being is also to be respected—a grandmother with Alzheimer's disease has not ceased being a person. A Christian philosophy that values human life over animal life would extend potential personhood also to retarded or otherwise deformed infants.[29] As creatures, even normal, healthy human beings are never through growing and changing, but always on the way, always dependent on others, always striving toward ideal humanity.[30] Thus there is a "fundamental contrast between man-as-he-happens-to-be and man-as-he-could-be-if-he-realized-his-essential-nature"; in other words, potentiality is an essential element of human *telos*.[31]

Respect for the Personhood of the Mother

If a human life with potential personhood is to be respected, which seems evident, the person who carries that life deserves at least equal respect. The controversy has often centered between the mother and the fetus, pro-choice focusing on the former and pro-life on the latter, as if the two are mutually exclusive. Defenders of abortion base their claim on the rights of the woman to her own body[32] and sympathy and forgiveness toward her.[33] Abortion is often advocated as the solution that best exemplifies a caring attitude toward the mother who is obviously in adverse circumstances.

The first two claims have to do with respect for persons and will be discussed in this section; the third will be discussed in the concluding section. The first viewpoint, that a woman has absolute rights to her own body, runs counter to Adventist theology which claims that our bodies are not our own, and it has been challenged on the grounds of secular ethics as well.[34] It further assumes that the pregnant woman is mature enough and independent enough in her own ethical framework so that her actions will not lead her into a "moral tragedy." Arthur Dyck defines moral tragedy as something that "occurs when, after you have acted in a certain way and reflected on how you have acted, you come to the conclusion that, upon reflection, had you thought about it before you acted, you would have acted differently."[35]

Considerable amount of research has been carried out attempting to assess the psychological effects of abortion on the woman, and many studies report data to prove the absence of harmful effects.[36] Studies on women's self-reported responses to abortion, however, show conflicting evidence, or perhaps more accurately, are used to prove contradictory points, since obviously both positive and negative reactions are present. One study of mostly married women shows that over fifty percent felt relieved after abortion, and negative responses were reported by less than twenty percent. During the months after the abortion, according to this report, there was increasing satisfaction in that women viewed their decision in "increasingly positive terms with the passage of time."[37] Another study of unmarried adolescents reports that more than eighty percent of the subjects would make the same decision again, whether that decision was abortion, single motherhood, or marriage. Among those who chose to abort, positive attitude toward abortion in general, consistent contraceptive use following abortion, and mother's higher educational attainment accounted for about twenty percent of the variance in satisfaction.[38] Family support has been found to be crucial in more than one study.[39] Obviously, married women had support in the context of their own nuclear families, whereas adolescents would need to receive it from their families of orientation.

There is a high number of women, however, who have admitted to having notable psychological problems after abortion. Some have experienced emotional and behavioral symptoms similar to "post-combat stress reactions" of soldiers returning from war.[40] Others have had symptoms of grief similar to the grief experienced after involuntary loss of an infant, and for many this grief reaction began with the decision to terminate the pregnancy.[41] In many cases nightmares, depression, and other kinds of trauma are experienced by the woman for years— periods as long as twelve years have been reported—and often the trauma emerges many years after the event, sometimes with the arrival of subsequent children.

Sometimes women may not consciously acknowledge such trauma for many years; as one young woman said, "I threw myself into my studies. . . . From the outside, you'd never guess how it hurt me."[42] It is doubtful that such hidden hurts will be reported accurately in quantitative studies in which the subjects often respond in socially acceptable ways. Certain justification of one's decision is also to be expected, which would explain some of the contradictory findings reported above.

Even when reactions are not dramatic, adolescents especially often experience ambivalence and conflict with their decision to terminate pregnancy. In one study, eighty-nine percent had engaged in some self-behavior blame.[43] The fact that about forty percent of the over one million pregnancies in females under twenty annually are terminated by induced abortions[44] shows the prevalence of this choice among adolescents. Studies have shown that abortions are most frequent among unmarried white women—in fact, this is the only group for which terminations of pregnancy outnumber births.[45] Strategies of coping with the accompanying conflicts differ, as do sources of social support. For advice, adolescents rely increasingly on peer groups rather than parents, but adolescents with low self-perceived competence and high conflict regarding the decision are more likely to involve parents in the decision.[46] More often than not, the matter seems less the freedom of choice and more the need of the frightened, confused woman for moral guidance.[47]

In the above situations, how is respect for the mother to be expressed? A common assumption seems to be that abortion is the answer.

But abortion is a cheap solution to a human crisis, a quick fix that is ugly, rude, and ruthless. Even many who hold it as a viable option feel an emotional repugnance toward it.[48] To be human is to be beautiful, to be guided by values, to take responsibility, to love, to sacrifice, to extend grace. To respect persons means to extend grace, and to expect them to extend grace in turn. Respecting persons does not mean leading them to evade responsibility but helping them carry it with grace.

Respect for Other Persons

In addition to the mother, there are other individuals whom the decision about a pregnancy concerns closely. The most obvious, of course, is the biological father. Although men's attitudes toward abortion are generally more liberal than women's,[49] disputes between couples in which the expectant father wants the fetus to be carried to term are not uncommon. Men's interest in pregnancies that women may define as unwanted has not received much research attention.

There are indications that men involved in the abortion experience also have psychological and emotional stress. In about half of the 1.5 million annual abortions in the United States, the women are accompanied by their male partners, but the clinics extend no assistance to the men who often feel shut out.[50] From time to time, the news media report cases of dispute between a man and a woman whose mutual offspring is on the way. Pro-abortion feminists usually welcome the woman's victory in such cases.[51] As some writers have noted, however, it would seem reasonable that biological fathers who oppose the abortion should have their rights weighed against the mother's rights.[52] Against the feminist argument it can be said that one wrong cannot be made right by another wrong; it is true that women have been discriminated against, but reverse discrimination cannot solve that problem.

Finally, a baby is born into an extended family and a community, however weak or inadequate that community may be. Respect for persons means respecting the feelings of even the more distant members of the community. If the people of the United States have a "collective right" to preserve a place like the Grand Canyon, they reason, why not a right to preserve the fetuses and infants for the good of society? On the basis of Rawlsian ethics, these writers question the right to property, and note that in today's technology, removal of the fetus from the woman's body and destruction of the fetus are inseparable, but only the first is justified by the principle of bodily autonomy. Thus the state's interest was considered in the *Roe v. Wade* case. Mark Tushnet and Louis Seidman conclude that the wishes of the mother, the father, and potential adoptive parents at the least should be considered in the decision. The third parties' rights must be questioned, however, if these parties do not invest in the child's welfare.[53]

Communal values and commitments are emphasized by many opponents of abortion. Sidney Callahan, for example, discusses the "primacy and the value of the collective human species" as a more appropriate basis for decisions about pregnancy than the usual, individualist claims about fetal rights. She also criticizes the idea of the rights of the family members in that such concepts emphasize possessive relationships. A new baby is a unique individual who should have an equal chance as a member of a community.[54] Lisa Cahill posits a similar theme, asserting that "the fetus is from conception a member of the human species" and entitled to protection.[55] It is noteworthy that Virginia Abernathy's pro-choice response to Cahill's article presents an entirely different conception of a community, one based on the evolutionary principle. To her, abortion is a sociobiological adaptation.[56] The problem with such an argument is that the evolutionary concept of community is based on the cruel idea of the survival of the fittest, a Spencerian, social Darwinist model that no serious social scientist today will take at face value. The Christian ideal is a caring community, and the pro-life side seems to be consistently more able to visualize such a community.

Abortion and the Church's Social Responsibility

As was discussed in the first part of this paper, any concern other than religious that a church may have is secularization, yet the separation of church and state—so highly prized—is to ensure that the secular and the religious remain separate. It would be easy to postulate that, since the church's function is spiritual and the government's function is practical, and since abortion is against the church's theology, the church can appeal to the division of labor and leave the government to do the dirty work. Much of Christian history appears to have proceeded with this model.[57] In the Adventist Church, this model has been followed with regard to war and military service—Adventists are pro-life when it comes to bearing arms, though not consistently so since medics help only their own side and thus indirectly aid in the war effort.

The challenge for the Adventist Church is to be consistent. In other, larger denominations, secularization has led to social action at the structural level, while the Adventist Church seems to have stayed at the individual level, with questions concerning lifestyle matters occupying our attention. The health emphasis provides an example: we worry about the harmful effects of smoking, but largely ignore the nuclear danger. Can the church extend its horizons and also address issues of structural health in our society and the world community? The question of abortion will never be solved as merely a personal, private trouble. Part of the prophetic mission of today's church is to critique contemporary culture, to be the conscience of the world, and to offer a better alternative, i.e., let Christ transform that culture.[58]

The church's role is spiritual, but it is the nature of holistic Adventist theology that spiritual matters have practical implications, and spirituality is expressed by practice in common, everyday life. Christians who do not believe in "cheap grace" should not believe in quick and dirty solutions to social problems. Should the church get involved in social issues? I believe it should, and that involvement should not be the popular, easy dispensing of services that are against its own spiritual principles. That involvement should address the cause of the problem at the structural level as well as the individual level. Abortion to eliminate unwanted pregnancies is like a war that is to end all wars—it is a short-sighted strategy that does not work in the long run. It does not remove the conditions of distress;

it treats the symptom, not the cause. On the other hand, to refuse abortion without offering a better alternative to help uplift the woman in distress is heartless dogmatism. It is blaming the victim. The problem needs to be addressed in its larger context.

It would be very difficult to turn the tide and completely stop the present liberal practice of abortion—even if a new ideology were to prevail, it could never be completely stopped. The focus of this chapter is not on legislation, but perhaps greater restrictions could be implemented in that arena as well. Presently, most decisions to abort appear to be viewed as birth control, yet the majority of Americans do not agree with this philosophy.[59] Although the American popular ethos denounces imposing one's own values on others, most would agree that in some cases this is not merely justifiable but the only moral cause to follow. The moral failure of the Western world in allowing Hitler's "final solution" to take place has been cited by both sides of the abortion debate to show that some values need to be imposed if human life is to be affirmed rather than destroyed.[60] Peter Singer traces this dictum back to John Stuart Mill's *On Liberty* and emphasizes the one qualification to this rule: no one is at liberty to harm others.

Whatever the societal practice may be, it is difficult to see abortion as part of the prophetic or service mission of the church, even if the church has become secularized to some degree. As long as the church places its medical mission within its spiritual mission and upholds the divine plan for humanity, it must treat people with respect and grace. Providing abortions can be justified only by complete acceptance of the theory of evolution, with both its biological and societal implications. When a church begins to merely mirror society rather than giving it moral guidance or even providing a haven from its problems, such a church has lost its primary reason for existence, whether as a church or as a sect.

Because of its spiritual resources, the church, better than any other institution, can have a reasoned, responsible, and loving approach that affirms the great value of the most helpless members of the human community and helps the people responsible for those members express their own essential humanity by caring and not destroying.

The church's approach to abortion is a concrete expression of its understanding of its mission in the secular society.

Endnotes

[1]Ernst Troeltsch, *The Social Teaching of the Christian Churches*, Vol. 1 (New York: Harper Torchbooks, 1960), 331, 338.

[2]One documentation of secularizaton is mentioned in Malcolm Bull, "The Medicalization of Adventistm," *Spectrum* 18 (February 1988):12-21. He views medicalization as an alternative explanation rather than part of secularization. Editor's note: Bull's ideas can be obtained and reviewed in the chapter "Doctors," published after Terian's chapter was produced. This is in a book he co-authored with Keith Lockhart, *Seeking a Sanctuary: Seventh-day Adventism and the American Dream* (San Francisco: Harper and Row Publishers, 1989).

[3]See, for example, Amos 5:15 and Isaiah 1:17. Amos 5:22-24 addresses the two sociological views of religion, with a definite preference for the second.

[4]One example is when Nathan rebuked David concerning Bathsheba and the killing of Uriah, then communicated pardon for his sin (2 Sam. 12:7-13); cf. Isaiah to Hezekiah (Isa. 38-39 and parallels).

[5]David Hill, *New Testament Prophecy* (Atlanta: John Knox Press, 1979).

[6]John Wilson, *Religion in American Society: The Effective Presence* (Englewood Cliffs, NJ: Prentice Hall, 1978), 196-211.

[7]Cf. Jon P. Gunneman, "Human Rights and Modernity: The Truth of the Fiction of Individual Rights," *The Journal of Religious Ethics* 16 (Spring 1988):160-189, where he notes that there is a plurality of "moral communities, and claims that this plurality can only be transcended by theology." Alasdair MacIntyre, *After Virtue: A Study in Moral Theory* (Notre Dame, IN: University of Notre Dame Press, 2nd ed., 1984), similarly notes the impossibility in our culture of reaching a rational agreement (p. 6) in moral matters such as chastity (p. 232).

[8]Leo Pfeffer, "The Legitimation of Marginal Religions in the United States," in Irving Zaretsky and Mark Leone, eds., *Religious Movements in Contemporary America* (Princeton, NJ: Princeton University Press, 1974), 9-26.

[9]Ian Gentles, "Good News for the Fetus: Two Fallacies in the Abortion Debate," *Policy Review* no. 40 (Spring 1987):50-54.

[10]E.g., Gary B. Melton, "Legal Regulation of Adolescent Abortion: Unintended Effects," *American Psychologist* 42 (January 1987):79-83, claims that such restrictions and obstacles to privacy induce embarrassment, anxiety, and family conflict; see also Henry P. David and Zdenek Matejcek, "Children Born to Women Denied Abortion: An Update," *Family Planning Perspectives* 13 (January-February 1981):32-24, a longitudinal study of over 200 children in Czechoslovakia who were born to mothers twice denied abortion and who showed some adverse psychological effects of rejection.

[11]Suzanne Staggenborg, "Life-Style Preferences and Social Movement Recruitment: Illustrations from the Abortion Conflict," *Social Science Quarterly* 68 (December 1987):779-97. A weightier point is made by Amy Fried "Abortion Politics as Symbolic Politics: An Investigation into Belief Systems," *Social Science Quarterly* 69 (March 1988):137-154, who claims that the controversy has to do with different worldviews that are narrowly focused and thus obscure possible commonalities.

[12]See also Elizabeth Fee and Ruth Finkelstein, "Abortion: The Politics of Necessity and Choice," a review article on *Abortion and Woman's Choice: The State, Sexuality, and Reproductive*

Freedom (Boston: Northeastern University Press, 1985), by Rosalind Pollack Petchesky, in *Feminist Studies* 12 (Summer 1986):368, reporting a point made by Petchesky that "The New Right's appeal to privatism. . .protects the corporation over its workers and the family over its members."

[13]Staggenborg, 783-784.

[14]See Michael Pearson's chapter in this book, point 7 under his section on "Sociological Determinants." Page 149 cites an edited version of this statement.

[15]Both were reprinted in *Ministry* 61 (January 1988):18-20.

[16]Pearson.

[17]Richard Fredericks, "Less Than Human," *Ministry* 61 (March 1988):15, cites such speakers. A paper presented at the 1988 Loma Linda Abortion Conference by John Stevens, "Abortion and Religious Liberty," made the same point.

[18]This point is implicit in Shane Andre's "Pro-life or Pro-choice: Is There a Credible Alternative?" *Social Theory and Practice* 12 (Summer 1986):223-240. According to data cited by David Cannon (with Victoria Sackett), "Split Verdict: What Americans Think about Abortion" *Policy Review* no. 32 (Spring 1985):18-19, "58 percent wanted abortion laws more restrictive than they are today," and "most people do not 'endorse abortion as a form of birth control.'" For the Adventist Church, the book by Malcolm Bull and Keith Lockhart, noted above, is revealing.

[19]Bull, 20.

[20]Churches are, in fact, accused by the opponents of abortion of not providing moral guidance to the world in this issue. Alan Clarke, "Moral Reform and the Anti-abortion Movement," *Sociological Review* 35 (February 1987):128.

[21]One example of a thorough discussion from this viewpoint is Fredericks, "Less than Human."

[22]Representatives on both sides of the debate have acknowledged this fact. See Peter Singer, *Practical Ethics* (Cambridge, MA: Cambridge University Press, 1979), 106; and an anonymous editorial, "When Life Begins," *Economist* 301 (November 15, 1986):15. The process is also briefly described by Gerald Winslow, "Abortion and Christian Principles." *Ministry* 61 (May 1988):14.

[23]The above-mentioned editorial, "When Life Begins," explains that since the first signs of the fetus appear 14-17 days after fertilization, a 14-day limit on embryonic experimentation has been imposed in Britain because that time shows whether an embryo will attach or not. See also Sidney Callahan, "Commentary to Chapter 12," on Daniel Callahan, "The Abortion Debate: Is Progress Possible?" In Sidney Callahan and Daniel Callahan, eds., *Abortion: Understanding Differences* (New York: Plenum Press, 1984), 309-324. Callahan points out the inconsistency of the prohibition of embryonic medical experiments without the consent of the institution's ethical review board when the same physician can perform an abortion with only the mother's consent.

[24]David Cannon, "Abortion and Infanticide" (p. 16), citing Sepp Schindler, an Austrian psychiatrist and endocrine researcher. Also, "The Mind," a documentary shown on National Public Television on Oct. 19, 1988, illustrates how the brain develops in the early weeks of pregnancy.

[25]E.g., Andre, "Pro-life or Pro-choice," 223-240.

[26]Arthur Dyck, *On Human Care: An Introduction to Ethics* (Nashville, TN: Abingdon, 1977), 81-91, presents an excellent argument for the ethics of "benemortasia" which, in the face of

inevitable death, "mercifully retreats to caring only" but refuses to deliberately induce death.

[27]"When Life Begins," 16. It would seem that this concept should fit Adventist theology since we believe in the unity of mind, soul, and body.

[28]Joseph Fletcher, *Humanhood: Essays in Biomedical Ethics* (Buffalo, NY: Prometheus Books, 1979), 12-16.

[29]Singer, chapters 3 and 4, would disagree with this since he sees preference for our own species over animals or other forms of life "morally indefensible."

[30]Richard Rice, *The Reign of God* (Berrien Springs, MI: Andrews University Press, 1985).

[31]MacIntyre, 52.

[32]This prevalent argument is espoused, along with that of the state's rights, by Rosalind Pollack Petchesky, *Abortion and Woman's Choice: The State, Sexuality, and Reproductive Freedom* (Boston: Northeastern University Press, 1985).

[33]Winslow, "Abortion and Christian Principles" (p. 13), brings this point, though I need not give a label to his carefully balanced view. He notes that even when "prepersonal human life" has to "yield to already established personal life, such decisions should never be made without regret" (p. 14). Compare this with the following statement by Fee and Finkelstein in their review essay: "As a social policy, abortion is a necessity. We must therefore stop apologizing for abortion, either as social policy or as individual decision" ("Politics of Necessity," 372).

[34]1 Corinthians 6:19-20 is one of the favorite prooftexts used by the church. For a secular challenge, see Mark Tushnet and Louis Michael Seidman's review article, "A Comment on Tooley's Abortion and Infanticide," *Ethics* 96 (January 1986):350-355.

[35]Dyck, *On Human Care*, 28.

[36]Gary Melton and Nancy Felipe Russon, "Adolescent Abortion: Psychological Perspectives on Public Policy," *American Psychologist* 42 (January 1987):69-72, assert that vulnerability to psychological harm from abortion is not supported by data, citing N. E. Adler and P. Dolcini, "Psychological Issues in Abortion for Adolescents," in G. B. Melton, ed., *Adolescent Abortion: Psychological and Legal Issues* (Lincoln: University of Nebraska Press, 1986), 74-95. This book contains the full report of the American Psychological Association's Interdivisional Committee on Adolescent Abortion.

[37]George M. Burnell and Mary Ann Norfleet, "Women's Self-Reported Responses to Abortion," *The Journal of Psychology* 121 (January 1987):71-76. This study surveyed 300 members of a prepaid health plan who had therapeutic abortions (randomly selected from 626). Over 50 percent of the subjects were married, and 44 percent were 30 years old or older.

[38]Marvin Eisen and Gail L. Zellman, "Factors Predicting Pregnancy Resolution Decision Satisfaction of Unmarried Adolescents," *The Journal of Genetic Psychology* 145 (December 1984):231-239. The subjects were interviewed six months after delivery or abortion.

[39]*Ibid.*, 237, reports that single mothers were more likely to be satisfied if they received support from their own mothers for their decisions to become mothers. Another study by Carmen G. Ortiz and Ena Vazquez Nuttall, "Adolescent Pregnancy: Effects of Family Support, Education, and Religion on the Decision to Carry or Terminate Among Puerto Rican Teenagers," *Adolescence* 22 (Winter 1987):897-917, found that those who decided to carry their babies to term had closer relationships with their mothers and more support from their families.

[40]Anne Speckhard, *The Psycho-social Aspects of Stress Following Abortion* (Kansas City, MO: Sheed & Ward, 1987). This book reports an in-depth study of 30 women who had such experiences.

[41]Larry G. Peppers, "Grief and Elective Abortion: Breaking the Emotional Bond?" *Omega: Journal of Death and Dying* 18, no. 1 (1987-88), 1-12.

[42]Quoted by Maggie Gallagher, "Abortion's Other Victims: Women Discuss Post-Abortion Trauma," *Policy Review* no. 32 (Spring 1985):20-22.

[43]Brenda Major, Pallas Mueller, and Katherine Hildebrandt, "Attributions, Expectations and Coping with Abortion," *Journal of Personality and Social Psychology* 48 (March 1985):585-599.

[44]Interdivisional Committee on Adolescent Abortion, American Psychological Association, "Adolescent Abortion: Psychological and Legal Issues," *American Psychologist* 42 (January 1987):73-78.

[45]Eve Powell-Griner and Katherine Trent, "Sociodemographic Determinants of Abortion in the United States," *Demography* 24 (November 1987):553-561. This study claims, however, that when other factors are controlled—such as increased access because of a metropolitan location and the mother's social circumstances, women are nearer the end of their childbearing age are more likely to abort than 15-19 year olds.

[46]Catherine C. Lewis, "Minors' Competence to Consent to Abortion," *American Psychologist* 42 (January 1987):84-88, citing R.H. Rosen, "Adolescent Pregnancy Decision-making: Are Parents Important?" *Adolescence* 15, no. 57 (Spring 1980):44-54.

[47]Ardyce Sweem, "Abortion's Effects," *Ministry* 61 (July 1988):14-16. See also Gallagher, "Abortion's Other Victims," who cites cases where pressure has been put on the woman to obtain abortion.

[48]Daniel Callahan, 311, a pro-choice advocate, confesses to such a repugnance, but some feminist writers, e.g., Fee and Finkelstein, "The Politics of Necessity," argue for an entirely positive approach to abortion.

[49]J. Blake, "Abortion and Public Opinion: The 1960-1970 Decade," *Science* (1971):540; Lloyd S. Wright and Robyn R. Rogers, "Variables Related to Pro-choice Attitudes among Undergraduates," *Adolescence* 22 (Fall 1987):517-524. See also Cannon, "Split Verdict," 19.

[50]"Men and Abortion," *Futurist* 19 (April 1985):60-62, commenting on Arthur B. Shostak and Gary McLouth with Lynn Seng, *Men and Abortion: Lessons, Losses, and Love* (New York: Praeger, 1984).

[51]"Hold a Baby" [a column], *Economist* 302 (February 28, 1987):74.

[52]Tushnet and Seidman, 352.

[53]*Ibid.*, 353-355. Some feminists also have noted the point that the language of rights is in the context of individualism, and while they support abortion, they see it as a social good rather than an individual right. See Rosalind Pollack Petchesky, *Abortion and Woman's Choice: The State, Sexuality, and Reproductive Freedom* (Boston: Northeastern University Press, 1985).

[54]Sidney Callahan, "Value Choices in Abortion," in Callahan and Callahan, eds., *Abortion: Understanding Differences*, 263.

[55]Lisa Sowle Cahill, "Abortion, Autonomy, and Community," in Callahan and Callahan, eds., *Abortion: Understanding Differences*, 263.

[56]Virginia Abernathy, "Commentary to Chapter 10," in Callahan and Callahan, eds, *Abortion: Understanding Differences*, 279-283.

[57]There is some merit to this claim since in a pluralistic society it seems necessary to have an objective, impersonal political order that makes justice its highest good. See Gilbert Meilaender, *Friendship: A Study in Theological Ethics* (Notre Dame, IN: University of Notre Dame Press, 1981). Whether the present U.S. government policy represents justice is another question.

[58]H. Richard Niebuhr, *Christ and Culture* (New York: Harper & Row, 1951).

[59]Cannon, "Split Verdict," 18-19.

[60]Fredericks, 13; Singer, 113.

15 Abortion and Public Policy

Michael Angelo Saucedo

The drafters of the U.S. Constitution could not foresee specific bioethical questions we face going into the 21st century. Subsequently, all sides of the moral debate extrapolate rules from hazy constitutional amendments or vague biblical verses. Resulting discussions are then reduced to confrontations of personal interpretations versus private opinions. In spite of this, certain legal and moral principles have emerged from the fires of conflict which are worth tracing through history so we may better perceive where this debate is heading in the future.

I. The Judiciary

The war on abortion has many legal battlefronts. Three are worth noting: (1) the woman's freedom to abort versus the fetus' right to existence, (2) the minor's right to physical self-determination versus the parent's right to control the minor, and (3) the woman's decision versus intervention by third parties.[1]

The most pivotal of the three is the woman's freedom to abort versus the fetus' right to existence. Here is our first inquiry, "When does the law consider 'life' to begin?" This permits us to try to distinguish the fine line between a legal medical act and medically induced homicide. Dr. John Pelt provides an incisive history of Christianity's role in attributing legal life to the fetus.[2] Early church fathers like Jerome and Augustine espoused beliefs strongly held even today of the sanctity of fetal life. Further, since most medieval courts had church sponsors and were staffed by ecclesiastical officials called chancellors, the church's view on fetal sanctity prevailed throughout Europe. But a sequence of historical events changed this view.

Beginning with King Henry VIII's break with Catholicism and continuing throughout the Reformation, ecclesiastical court officers found both their power and input diminishing. Then rational tools of analysis, based in the Enlightenment's scientific explosion, were gradually adopted in England by the King's legal courts. Now the courts, freed from the traditional structure of unthinking dogmatic outcomes, used this new form of analysis to break down legal questions in the same way their scientist colleagues solved problems in physics and mathematics. In other words, there were no pre-set conclusions.

Eventually, under English common law, the fetus was considered alive if (1) it was fully expelled from the womb, and (2) had an independent circulation. Lord Edward Coke (1552-1634), an English jurist, redefined in 1631 the criminal culpability of individuals towards the fetus. He regarded abortion as murder only if the fetus was (1) quickened, (2) born alive, (3) lived for a short time, and (4) then died.[3] "Quickening" referred to the fetus' movements observed after the 16th-18th week of pregnancy. Hence, English common law accepted these views as being authoritative on cases involving abortion.[4]

In the mid-19th century, a succession of abortion prosecutions were brought in English courts. In each, a woman or her accomplice was accused of killing a newborn by inducing premature labor, and it was always declared that a murder verdict couldn't be returned unless the infant was born alive. Thus, in *Rex v. Brain* (1834), the court instructed the jury that a murder charge would lie only if the child had been "wholly" born alive.[5] By 1850, this rule had been accepted in the United States. However, in that year it was modified by the California Legislature as Penal code section 187. It stated that a murder charge would lie for the killing of a fetus, giving an impression that the statute was more protective of the fetus than was the common law.

But 120 years later in *Keeler v. Superior Court* (1970), Justice Mosk's majority opinion limited the scope of the statute's legislative intent to mean it doesn't include the killing of an unborn fetus,[6] though it did intend to include the killing of a viable fetus in the process of being born.[7] In general, though, most abortions were criminally proscribed by statute in most states. But legal America was soon to be convulsed.

Two U.S. Supreme Court cases, *Roe v. Wade* (1973) and *Doe v. Bolton* (1973), addressed the constitutionality of criminal abortion codes by overturning them.[8] *Roe* overturned a Texas statute by saying the decision was within a woman's "right of privacy," whether based in 14th Amendment concepts of personal liberty and restrictions on state, or in 9th Amendment reservations of rights to the people.[9] *Roe* also outlined the trimester system medical model which established interest levels of both the woman and the state during different periods of the pregnancy.[10] *Doe* overturned a Georgia statute by finding it too restrictive of the physician's judgment and also emphasized the privacy of the doctor-patient relationship in making abortion decisions.[11]

The second battlefront boils down to the minor's right to physical self-determination versus the parent's right to control the minor. What role, if any, do parents have in forcing their minor to abort or not to abort? Many states try to allow parents to impact this decision. In *Belotti v. Baird* (1979), Massachusetts enacted a law requiring both parental notice and consent to perform an abortion.[12] Justice Powell's majority opinion overturned it. He held it unduly burdened the minor's right to seek an abortion. The judicial proviso allowing a parental bypass wasn't adequate since it allowed the judge to withhold abortion authorization even if the minor was found mature and fully competent by the court to make this decision independently.[13] Justice Stevens' concurrence went further by criticizing Powell for still including the state in the decision-making since states are as much a burden as parental consent.

Stevens suggests a constitutionally mandated biological mature minor rule: if a female is old enough to get pregnant, she is old enough to decide on abortion. Thus *Bellotti* lets mature minors decide on abortion and whether or not to inform their parents.[14] But Chief Justice Burger's majority opinion in *H.L. v. Matheson* (1981) attempts to limit the scope of the minor's autonomy by finding simple "notification" statutes as constitutional.[15] Still, Justices Marshall, Brennan and Blackmun dissented, finding it unrealistic when most pregnant minors come from troubled families.[16] More broadly put, parental notification hardly seems a legitimate state purpose when (1) the pregnancy resulted from incest, (2) an abusive parental response is assured, or (3) fears of such an abusive response deter the minor from the abortion she wants.

The third battlefront queries, "When can others intervene in abortion decisions on behalf of protectable interests?" Parental relationships were already dealt with since they are more convoluted. But other parties may have reasons to be involved in the abortion decision. In *Planned Parenthood v. Danforth* (1976), besides parental consent, the targeted statute required prior written consent of the spouse.[17] The argument goes that any change in family status should be decided jointly by the marriage partners. However, the court quickly discarded this argument on grounds that it violated personal autonomy. Also, if the husband can veto the wife's decision, the goal of fostering trust and strengthening the marriage relationship hardly results. More importantly, the state cannot delegate to the husband a right he does not already have.

However, the state can control the environment around which women get abortions. In *Doe*, the state compelled women to seek abortions only from licensed physicians.[18] In *Danforth*, the state chose abortion procedures which reasonably related to protecting the woman's health.[19] But, obviously, state interests are not limited to just protecting the woman's health.

Controversy erupts when states intervene to protect the fetus. In *Akron v. Akron Center For Reproductive Health* (1983), a statute required hospitalization starting with second trimester abortions.[20] Justice Powell's majority opinion held this unconstitutional. But this triggered a sharp dissent by Justice O'Connor and the two original *Roe* dissenters, Justices White and Rehnquist. Their attack went to the heart of the *Roe* medical model.

O'Connor feels that the growing quality of biotechnology dates the *Roe* trimester model. Since there may be a chance to save viable fetuses by having abortions in fully equipped hospitals, she detects a collision course between the time moved back in which to have a safe abortion, and the time moved up in which a fetus may be viable.[21] Whether an apt metaphor, it is true that in adopting an analysis making present-day medical facts so critical, *Roe* did ensure that advancing technology impacts on the law. The tenacity of these dissenters is influential. Already, *Roe* is being eroded away in lower courts as analyses expose an old unarticulated assumption underlying most abortion discussions: that abortion necessarily includes both termination of the pregnancy and termination of the fetus.[22] For now, courts grudgingly allow both terminations. Yet states, acting as guardians of perceived innocents, are not powerless to demonstrate where they draw the line on abortion.

Medicaid pays for most states' indigent medical assistance costs. To receive funding, states make reasonable standards to determine the extent of assistance. Many states allow funding to medically necessary incest and rape abortions. However, states are not obligated by federal law to do this and in *Maher v. Roe* (1977), the Court allowed Connecticut's program to prioritize funding towards childbirth and away from abortion.[23] Yet Justice Brennan's dissent stated that an inducement for a funded childbirth interfered with free choice.[24] Is this similar to a statute allowing reimbursement of voting costs (child care, transportion, etc.) only for those who vote for Democrats? Maybe. But for now, states control the money and so legally may make the decisions.

II. The Legislatures

Through it all, the U.S. Supreme Court has operated with grace while under intense pressure. Legislatures are the forums where abortion should be debated.

Yet they continue to throw undefined abortion issues to the courts, who, in all courtesy, should be receiving a more refined legal product.[25] But our elected politicians, fearful of alienating big blocs of their constituents wherever they come down on abortion, shrink away from the direct engagement of it. Instead, there have been only the most general abortion discussions within the political process. Only politically conservative legislators from areas with majority voting blocs of single-issue pro-lifers feel secure enough to publicly discuss abortion and propose statutory resolutions. Many of them attempt to overrule *Roe* by redefining the word "person" in the 14th Amendment's due process clause to include the unborn fetus. Other proposed amendments would flatly prohibit abortions. Many declare abortion rights are not secured by this Constitution. A few object on moral grounds and others object on grounds of federalism.[26] However, such one-sided proposals by no means indicate the legal direction we are about to take, but rather show our ship of state quickly steaming nowhere and about to capsize on this issue.

At this point, an obvious query would be, "Are our legislatures effective in legislating legal answers to moral conflicts?" Is the answer "No?" If so, Why? What is society doing differently that causes legislative bodies, who generally frame our public policies, to seemingly become morally impotent? Yet in all fairness, is abortion a simplistic black-and-white issue that allows legislators to easily distinguish it? Can it be said that of the two competing interests, women's autonomy and fetal rights, one will always be paramount? At this time, there are no simple answers. But it is important that some sort of resolution be found.

Abortion fluctuates between various hues of gray as it is impacted by national moral trends or the fractious legal relationship between the states and Washington, D.C. Since laws represent pluralistic compromises of competing concepts of morality, our nation's abortion policy is like a Savings and Loan where moral concepts are accounted for. As shareholders, we contribute to the S&L capital fund. Its officers, our legislators, use the capital to implement public policies. Lately, however, there's a rumor the S&L is about to go bankrupt. Deposits are getting more scarce. The officers try to carry on business as usual, but unless the S&L is reinvigorated it will go under.

In plainer terms, the last couple of decades have seen a determined eradication of religious icons from the public domain.[27] This may be desirable because nobody wants one particular religious philosophy to dominate any aspect of public life. But now when our political leaders need moral input on which to premise a more balanced public policy, they hesitate to participate in any moral arena for fear of showing religious favoritism. We must first understand their fear before we can correct it.

Up through the 20th century, our nation had a *de facto* semi-establishment of one religion: a generalized Protestantism with dominant national status.[28] Though Protestants approved, Catholics and Jews did not. Partly in reaction, the constitutional jurisprudence pendulum swung toward the *de facto* semi-establishment of secularism. Ironically, secularists are as unconcerned about this as were Protestants during their heyday. So now we see exclusion of teaching about the needed role of religion in society.[29] In their hurry to throw prayer out of school and keep nativity scenes off public land, zealous amoralists helped throw off our nation's moral compass. More specifically, a moral void haunts our nation's abortion policy.

III. Bridging the Gap

When elected leadership fails, other groups provide solutions. In the early 1960s, law professors attending American Law Institute (ALI) forums drafted Model Penal Code Section 230.3. It justified abortions if: (1) substantial risk in continuing the pregnancy would gravely impair the mother's physical or mental health; (2) the child would be born with grave physical or mental defect; or (3) the pregnancy resulted from rape, incest, or other felonious intercourse.[30] Law professors make no pretense about being moral experts. Yet where legislators fumbled abortion issues to judges on regular bases and no communicable reasoned dialogue emerged from the moral community, ALI's Model code was well received later by policy-makers. For example, it was adopted in California as the Therapeutic Abortion Act which reduced the Penal code's harshness by making abortion a justified exception to homicide.[31]

Behavioral scientists also contribute to and impact the law. Henry P. David of Transnational Family Research Institute in Bethesda, Maryland, with three Czechoslovakian colleagues, studied 440 Czech children while taking advantage of Prague's strict abortion controls during the 1960s.[32] They found psychological and social problems more prevalent among children born to mothers who sought an abortion, were refused, then appealed, and were refused again.[33] The 220 children born to these "twice-refused" mothers were compared with 220 children of similar backgrounds but who were clearly wanted by their parents. The unwanted children by age 21 had more than twice the psychiatric and social disorders and more than twice as many criminal convictions and usually for more serious crimes. A mere study? Hardly. The research changed the law: a first-term abortion is now available on demand in Czechoslovakia.[34] It also shows that unwanted babies should be given up to adoption. But in essence, no one can doubt now that many unwanted pregnancies result in very unwelcome babies.

And what contributions can be made by the moral community? Here is where our church has an opportunity to provide moral leadership in an arena in desperate need of it.

IV. Procedural Observations

We need to employ procedural methods which bring together the different parties and their ideas in the abortion debate. Recently, as has been evidenced by inadequate abortion policies and laws, there have not been effective channels by which we can get our moral input to policy-makers. But before we even move into that arena, we must first successfully come to terms with this issue within our own Adventist community.

A. A Specific Inquiry For Our Denomination

"Should our church develop an abortion policy as a test of membership or worthiness of church office?" "No," for two reasons. The first is simple because of the state of the law: abortion is legal.[35] The second is more complex because of the question of unity or lack of it: abortion divides our church. Since this issue has high negative ratings on each side of the debate, we would probably risk alienating up to two-fifths of our membership on this issue whether we declared a pro-life or pro-choice policy. As long as present circumstances remain static, it would be reckless to initiate a policy.

The legal issue is simple, since if the law changes by restricting abortions, then the issue would be taken out of our hands and rendered moot. However, the unity issue is tougher. My mind is drawn to the abolition movement's reaction to the *Dred Scott* decision.[36] When it came down from the U.S. Supreme Court in 1857, requiring the return of escaped slaves, Ellen G. White placed morality above that law and encouraged the church not to observe it.[37] This was, remember, a unifying policy throughout our church that garnered a strong majority support. The same does not hold true today of abortion.

On balance, there is no question that the life of freedom for a slave far outweighed the minor economic benefits a slaveowner gained by subjugating that slave. Here, the personal civil rights of an individual (the slave) are adversely affected by slavery whereas the personal civil rights of the other individual (the slaveowner) are *not* adversely affected by freeing the slave, since no person has any moral or legal right to maintain a property interest in another individual.

But the moral balance is not as decisive when weighing the right for a fetus to exist against the personal autonomy, privacy and health of a woman. Here there is the trauma of choosing between two entities where one will have adversely affected civil rights, however we decide. In this dilemma no unified perspective exists within our church. This makes the question of church policy, if anything, more difficult to surmise.[38] When achieved, our church will be ready to take on the public arena of abortion.

B. When Disciplines Collide

It's unfortunate the "moral debate" on abortion, the "constitutional debate" on abortion, and the "medical debate" on abortion are most often three separate and often conflicting discussions. In fact, they are often reduced to name calling or character assassinations of each other. This was vividly portrayed when the U.S. Supreme Court ruled on *Roe*. It subsequently triggered vehement religious moral offensives where effigies of the court were burned and abortion clinics were bombed. But many hospitals and doctors also cried foul because their autonomy in developing working abortion protocols would be increasingly usurped by lower-court judges, who aren't even well versed in the medical issues and yet would be responsible as the final legal arbiter for making these decisions.

Of all the debates, the moral debate is most important. Through institutional vehicles of organized religion and through individual members, the moral debate is energized and gives moral input into our civil morality. From here, all other debates draw values for interdisciplinary conventional points of reference. But some religions choose to opt out of using constructive conventions of communication within our civil morality. Instead, some organized memberships try to persuade changes in law by shouting at judges, calling them "sexist pigs" and "women oppressors," or "baby killers" and "murderers,"[39] depending on their view. Then campaigns are mobilized with a single-issue mentality to unseat politicians, harass medical professionals and/or obstruct access to clinics.[40]

Because of the failure of some churches to become rational legal actors, the courts will continue to view many religious participants in the abortion debate as fanatical and extreme.[41] Changes in laws are predicated upon the petitioner bearing the burden of production and the burden of persuasion. If religion wishes to communicate effectively, it must show that change is warranted by substantial moral methodologies and by expressing these in shared terms of social realism. Otherwise the burden of proof is not met and instead of principled communication, confusion erupts. We must recognize procedural methods that are ineffective so we may avoid their pitfalls.

C. "Ethical Feudalism"

A notoriously ineffective procedural methodology is ethical feudalism. This describes how moralists of every persuasion stumble into siege mentalities by isolating themselves from the pointed, contradictory challenges to their moral thinking that lie beyond their doctrinal walls. And what lies beyond? Both the pragmatic realities of social realism and the courts. Feudal lords succeed in harboring their belief systems. But with their defenses and a shut drawbridge to the mind, they prevent themselves from engaging in relevant decision-making discussions aiming to resolve the abortion debate.[42]

Feudal lords who do come down from their ivory towers to joust in the field of issues become ethical "White Knights." But mostly we see edicts being issued: full of statements of conduct, devoid of practical insights in the abortion debate, and showing a feudal lord as tragically out of touch with the common people as that monastary on the next hill. Then the word goes out: mobilization! The feudal lords with their ignorant troops and with cooperation from the church take on a single-issue crusade to combat courts and targeted politicians on levels defying any sense of decency or understanding.

Don't deteriorate into a feudal lord. It isn't productive and it alienates. Instead, choose an approach that allows a positive on-going conversation with our policy-makers. Some modest procedural suggestions and recommendations will follow. These will help reinforce our ability to find answers.

D. Multi-institution Cooperation and Other Models for Success

Hospitals, clinics, legislatures, courts, nursing associations, doctor-groups, and churches need to come together and integrate their discussion. Ongoing conflict results from keeping members of the different debates from each other. However, in the world of Adventism, we see a close and productive relationship between our hospital systems and the church: often our medical and moral debates on abortion are the same. But this is not true of most hospitals and most churches. With this in mind, the following observations and reaffirmations are made to promote good policy.

1. Develop Bioethics Awareness Within our Membership

We must educate our membership with the facts. "Adamant innocence" is a virulent form of aggressive ignorance that needs to be combated. There is no justification for certain members to continue harboring misconceptions that suit particular extrinsic motivations (either political or ideological) to maintain pet beliefs. Integrity demands continual, honest appraisals.

2. Sensitize our Membership to Constructive Issue Engagement

To become rational legal actors in the abortion debate, we need to engage in non-Adventist forums using shared terms of social realism that can be understood by non-Adventists. Our civil morality obliges us to take care in using words and casting issues.[43] Using terms like public, secular, and religious should be free from discriminatory bias.[44] "'Secular purpose,' for example, should not mean 'non-religious purpose' but 'general public purpose.' Otherwise, the impression is gained that 'public is equivalent to secular and religion is equivalent to private.' Such equations are neither accurate nor just. Similarly, it is false to equate 'public' and 'government.' In a society that necessarily limits government's role, there are many spheres of life that are public but non-governmental."[45]

3. Expand Roles of our Bioethics Centers

Our ethics centers should not be think-tanks only relied on by the General Conference or Adventist Health Systems, but also a practical resource to be drawn on by legal, medical, and social professionals looking for answers. Sponsoring seminars, conventions and hotlines allows them to expand their community role.

4. Promote Presentations of Ethicists in Church Forums

Ethicists are representatives of our ethics centers. As such, they are a mobile research resource that may be drawn on by in-house committees and our churches to answer questions on moral issues.[46] More importantly, they would advance a consistent perspective among all Adventist bioethics groups and they would have fingers on many different Adventist bioethical pulses.

5. Advance the Work of Laypersons

If at times we need to use only laypeople to prevent defensive posturing by

230

policy-makers, then the church must utilize them. As previously noted, not all religions are well regarded and, unfortunately, their negative associations tend to rub off on even a worthy denomination's theologians.

6. Establish and Broaden Roles of Bioethics In-House Committees

These committees initially allow for in-house consultations. Yet their roles can expand into including liaison functions with a greater inter-community bioethics forum made of constituent members from each area-hospital's bioethics advisory committee.[47] Thus routine consultations of liaisons to our ethics centers informs them of bioethical evolution in different communities.

7. Create Judicial Advisory Committees

Judges don't have all the answers and often appreciate help in finding them. Let them know they can count on you as a resource providing data on bioethical questions. Whether a hospital in-house committee or an ad hoc sub-committee of an inter-community forum, be retained by judges on particular issues. In any event, public policy is better served when legal decisions are premised on accurate and balanced information.

8. Improve Facilitation to all Policy Makers

Policy makers, from federal down to the local level, from medical to social to moral, must have opportunities to attend and participate in our debates. This not only provides the policy maker with invaluable input and perspectives, but also enhances our church's role in providing needed community debates on abortion. Of course this assumes we have worked out some moral methodologies in shared terms of social realism that policy-makers may be persuaded by, such as the emphasis on values we share.

9. Provide Feasible Abortion Alternatives

We should call for any combination of laws that promote: (1) insured pre-natal care for all women; (2) paid maternity leave, (3) less expensive birthing alternatives; (4) full-coverage medical care for mother and infant child;[48] (5) child-care credits for targeted socioeconomic families needing financial help;[49] (6) the criminalization of discrimination against single mothers that injures them in any capacity; (7) greater protections for abused children and/or abused mothers; (8) school lunches; (9) upgrades of sex education/family planning to include a value-system derived from our civil morality;[50] (10) guaranteed short-term foster care if parents have exigencies that won't allow them to presently devote their wherewithall to the child; (11) effective and smoother adoption and foster care procedures;[51] (12) forced birth control/sterilization of individuals where their non-restrictive procreative histories establish a pattern of abuse of the social welfare system, and where population-density control is being jeopardized;[52] (13) putting more teeth into statutes promoting child support collections from the child's father and/or his family;[53] and (14) free dissemination of contraception information and devices, especially to promiscuous teenage females. Preventing pregnancy is best; but if we must have babies, we had better protect them.

If society is not willing to foot the bill for any of these options within this wide spectrum of alternatives, abortion is indeed an inexpensive route. If society decides to criminalize abortion and still not provide any reasonable protections or options for the woman, then it heralds in more evils such as increased infant mortality and abandonment, and even expanded black markets for babies (mothers who cannot afford to keep babies are a market waiting to be exploited). We must get involved to impact public policy.

E. Bioethics as a Judicial Specialty

Finally, we must recognize the need for legal specialists with a firm grounding in medicine and ethics to judge these cases. Precedent is based on the legal system's establishing specific issue courts like bankruptcy, probate, family law, juvenile, small claims, criminal law and civil law when the need existed for judicial specialization. Now we need biomedical courts. With the increasing role that issues of medicine, healthcare, genetic engineering and other forms of medical and drug research play in our lives, only judicial specialists in bioethics will sufficiently stay on top of the multiplicity of proliferating issues such as fetal tissue experimentation, euthanasia, anencephalic harvesting, blood patents, surrogacy and, of course, abortion.

V. Adventists as Public Stewards

Adventists have important roles to play in society, not only in terms of an eschatological world mission, but on more practical levels by enriching society with our moral methodology, sharing it in ways society can comprehend. Moralists who speak in terms that only an "in-group" understands are a dime a dozen. But by choosing to be involved in this debate, we, as Christian stewards, need to articulate Christian morality in terms the public understands since "Christians with a vivid vision of the future promise can still act responsibly in the present, contributing to the betterment of this world while hoping for the next."[54]

Endnotes

[1]More experimental controversies include sperm/ovum DNA coordination, robotized embryo creation, woman/fetus compatibility selection processes, artificial implantation, fetal tissue research, fetal cloning, in vitro abortions, anencephaly harvesting, etc. These elicit criticism in view of associations made to similar experiments conducted by war criminals. See Michael Saucedo, "The Nuremberg War Trials: A Lecture by Professor Edgar Bodenheimer," *The Advocate* (November 23, 1987):6.

[2]John Pelt, *The Soul, the Pill, and the Fetus* (Philadelphia: Dorrance & Company, 1973), 83.

[3]See Means, "The Law of New York concerning Abortion and the Status of the Fetus, 1664-1968: A Case of Cessation of Constitutionality," 14, N.Y.L.F. (1968):420. Stern, Abortion: Reform and the Law. 59 J.Crim. L., C. & P.S. (1968):52-60.

[4]Sir Matthew Hale (1609-1676) and Sir William Blackstone (1723-1780), two successive English jurists, reiterated and expanded upon Lord Coke's requirement that an infant be born alive to be the subject of homicide. See Stephen, *A History of the Criminal Law of England* (London: MacMillian, 1883), 52-60.

[5]*Keeler*, at pp. 2,3.

[6]*Keeler v. Superior Court*, 2 Cal. 3d 619 (1970).

[7]*People v. Chavez*, 77 Cal. App. 2d 621 (1947).

[8]*Roe v. Wade*, 410 U.S. 113 (1973); *Doe v. Bolton*, 410 U.S. 179 (1973).

[9]*Roe*, at 153.

[10]The trimester system balances both physical risks and the interests different entities have: (1) during the first trimester it is easier and safer to have an abortion than to give birth, the woman and the doctor are the only parties who participate in the abortion decision, and no state interest is yet present; (2) during the second trimester, though an abortion is still feasible, the state can require certain procedures that will protect the woman's health and safety; and (3) during the third trimester, the viability of the fetus is greater and so the interest of the state is stronger to protect it.

[11]*Doe*, at 179.

[12]*Bellotti v. Baird*, 443 U.S. 622 (1979).

[13]*Ibid.*, at 623.

[14]But cf. *Planned Parenthood v. Ashcroft*, 462 U.S. 476 (1983). (The U.S. Supreme Court upheld a Missouri statute outlining judicial proceedings for the minor seeking an abortion. Attackers of the statute felt it violated *Bellotti* by failing to protect a mature minor's decision for abortion. However, the Court determined that a subsection of the statute *would initially* require a finding that the minor wasn't mature enough to make the decision and that it wasn't in her best interests before a judge would go on to deny an abortion.)

[15]*H.L. v. Matheson*, 450 U.S. 398, 411-13 (1981).

[16]*Ibid.*, at 448.

[17]*Planned Parenthood v. Danforth*, 428 U.S. 52 (1976).

[18]*Doe*, at 192.

[19]See *Danforth*, at 75.

[20]*Akron v. Akron Center For Reproductive Health*, 462 U.S. 416 (1983).

[21]*Ibid.* at 462 U.S. 430.

[22]See *Danforth*, 428 U.S. at 83.

[23]*Maher v. Roe*, 432 U.S. 464 (1977).

[24]*Ibid.* at 484-88.

[25]See *Gregg v. Georgia*, 428 U.S. 153 (1976).

[26]Pearson & Kurtz, *The Abortion Controversy: A Study in Law and Politics*, 8 Harv. J.L. & Pub. Poly 427 (1985).

[27]*The Williamsburg Charter* (Williamsburg Charter Foundation, 1988), 14.

[28]*Ibid.*

[29]*Ibid.*

[30]American Law Institute Forum, *Model Penal Code*, Official Draft, Sub-section 230.2 (Philadelphia: The American Law Institute, 1962).

[31]See Cal. Penal Code Sub-section 187 (West 1985).

[32]Terence Monmaney, "When Abortion Is Denied," *Newsweek* (August 22, 1988):64.

[33]*Ibid.*

[34]*Ibid.*

[35]For those who subscribe to the moral methodology of authority, Romans 13:1-7 could be used to support adherance to the state of law.

[36]*Dred Scott v. Sandford*, 19 Howard, 393 (1857).

[37]Ellen G. White, *Testimonies for the Church*, Vol. 1, (Mountain View, CA: Pacific Press Publishing Association, 1948), 201-2; Ellen G. White, "Slavery and the War," *The Review and Herald* 18 (August 17, 1861):13, 27.

[38]Would policy be made on a division by division basis or would we allow individual churches and conferences to set up their own individual guidelines?

[39]U.S. Supreme Court Justice Brennan experiences the brunt of anti-abortion forces wherever he goes.

[40]Martz, supra.

[41]California Supreme Court Justice Cruz Reynoso stated religious groups each have their own truths, but each sees itself exclusively as interpreter of God's will on earth which leads

them to think they can transcend necessary human channels to promote social change. But they won't succeed outside the legal system. Cruz Reynoso, interview by author, April 12, 1987.

[42]There are universal rights and responsibilities derived from guidelines for conducting public debates involving religion in a manner that is democratic and civil. *The Williamsburg Charter*, 22-26.

[43]Carl George, *Empty Pews, Empty Streets* (Columbia, MD: Columbia Union Conference Publishers, 1988), 76. Also, *Ibid.*, 72.

[44]*The Williamsburg Charter*, 15.

[45]*Ibid.*

[46]David Larson, "Medical Termination of Life/Existence: Legal Act, Homicide or Both?" featured speaker at Sacramento Adventist Forum, October 29, 1988.

[47]Sacramento Bioethics Forum serves as a community resource where bioethical issues are discussed and sometimes debated by local doctors, state legislators and aides, nurses, hospital personnel, medical social workers.

[48]Senator John Kerry, D.MA. argued this need.

[49]*Ibid.*

[50]Value-neutral sex education is the trend. However, this seems to deny the national importance we put on our civil morality. We should include at least some basic morals in sex education.

[51]See Melinda Beck, "Willing Families, Waiting Kids," *Newsweek* (September 12, 1988):64.

[52]See L. Barnett, *Population Policy and the U.S. Constitution* 3-6 (1982).

[53]See Mickey Kaus, "Is It Hype or True Reform?" *Newsweek* (October 10, 1988):45.

[54]John Brunt, *Now & Not Yet* (Washington, DC: Review and Herald Publishing Association, 1987), 81.

16   Abortion Policies in Adventist Hospitals

Gerald R. Winslow

Introduction

What policies, if any, should govern the practice of abortion in Seventh-day Adventist hospitals? This question is on the minds of many Adventist hospital administrators. It also concerns Adventist Church leaders, health care professionals, and a large number of laypersons. If the various "right-to-life" groups do what they have promised and stage increasingly strident protests at facilities providing abortion, then the abortion policies of hospitals, including Adventist ones, are likely to come under more public scrutiny.

The time seems right, then, for another look at Adventist abortion policy. In what follows, I describe briefly what has led to the current variety of Adventist hospital policies, analyze the results of a small survey of Adventist hospitals on the matter, and offer some reflections on the shape that hospital policy might take if general principles of Christian ethics are foundational. But first a short word about policy and ethics.

It is not uncommon to feel a certain uneasiness about the relationship between policy and ethics. Maybe it is because policy carries the scent of the coercive. After all, the English word most resembling "policy" is "police." The mere slip of a letter evokes the faint sound of sirens (though, I understand, both words take root in that ancient and noble word for human community, the "polis"). Perhaps the uneasiness with the conjunction of policy and ethics stems from the fact that policies are bureaucratic instruments that tend to be highly pragmatic, very specific, and distressingly inflexible. Many of us prefer our ethics loftily principled, with plenty of room for individual interpretation.

Whatever the causes for uneasiness, it is important to diminish barriers between thinking about ethics and formulating policy. Policies are, in so many ways, ethics made visible. The rules that we make to govern our social institutions, the exceptions that we grant, the procedures that we establish, the penalties that we propose, all tell us about the values that we hold. Failure to state a policy, especially on matters as important as abortion, does not mean that an unwritten policy does not exist. For at the institutional level, some decisions for or against the practice must be made. Good policies, well-considered and well-written, can nourish the institutional virtues that we deem to be central. Poor policies can do precisely the opposite, and produce endless confusion at the same time.

Some Background

How have Adventist institutions arrived at the current variety of policies, including, in some cases, no policy? Most of the story has been told, in some detail, elsewhere.[1] But a few points will serve here as useful background.

By the late 1960s and early 1970s, the issue of abortion was receiving increased attention and debate in American society. Some states, such as New York and Washington, had begun the process of liberalizing their abortion laws. Highly publicized cases, such as those involving pregnant women seeking abortion after taking the teratogenic drug thalidomide, caused nationally felt distress. It became ever more clear that social policies on abortion were headed toward major reconsideration.

On May 13, 1970, the General Conference officers, in consultation with the General Conference's Department of Health, adopted what were called "suggestive guidelines" for therapeutic abortions performed in Adventist hospitals in the United States (the officers stated clearly that they did not intend to formulate guidelines for all Adventist institutions everywhere in the world). The guidelines were circulated first in a mimeographed form, then published in 1971 in *Ministry*, a publication for Adventist ministers.[2]

In a brief preface to the published statement, it was made clear that no answers were being attempted to questions such as: "When does actual life begin, or when does the product of conception come to possess a soul?"[3] The only stated theological foundation for the guidelines was given in the following two sentences:

> The basis for these guidelines exists on the person-image concept, which is governed by a system of priorities with an ascending scale of values. It is believed that this person-image concept is the biblical basis enjoined upon the church, is one that can be defended, and is one that we should support.[4]

Neither the preface nor the guidelines sought to clarify the "person-image concept." But in an article accompanying the guidelines, R. F. Waddell, then-secretary of the Department of Health, offered his perspective. Waddell suggested that the "basic problem that needs to be considered in analyzing the rightness or wrongness of abortion...[is] appreciation of the human image or person image."[5] To respect this "person image" is to acknowledge that human beings are children of God, made in God's image.

Waddell did not say exactly when a fetus becomes a "person image." But as he saw it, the fetus had no such status during first trimester when, in his words, the fetus "has not reached a stage where it can be considered an identity."[6] Thus, if abortions are necessary for therapeutic reasons, Waddell contended, it is preferable to do them during the first trimester. After that time, the "person-image" gradually develops, making abortion less and less acceptable.

The guidelines built on this "person-image concept" called for Adventist hospitals to ensure that therapeutic abortions be performed in accordance with state laws, by qualified medical practitioners, in consultation with two other physicians, during the first trimester of pregnancy, with the written consent of the patient, and with respect for the conscientious objection of hospital employees who choose not to participate. The hospitals were also asked to establish standing committees that would oversee the practice of abortion, including a review of all cases. The guidelines concluded with a list of three "established indications" for therapeutic abortions:

1. When continuation of the pregnancy may threaten the life of the woman or seriously impair her health.

2. When continuation of the pregnancy is likely to result in the birth of a child with grave physical deformities or mental retardation.

3. When conception has occurred as a result of rape or incest.

The publication of these guidelines must have come as a surprise to some observers of Adventism. Here was a church, known for relatively conservative theological and ethical views, stating what was, at that time, a relatively liberal position. In fact, the guideline's indications for therapeutic abortion were nearly identical to the cautiously liberal reforms then being advocated by the American Law Institute in its Model Penal Code.[7]

Even more surprising was a subsequent "Statement of Principles" on "the intentional interruption of pregnancy" that was sent to Adventist hospitals later in 1971. It proposed what, in the eyes of many, was an even more liberal position. This second mimeographed statement, which was sent by the General Conference officers to Adventist hospitals in the United States, opened with these lines:

"The intentional interruption of pregnancy involves complicated, subtle, and sometimes morally obscure issues. Because of this, no set of moral generalizations can substitute for individual conscience."[8]

What followed was a list of five theological bases for the stated guidelines. First, the Adventist concept of "soul" is functional; the soul develops as people develop rationality and morality. Therefore, in its earliest stages, the fetus cannot be considered a human soul. But the human investment in the fetus is such that, at about twenty weeks' gestation, the fetus should be the subject of complete protection so that only risk to the life of the pregnant woman could be considered weighty enough to justify an abortion. Second, the right of a human being to life is based solely on his or her being a unique child of the Creator, and not on his or her value to other humans. Third, there is no explicit biblical passage about abortion, but Exodus 21:22-25 teaches that ending fetal life should not be considered the same as killing a person. Fourth, some life, such as fetal life, may not be functionally human, but it may symbolize human life. Such symbolic life should never be ended carelessly, but only when demanded, "for some reason," by the needs of functional human life. Fifth, Adventists should remain "prophetic" and resist the incursions of dehumanizing and demoralizing influences of the world.

Most of this second statement's specific guidelines were similar to those already published in *Ministry*. However, instead of limiting therapeutic abortions to the first trimester, as was the case in the earlier guidelines, the second statement said that abortions "should be performed as early as possible, preferably during the first trimester of pregnancy." The first guidelines' indication for therapeutic abortion, that the pregnancy represents a threat to "seriously impair" the woman's health, was changed by dropping the word "seriously." And the earlier indication that spoke of the likelihood of the birth of a child with "grave physical deformities or mental retardation" was modified by omitting "grave." Finally, in addition to the now-modified list of three indications for therapeutic abortions were added two more:

4. When the case involves an unwed child under 15 years of age.

5. When for some reason the requirements of functional human life demand the sacrifice of the lesser potential human value.[9]

The fourth indication is not without potential for controversy. But the fifth is truly remarkable. It would appear, on the face of it, to be so vague as to make stating the first four indications quite unnecessary. After all, what *could not* be included under the rubric of "some reason?" Though this last indication is obviously based on the statement's fourth theological rationale, described above, it is impossible to say with certainty what its authors had in mind (a theologian who was prominent in the process of formulating the statement once told me that he thought the fifth indication was written by someone who had heard a paper that the theologian gave, but had misunderstood it). Given the contrast between the relative precision of the first four indications and the last indication's opaqueness, it is powerfully tempting to wonder if the lack of clarity was intentional. In any case, there can be little doubt that the fifth indication's language of "some reason" introduced a large degree of uncertainty among Adventist hospital administrators faced with the practical application of the guidelines.

During the rest of the 1970s and 1980s, Adventist hospitals gradually formulated their own abortion policies. As we shall soon see, very few of the hospitals in the present survey have relied totally on the General Conference guidelines. Nor, it seems, was strict adherence ever the expectation. The guidelines were sent to the hospitals "as counsel," and most administrators and their boards exercised judgment about the degree to which the guidelines were applicable in their facilities.

For example, in a memo to hospital administrators in his area, the president of one of the Adventist Health System's divisions cautioned his colleagues against allowing their hospitals to become "abortion mills." He attached a copy of the General Conference's 1971 guidelines (with the *five* indications for therapeutic abortion) and added:

> I think it would be wise for you, insofar as possible, to endeavor to have your hospital practices in line with these guidelines. I recognize there may be some hospitals that are not following these guidelines entirely. We suggest that as opportunity presents itself you endeavor to get as closely in line with the guidelines as possible.[10]

Since 1971, so far as I am aware, the General Conference has not chosen to issue additional statements of policy guidelines. It has, however, continued to consider the matter of abortion. In 1979, for example, abortion was included, along with a number of biomedical topics, in the work of a General Conference task force.[11] And, beginning early in 1989, another large committee on abortion began work for the General Conference.[12]

Meanwhile, Adventist hospitals have continued to develop an interesting array of hospital policies. It is to this diversity that we now turn.

Survey of Adventist Hospitals

In August, 1988, short questionnaires concerning abortion policies were sent to the chief executive officers of the 51 Adventist hospitals in the United States whose addresses are listed in the *Seventh-day Adventist Yearbook*.[13] Responses were received from 26 administrators. This is a response rate of 51 percent, which is generally considered good for this type of survey.

Responses came from the entire range of hospital sizes, including eight of the largest "flagship" hospitals. The responses were scattered throughout all areas of the United States. Though sampling bias is a perennial problem of such surveys, it would appear that the 26 responding institutions are a representative sample of Adventist hospitals in the United States.

Of the responding administrators, 16 (64 percent) were presidents, seven (28 percent) were vice presidents, one was a director of nursing services, and one was a chaplain who is vice-chairman of his hospital's ethics committee. The average length of experience in hospital administration was 12.2 years.

Here are key questions from the questionnaire and the results:

Does your hospital currently have a policy concerning abortions performed in the facility?

Yes = 23 (88 percent)   No = 3 (12 percent)   No answer = 0

Of the three who responded "No," one explained that the hospital has no obstetrics department at this time, but will be adding such a department and plans to develop an abortion policy. Another stated tersely, "It has not been discussed." The third did not comment, but indicated that there was no plan to develop a policy and that only one abortion had been performed at the facility in 1987.

Most of the respondents (18, or 72 percent) included copies of their hospitals' abortion policies with the returned questionnaires.

Are elective abortions currently permitted in your hospital?

Yes = 5 (19 percent)   No = 21 (81 percent)   No Answer = 0

The choice of the word "elective" may have introduced an unfortunate degree of ambiguity. The intention was to distinguish between "therapeutic" and "elective" abortions. The problem, of course, is that almost all abortions are "elective" in the sense that they are not "emergency" procedures. In the case of at least two respondents, this ambiguity probably led to confusion, because "Yes" was checked but the words "therapeutic only" or "therapeutic" were written beside the checks. Another respondent, representing a very large hospital, checked "Yes" but then commented that the hospital had performed only one abortion in 1987. Yet another respondent marked "Yes" but then attached his hospital's policy which limits abortion according to therapeutic indications specified in the General Conference guidelines. In other words, *nearly all of the surveyed Adventist hospitals limit abortions to those that they consider "therapeutic."*

Indeed, a close reading of all the questionnaires and their accompanying policy statements reveals that *only one Adventist hospital of the 26 responding appears officially to permit elective abortions without restrictions.* (This hospital only limits abortion after the twentieth week of gestation.) Thus, if an unbridled practice of abortion is occurring in many (or most) Adventist hospitals, as some have worried, it is not because of the announced policies of those hospitals.

As a matter of fact, six of the respondents (23 percent) clearly have policies more restrictive than the General Conference guidelines. Four (15 percent) stated that *no* abortions whatsoever are permitted in their facilities. Two others stated that the only permissible indication for therapeutic abortion is that the pregnancy clearly threatens the physical life of the mother. One of these even insists on two physicians' consultations to confirm that level of medical need.

The large majority of respondents, however, are attempting officially to hold the moderate, middle ground, allowing some abortions but using a number of stipulated procedures and indications to limit the practice to therapeutic abortions. In this category are 19 (73 percent) of the responding facilities. Typical, for example, is one respondent who answered the question about allowing "elective" abortions by checking "No" and adding the comment: "The abortions we would perform are 'therapeutic' in nature and would be done under very limited, non-elective circumstances."

This is the basic pattern called for by the General Conference guidelines. However, only seven (27 percent) hospitals actually state as their policy an unreconstructed version of all or part of the General Conference guidelines. Of these, six incorporate in their policies the second set of indications for therapeutic abortions, including the fourth and fifth indications that were added in 1971. Only one facility uses the original guidelines with their three indications for abortion, as circulated in 1970.

The other 12 hospitals (46 percent) taking the middle way have evolved an interesting range of policies, from the highly elaborate to the very simple.

On the elaborate end is one hospital whose abortion policy fills over three pages of relatively fine, single-spaced print. This policy stipulates that therapeutic abortions should not be performed "without serious consideration of the implications." It includes a list of "bases" for first-trimester abortions that is nearly identical to the five indications circulated by the General Conference. However, in place of the General Conference's vague fifth indication, this hospital's policy states: "When continuation of the pregnancy may significantly threaten the psychological health of the woman." The policy also includes the curious statement that "only intentional interruptions based on termination of pregnancy for socio-economic reasons is [sic] prohibited. . . ." Second-trimester abortions, except in cases of rape or incest, are permitted only if two consulting physicians agree that they are medically indicated. And third-trimester abortions are forbidden except in cases of very serious threat to the pregnant woman's life or health, as confirmed by two consulting physicians in writing. Further stipulations include a rule protecting potentially viable aborted fetuses, a number of rules regarding proper record-keeping, and a standing committee to review all cases retrospectively.

Most hospitals' policies were considerably shorter and simpler. For example, one manages to state its policy in a mere three sentences:

> _____ Hospital Medical Staff takes the position that in order to preserve regard for the sanctity of life, and yet have concern for people, abortion shall not be done without serious consideration of the indications. An approach which will minimize the need for abortions as a form of medical therapy is favored and abortion is opposed except on adequate medical grounds, and being a last resort measure. When indicated interruptions of pregnancy are done, they should be performed as early as possible, preferably during the first trimester of pregnancy.

The brevity of this policy might leave the impression that much flexibility exists in its application. However, the hospital's responding administrator states flatly that there is no debate about this policy, "because we do not do abortions."[14] Another example, interesting for more than its brevity, says:

> Abortions will be performed for medical reasons (pertaining or relating to the mother) only and will require two consultations: from the department which relates to the medical reason, and from another surgeon or OB/GYN person on the Active Staff not associated in practice with the surgeon doing the abortion. No abortion will be performed for fetal reasons other than anencephaly. (The above does not pertain to known fetal demise where an evacuation of the uterine contents is indicated.)

Most of the policies of the middle type are somewhat more detailed than the previous two examples. Typically, they insist that the abortions performed in the facility be "therapeutic," they specify a brief list of indications for such abortions (usually close to the first four of the General Conference's 1971 statement), they call for two medical consultations, they require some type of committee review, and they make provision for employees' conscientious objection to participation in abortions.

If your hospital has a stated policy, is there any plan, at present, to revise it?

Yes = 2 (8 percent)   No = 18 (58 percent)
No answer or not applicable = 6 (23 percent)

Many respondents stated that their policies are given routine reviews annually. One person wrote: "[We] need to revise and update current policy—10 + years old." Another said that his hospital is currently rewriting its policy. However, it appears that most hospitals have no plan to change policies in the near future.

Do you presently sense any debate on the part of those connected with your hospital (for example, the medical staff, hospital personnel, or constituency) concerning abortion at the facility?

Yes = 5 (19 percent)   No = 18 (69 percent)
No answer = 3 (12 percent)

One respondent commented that "There is considerable debate possible within the Medical Staff and Board relating to the issue. . . ." But he went on to say that most of the members of the obstetrics department were unified. Another said: "There is definitely a variety of opinions." But most of the respondents indicated that there is no significant debate. Some added that difficulties with their hospital personnel were eased by a policy granting employees the right to refuse involvement. Given the conflicted nature of the issue in society and in the church at large, the widely reported absence of debate within most Adventist facilities seems somewhat surprising.

Do you think that it would be a good idea for the Adventist church to take an official stand on abortion and insist that all Adventist facilities abide by that position?

Yes = 11 (42 percent)   No = 14 (54 percent)
No answer = 1 (4 percent)

This question prompted the most vigorous comments by the respondents. And it plainly split the group. Those on the "Yes" side offered comments like these:

> An absolute ban on abortion in our facilities would be easy to administer and remove us from the spotlight of the religious right, [but] it would not allow for an objective evaluation of cases on an individual basis. Once an official position is adopted, however, Adventist facilities should abide within that position.

> A general policy, with some latitude, should be developed to insure that no elective abortions take place at Seventh-day Adventist hospitals.

> Something this critical and sensitive should not be a 'local options' issue.

> Yes on official stand, but what are the implications of enforcement—can the church police it well?

On the other side were comments such as these:

> This would be very difficult for the church and possibly for hospitals to follow the 'letter' of the law.

> That decision is best made by each hospital.

> The current position works for us.

> Abortion prior to 20 weeks is a personal choice by law and a matter of conscience spiritually. The Adventist hospitals cannot take a stronger stand than the Church on this issue. I would hope our Church doctrines never mandate an individually responsible choice.

The fact that a slim majority of the surveyed administrators would not want to see a definite position taken by the church and the fact that even those who favor a more definite position often express doubts about its practicality would seem to indicate that the impetus for such a move will not come from this quarter.

A Principled Approach to Policy

Some years ago, in an essay on Adventists and abortion, I wrote: "No one would be more dismayed than I if our present efforts to address the moral questions in human biology and medicine were to result in attempts to produce moral conformity through policy-making."[15] I am of the same opinion still. But I hope that I am now more sensitive to the needs of Adventist hospital administrators who must explain to their boards, constituencies, medical staffs, employees, and often to the press just what their hospital's policy is. I believe that the way to proceed is for the church to assist its hospitals by stating more clearly than in the past the *broad principles* that should govern Adventist abortion policies, and by suggesting how those principles could be applied in a model policy. Each hospital, in my view, should then continue to develop its policies within the bounds of the broadly stated principles and in consideration of the model policy.

I do not wish to propose the details of a model policy. I think that a representative group, such as the General Conference's Christian View of Human Life Committee can best do this work. But I would like to offer some thoughts on the principles that should inform such a policy.[16]

1. *Publicity.* A formal requirement of any sound abortion policy is that its provisions be open to public view. The moral principle of publicity enjoins that the rules which govern social institutions be subject to public knowledge. There are many good reasons for this principle. Scrutiny of policies opens the way for possibly needed revisions. It permits participants in social institutions to know the rules and make appeals if they believe they have just cause. And it provides a way of assessing whether actions fit expressed convictions. The abortion policies proposed by the church and adopted, with whatever modifications, by church institutions should be open to all interested church members, to all other participants in those institutions, and to the general public. It is my impression that such has not been the case with Adventist policy in the past. It is also my impression that the reason for this lack of openness is that neither the official guidelines of the past nor the process that led to them would bear such publicity.

2. *Respect for Human Life.* Adventists have stood on the side of life in its wholeness. Whatever policies we generate, they should bear evidence of our respect for God's gift of human life, including fetal life. With the special instruction that Adventists have received regarding the protection of life during the prenatal period, it is inconceivable that any position which completely minimizes the significance of prenatal life could be the basis for Adventist policy. Adventists should neither condone, nor provide, abortions for trivial reasons. Nor should we be reticent to state with more clarity than the "some reason" indication of the 1971 guidelines what types of conditions justify therapeutic abortions. In my opinion, these conditions include serious threats to the pregnant woman's life or health, the very most serious defects (such as anencephaly) clearly diagnosed in the fetus, and pregnancies resulting from rape or incest. When, under tragic

circumstances, abortions are deemed necessary, they should be performed as early as possible so that the increasing significance of the developing fetal life is acknowledged.

3. *Respect for Personal Conscience*. Adventists have also stood on the side of liberty. Our policies should reflect our commitments to respect the personal convictions of others. But there is much confusion on this matter. We should, as I see it, acknowledge that the one who should make the final decision about whether or not to *seek* an abortion is the person most affected by that decision, the pregnant woman. We should not lobby for political intrusions into these highly personal decisions. But the legal right to seek an abortion in no way obligates any institution or health-care professional to perform abortions. It is a specious line of reasoning which states that, because abortion is legal in our society, and because we believe in obeying the law, we are obligated to perform abortions without assessing the reasons for them. The fact that it is specious does not mean that such "reasoning" is not encountered with distressing frequency. Adventist abortion policies should incorporate not only respect for the preferences of pregnant women (none, for example, should be forced to have an abortion) but also respect for both the integrity of the institution and its individual employees. It is also in the service of personal freedom if our institutions make known and, to the extent possible, make available alternatives to abortion.

4. *Due Process*. The strength of moral principles is often buttressed by the provision of adequate institutional processes. These should not be so cumbersome that they collapse from their own weight. They should be sufficient, however, to ensure that the other provisions of the policy can be carried out with a measure of integrity. It is not my purpose here to say what sorts of consultations, record-keeping, review, and the like should be incorporated in a model policy (others with far more and better experience can lead the way). It should be obvious, however, that careful attention to the necessary procedural elements that allow for the contingencies of individual cases while preserving institutional integrity must be a central feature of any successful policy.

5. *Equity*. People deserve to be treated in an equitable and impartial way. It has often been observed that the abortion policies of the past were not always applied in evenhanded ways. No policy by itself can eliminate all the forms of unfair discrimination to which human brings are often prone. But we can try. We should, for example, ensure that women who seek abortion are not treated

differently simply because they are poor or lack education or other standard indicators of social power.

Conclusion

No policy can substitute for the refined moral judgment of those who must decide whether or not to seek an abortion and of those who must decide whether or not to do an abortion. To Christians, Jesus has promised the Spirit. I am aware of no promise of policies. These we will have to make and change together, as a community of faith, using the principles that the Spirit has led us to discover.

Endnotes

[1]The best historical and sociological account of Adventists on abortion, so far as I know, has been produced by Michael Pearson, *Millennial Dreams and Moral Dilemmas* (New York: Cambridge University Press, 1990).

[2]General Conference Officers, "Abortion Guidelines," May 13, 1970 (mimeographed); published as General Conference Officers, "Abortion Guidelines," *Ministry* (March, 1971):10-11.

[3]*Ibid.*, 10.

[4]*Ibid.*

[5]Ralph F. Waddell, "Abortion Is Not the Answer," *Ministry* (March, 1971):8.

[6]*Ibid.*, 9.

[7]American Law Institute, *Model Penal Code* (Philadelphia: American Law Institute, 1962), Section 230.3.

[8]General Conference Officers, "Interruption of Pregnancy (Recommendations to SDA Medical Institutions): Statement of Principles," August 10, 1971 (mimeographed). My copy of this statement bears, at the top, the following background information: "The Officers received from the appointed representative committee of theologians, physicians, nurses, teachers, psychiatrists, laymen, etc., who met at Loma Linda, California, January 25, 1971, a report of opinion on intentional interruption of pregnancy. The report, slightly amended by the Officers is the following. . . ." A curious fact that I cannot explain is that these later guidelines were actually being developed over two months before the previous set of guidelines were first published in *Ministry*. However, the second set of guidelines was not circulated among the hospitals until five months after the *Ministry* publication.

[9]*Ibid.*, 1-2.

[10]Donald W. Welch, Memo to Hospital Presidents Regarding Abortions, Adventist Health System/Sunbelt, December 13, 1982.

[11]The results of this task force's work were published as General Conference of Seventh-day Adventists, Department of Health, *Seminar on Genetic Engineering*, mimeographed, Janu-

ary, 1979. Despite the limited title, the collected papers from this task force include a wider range of topics, including abortion.

[12]"General Conference Appoints Committee on Human Life," *Ministry* (November 1988):20-21. The committee, called "Christian View of Human Life Committee," is charged with study of a number of biomedical topics in addition to abortion.

[13]*Seventh-day Adventist Yearbook* (Hagerstown, MD: Review and Herald Publishing Association, 1988), 65-67.

[14]For the purposes of this survey, however, I have not included this facility among those that forbid all abortions, since the hospital's official policy, which is the primary concern of this study, does not prohibit all abortions.

[15]Gerald Winslow, "Adventists and Abortion: A Principled Approach," *Spectrum* 12, no. 2 (December 1981):6-17.

[16]In addition to the previously cited article, see for example my "Abortion and Christian Principles," *Ministry* (May 1988):12-16.

Appendix

Seventh-day Adventist Abortion Guidelines

This appendix contains guidelines presented by the Seventh-day Adventist Church. The first section contains the 1970 and the 1971 guidelines. The second section contains the most recent recommendations voted by the General Conference Annual Council on October 12, 1992. The last section contains guidelines for healthcare facilities.

1970 Abortion Guidelines

Agreed, To accept the following as suggestive guidelines for therapeutic abortions which might need to be performed in denominational hospitals in the United States.

The Seventh-day Adventist Church's position on specific programs in any country must relate to its world involvements. Thus, the church has taken no position establishing general regulations governing the performing of abortions in church-controlled medical institutions everywhere. This does not mean that the church does not favor and does not uphold standards, nor that it does not establish regulations; but rather that these standards and regulations are established in the various countries in which the church conducts hospitals.

The church is cognizant that attitudes and laws relating to permitted abortions are changing in the United States of America today. It opposes a laxity of regulations and practice which might contribute primarily to the lowering of moral standards of society. It is the position of the church that regulations relating to the performing of abortions are the proper business of responsible medical staffs of hospitals, such regulations to be approved by the hospital's controlling board, and always to be in harmony with the laws of the state.

The termination of pregnancy by therapeutic abortion is a surgical procedure and should be performed only by qualified and licensed practitioners in accredited hospitals.

This procedure may be performed only with the informed written consent of the patient and her husband, or herself if she is unmarried, or her nearest responsible relative if she is under the age of consent. Under no circumstances should a patient be compelled to undergo, or a physician to perform, a therapeutic abortion if either has a religious or ethical objection to it.

In the consideration of the indications for a therapeutic abortion the consultative opinion of at least two licensed physicians other than the one who is to perform the procedure must be obtained and on file. This opinion must state that the procedure is medically indicated, except in case of rape or incest. One consultant should be a qualified obstetrician-gynecologist and one should be recognized as having special competence in the medical area in which the indications for the procedure reside.

The hospital in which the procedure is to be done should have a standing committee, selected by the staff according to a method approved by the board, that is empowered to deal with abortion problems, to receive and pass on the consultative opinion relating to a proposed procedure, and to review all cases, including physicians who have requested and have carried out such procedures.

The board of trustees of a Seventh-day Adventist-sponsored institution should insist that the performing of therapeutic abortions be well controlled, that the practice and clientele of the institution not be placed in jeopardy by the abuse of the privilege, and that in all cases the staff act in accordance with the laws of the state, acceptable social standards of the community, and the moral principles taught by the sponsoring church.

It is believed that therapeutic abortions may be performed for the following established indications:

1. When continuation of the pregnancy may threaten the life of the woman or seriously impair her health.

2. When continuation of the pregnancy is likely to result in the birth of a child with grave physical deformities or mental retardation.

3. When conception has occurred as a result of rape or incest.

When indicated therapeutic abortions are done, they should be performed during the first trimester of pregnancy.—*General Conference Officers, May 13, 1970.*

1971 Abortion Guidelines

(The officers received from the appointed representative committee of theologians, physicians, nurses, teachers, psychiatrists, laymen, etc., who met at Loma Linda, California, January 25, 1971, a report of opinion on intentional interruption of pregnancy. The report, slightly amended by the officers, is the following:)

Interruption of pregnancy

(Recommendations to SDA medical institutions.)

Statement of principles

The intentional interruption of pregnancy involves complicated, subtle, and sometimes morally obscure issues. Because of this, no set of moral generalizations can substitute for individual conscience. The following statement is intended to provide a measure of guidance by clarifying the questions and by emphasizing the general principles and values with which specific actions should be consistent.

An Adventist position must, first of all, be conditioned by the Bible's teaching on the nature of man. According to the Bible, man's soul is a functional, rather than an objective, reality. Man does not have a soul; man is a soul. The soul is not infused in a "thing" at a specific moment in life such as at the time of conception. It is rather a human capacity to function rationally and morally, achieved fully through growth and development and an increasing investment of human life; at the time of fetal viability (the ability to live after birth— approximately 20 weeks) and thereafter, that development and investment are such that only another human life could balance the scale.

Second, the Adventist position does not measure a human being's right to live primarily in terms of happiness, utility, functional viability, or the desires of the mother, the family, or the society, but rather in terms of a human being's uniqueness as a child of the Creator. Humanity is first a God-given endowment, then an achievement.

Third, the Adventist position recognizes that no Bible passage expressly condemns abortion or speaks of man as fully human before birth. The Mosaic law is relatively thorough and explicit in dealing with all areas of sexual ethics, but it fails to mention abortion—though abortion was common in ancient times and some other legal codes severely condemned it. One relevant scripture is Exodus 21:22-25, which reads as follows (*Jerusalem Bible*): "If, when men come to blows, they hurt a woman who is pregnant and she suffers a miscarriage, though she does not die of it, the man responsible must pay the compensation commanded of him by the woman's master; he shall hand it over, after arbitration. But should she die, you shall give life for life, eye for eye, tooth for tooth, hand for hand, foot for foot, burn for burn, wound for wound, stroke for stroke."

It is to be noted that the fetus was not considered a human life to the point where "life for life" was to be demanded. Thus a distinction is made between the destruction of a fetus and the killing of a person.

Fourth, the Adventist position must be conditioned by the Bible's exalted sensitivity for life in general and for human life in particular. This includes a protective regard for what is "not yet" or "no longer" functionally human but "means" (symbolizes) human, as well as for those social institutions such as the family that serve to nurture and preserve "humanness." Any act that immediately or potentially threatens such real or symbolic values or institutions must never be carried out lightly. Even when for some reason the requirements of functional human life demand the sacrifice of the lesser real or symbolic human values, this must never be done for trivial or self-serving reasons or carried out in such a manner as to diminish respect for them lest reverence for the prior human values to which they point be also sacrificed.

Fifth, the Adventist position must be conditioned by the prophetic function of the church and its members, that is to say, by their vocation to "stand for" something in the world. The church has something to say to the world regarding the value of human existence and of the social institutions designed to preserve it. Its members and institutions should at all times govern their actions so as to maximize resistance to the dehumanizing and demoralizing pressures that so often characterize our contemporary society.

It is in this spirit that the following guidelines have been developed:

Guidelines

The intentional interruption of pregnancy is a surgical procedure and should be performed only by qualifed and licensed practitioners in accredited hospitals.

Under no circumstances should a patient be compelled to undergo, or a physician, nurse, or attendant personnel be forced to participate in, an interruption of pregnancy, if he or she has a religious or ethical objection to it.

To preserve regard for the sanctity of life and yet have concern for people, abortion shall not be done without serious consideration of the indications. Consultation shall be obtained as required by hospital rules.

The hospital in which the procedure is to be done should have a standing committee, selected by the staff according to a method approved by the board, that is empowered to deal with interruption of pregnancy problems, to receive and pass on consultative opinions relating to a proposed procedure. This committee should review all cases, including the records of physicians who have requested and have carried out such procedures.

The board of trustees of a Seventh-day Adventist-sponsored institution should insist that interruptions of pregnancy be well controlled by the highest medical, ethical, and professional requirements of the hospital council and/or the medical community; that the operation and clientele of the institution not be placed in jeopardy by the abuse of privilege; and that in all cases the staff act in accordance with the principles taught by the sponsoring church.

It is believed that interruptions of pregnancy may be performed for the following established indications:

1. When continuation of the pregnancy may threaten the life of the woman or impair her health.

2. When continuation of the pregnancy is likely to result in the birth of a child with physical deformities or mental retardation.

3. When conception has occurred as a result of rape or incest.

4. When the case involves an unwed child under 15 years of age.

5. When for some reason the requirements of functional human life demand the sacrifice of the lesser potential human value.

When indicated interruptions of pregnancy are done, they should be performed as early as possible, preferably during the first trimester of pregnancy.

Abortion Guidelines Voted by the
Annual Council of the Seventh-day Adventists
October 12, 1992

Many contemporary societies have faced conflict over the morality of abortion.[1] Such conflict also has affected large numbers within Christianity who want to accept responsibility for the protection of prenatal human life while also preserving the personal liberty of women. The need for guidelines has become evident, as the Church attempts to follow Scripture, and to provide moral guidance while respecting individual conscience. Seventh-day Adventists want to relate to the question of abortion in ways that reveal faith in God as the Creator and Sustainer of all life and in ways that reflect our Christian responsibility and freedom. Though honest differences on the question of abortion exist among Seventh-day Adventists, the following represents an attempt to provide guidelines on a number of principles and issues. The guidelines are based on broad biblical principles that are presented for study at the end of the document.[2]

1. Prenatal human life is a magnificient gift of God. God's ideal for human beings affirms the sanctity of human life, in God's image, and requires respect for prenatal life. However, decisions about life must be made in the context of a fallen world. Abortion is never an action of little moral consequence. Thus prenatal life must not be thoughtlessly destroyed. Abortion should be performed only for the most serious reasons.

2. Abortion is one of the tragic dilemmas of our fallenness. The Church should offer gracious support to those who personally face the decision concerning an abortion. Attitudes of condemnation are inappropriate in those who have accepted the gospel. Christians are commissioned to become a loving, caring community of faith that assists those in crisis as alternatives are considered.

3. In practical, tangible ways the church as a supportive community should express its commitment to the value of human life. These ways should include: (a) strengthening family relationships, (b) educating both genders concerning Christian principles of human sexuality, (c) emphasizing responsibility of both male and female for family planning, (d) calling both to be responsible for the consequences of behaviors that are inconsistent with Christian principles, (e) creating a safe climate for ongoing discussion of the moral questions associated with abortion, (f) offering support and assistance to women who choose to complete crisis pregnancies, and (g) encouraging and assisting fathers to participate responsibly in the parenting of their children. The Church also should commit

itself to assist in alleviating the unfortunate social, economic, and psychological factors that may lead to abortion and to care redemptively for those suffering the consequences of individual decisions on this issue.

4. The Church does not serve as conscience for individuals; however, it should provide moral guidance. Abortions for reasons of birth control, gender selection, or convenience are not condoned by the Church. Women, at times however, may face exceptional circumstances that present serious moral or medical dilemmas, such as significant threats to the pregnant woman's life, serious jeopardy to her health, severe congenital defects carefully diagnosed in the fetus, and pregnancy resulting from rape or incest. The final decision whether to terminate the pregnancy or not should be made by the pregnant woman after appropriate consultation. She should be aided in her decision by accurate information, biblical principles, and the guidance of the Holy Spirit. Moreover, these decisions are best made within the context of healthy family relationships.

5. Christians acknowledge as first and foremost their accountability to God. They seek balance between the exercise of individual liberty and their accountability to the faith community and the larger society and its laws. They make their choices according to Scripture and the laws of God rather than the norms of society. Therefore, any attempts to coerce women either to remain pregnant or to terminate pregnancy should be rejected as infringements of personal freedom.

6. Church institutions should be provided with guidelines for developing their own institutional policies in harmony with this statement. Persons having a religious or ethical objection to abortion should not be required to participate in the performance of abortions.

7. Church members should be encouraged to participate in the ongoing consideration of their moral responsibilities with regard to abortion in the light of the teaching of Scripture.

---

[1]Abortion, as understood in this document, is defined as any action aimed at the termination of a pregnancy already established. This is distinguished from contraception, which is intended to prevent a pregnancy. The focus of the document is on abortion.

²The fundamental perspective of these guidelines is taken from a broad study of Scripture as shown in the following "Principles for a Christian View of Human Life."

Introduction

"Now this is eternal life: that they may know you, the only true God, and Jesus Christ, whom you have sent" (John 17:3, NIV). In Christ is the promise of eternal life; but since human life is mortal, humans are confronted with difficult issues regarding life and death. The following principles refer to the whole person (body, soul, and spirit), an indivisible whole (Gen. 2:7; 1 Thess. 5:23).

Life: Our valuable gift from God

1. God is the source, giver, and sustainer of all life (Gen. 1:30; Job 33:4; Ps. 36:9; John 1:3, 4; Acts 17:25, 28).

2. Human life has unique value because human beings, though fallen, are created in the image of God (Gen. 1:27; John 1:29; Rom. 3:23; 1 Peter 1:18-19; 1 John 2:2; 1 John 3:2).

3. God values human life not on the basis of human accomplishments or contributions but because we are God's creation and the objects of His redeeming love (Matt. 5:43-48; John 1:3; 10:10; Rom. 5:6, 8; Eph. 2:2-9; 1 Tim. 1:15; Titus 3:4-5).

Life: Our response to God's gift

4. Valuable as it is, human life is not the only or ultimate concern. Self-sacrifice in devotion to God and His principles may take precedence over life itself (1 Cor. 13; Rev. 12:11).

5. God calls for the protection of human life and holds those who destroy it accountable (Gen. 9:5, 6; Ex. 20:13; 23:7; Deut. 24:16; Prov. 6:16-17; Jer. 7:3-34; Mic. 6:7; Rev. 21:8).

6. God is especially concerned for the protection of the weak, the defenseless, and the oppressed (Ps. 82:3-4; Prov. 24:11-12; Mic. 6:8; Luke 1:52-54; Acts 20:35; James 1:27).

7. Christian love (agape) is the costly dedication of our lives to enhancing the lives of others. Love also respects personal dignity and does not condone the oppression of one person to support the abusive behavior of another (Matt. 16:21; 22:39; John 13:34; 18:22-23; Phil. 2:1-11; 1 John 3:16; 4:8-11).

8. The believing community is called to demonstrate Chrisitan love in tangible, practical, and substantive ways. God calls us to restore gently the broken (Isa. 61:1-4; Matt. 1:23; 7:1-2; John 8:2-11; Rom. 8:1, 14; 12:20; Gal. 6:1, 2; Phil. 2:1-11; 1 John 3:17-18).

Life: Our right and responsibility to decide

9. God gives humanity the freedom of choice—even if it leads to abuse and tragic consequences. His unwillingness to coerce human obedience necessitated the sacrifice of His Son. He requires us to use His gifts in accordance with His will and ultimately will judge their misuse (Gen. 3; Deut. 30:19, 20; Rom. 3:5-6; 6:1, 2; Gal. 5:13; 1 Peter 2:24).

10. God calls each of us individually to moral decision making and to search the Scriptures for the biblical principles underlying such choices (Acts 17:11; Rom. 7:13-25; 1 Peter 2:9).

11. Decisions about human life—from its beginning to its end—are best made within the context of healthy family relationships and the support of the faith community (Ex. 20:12, Eph. 5, 6).

12. Human decisions should always be centered in seeking the will of God (Luke 22:42; Rom.12:2; Eph. 6:6).

Abortion: Guidelines for Adventist Healthcare Facilities for Intentional Termination of Pregnancy

Draft, November 2, 1989

The following statements are intended to serve as guidelines to assist the leadership of Adventist healthcare facilities in the development and implementation of institution-specific policies regarding abortion—the intentional termination of pregnancy.

Guiding Principles

Prenatal human life is a magnificent gift of God and deserves respect and protection. It must not be thoughtlessly destroyed. Since abortion is the taking of life, it should be performed only for the most serious reasons. Among these reasons are:

- Significant threat to the pregnant woman's life or health.
- Severe congenital defects carefully diagnosed in the fetus.
- Pregnancy resulting from rape or incest.

Abortion for social or economic reasons including convenience, gender selection, or birth control is institutionally prohibited.

Notification and Referral

Attending physicians and patients requesting an intentional termination of pregnancy prohibited by policy should be so informed and may be referred to other community agencies for care.

Review committee

A standing committee appointed by the President of the Medical Staff in consultation with the Chairman of the Department of Obstetrics and Gynecology,* should be charged with *prospectively reviewing* all requests involving an intentional termination of pregnancy.

Standing committee members should be qualified to address the medical, psychological, and spiritual needs of patients. There should be an equal representation of women on the standing committee.

Abortions deemed appropriate should be performed only after a recommendation to do so is approved by the standing committee following consultation with the patient's primary physician. A satisfactory consultation includes: examination of the patient if indicated; review of the chart; and a written report of findings and recommendations signed by the primary physician and each member of the standing committee.

In the event that a standing committee member is the patient's primary physician requesting an intentional termination of pregnancy, she or he should declare a conflict of interest and an alternate qualified member of the medical staff should be appointed.

When an institution lacks sufficient medical staff structure or subspecialty depth, standing committee functions may be performed by telephone with external consultants.

Counseling

When an intentional termination of pregnancy is requested, the interests of both the woman who is pregnant and the fetus must be considered. When available, professional counseling regarding those interests should be provided and alternatives to the intentional termination of pregnancy should occur before a final decision to proceed is reached by the pregnant woman. Such alternatives include parenting and adoption. The availability or non-availability of support systems should also be considered when reviewing options.

Under no circumstances should a woman be compelled to undergo, or a physician, nurse, or attendant personnel be forced to participate in an intentional termination of pregnancy if she or he has a religious or ethical objection to doing so. Nor should attempts to coerce a woman to remain pregnant be permitted. Such coercion is an infringement of personal freedom, which must be protected.

A minimum period of twenty-four (24) hours should elapse between counseling and the choice to proceed with an intentional termination of pregnancy, except in emergent situations.

Available professional counseling should continue to be made available to *support* the woman in her choice to parent, adopt, or intentionally terminate pregnancy.

Intentional termination of pregnancy during viability

If an intentional termination of pregnancy is medically indicated after viability begins, the medical treatment of an infant prematurely born during the course of termination of pregnancy should be provided the same level of care and life support efforts by the medical staff and hospital personnel as would be provided any other similar live born fetus. Viability means that stage of fetal development when the life of the unborn child may, with a reasonable degree of medical probability, be continued indefinitely outside the womb.

Notwithstanding the above, the woman's life and health should constitute an overriding and superior consideration to the concern for the life and health of the fetus, when such concerns are in conflict.

Reporting

The hospital shall maintain a record of all intentional terminations of pregnancies. The record shall include:

- Date
- Procedure performed
- Reasons for procedure
- Period of gestation at the time procedure performed.

A summary report containing the above information should be forwarded annually by the Quality Assessment Committee of the hospital to the Board of Directors for their review.

*When defined by medical staff structure.

INDEX OF SCRIPTURAL REFERENCES

Genesis

1 . . . . .34, 173
1:3 45
1:24 62
1:26 . . . . .43, 44
1:27 . . . . .62, 260
1:28 176
1:29 119
1:30 260
2 . . . . .102, 173
2:4-5 48
2:7 . . . . .31, 34, 43, 46, 57, 62, 260
2:19 62
2:21 46
2:24 44
3 259
3:5 134
3:16 46
3:18 119
5:1-3 47
4:1 . . . . .30, 44
7:2 119
9:2-6 . . . . .119, 123
9:3 181
9:5-6 260
9:6 29
11:30 47
12:2 47
16:1 47
16:4 45
16:11 30
18:15-21 48
19:36 30
21:2 45
24:60 47
25:21 .45, 47
25:25 48
27:45 48
28:14 47
29:2 47
29:31 47
30:1, 2 47
31:38 48
35:17-19 47
37:33-35 51
38:27-30 48
38:28 47
42:4 50
42:36 48
43:33 48
44:29 50

Exodus

1:15, 19 47
1:16, 22 51
2:2 45
4:11 63
20:12 261
20:13 . . . . .29, 30, 129, 159, 260

Leviticus

10:9 63
17:10-14 57
24:18 32
26:22 48

Numbers

6:3 63
12:12 .45, 48

Deuteronomy

5:17 159
7:14 . . . . .47, 48
10:17-19 . . . . .34, 197
12:23 57
13:10 181
14:26 68
23:15 64
24:16 . . . . .129, 157, 260
30:19 34
30:19-20 .260
32:25 48

Judges

13:2 48

I Samuel

1:8 48
1:5 44
1:19-20 48
2:6 163
4:20 47
31:3 52
31:4-5 181

2 Samuel

12:7-13 216
12:15-18 . . . . .47, 51
18:33 51

I Kings

16:34 51
17:17 51
19:4 52

2 Kings

2:19-21 8
8:12 36
15:16-18 36
16:3 51
17:16 51

Job

1:21 48
3:1-26 59
3:3-6 48
3:11 . . . . .48, 50
3:3-19 52
10:8-11 . . . . .44, 46
10:8-12 56
10:10 56
10:18-19 59
21:10 48
27:3 57
31:1-5 56
31:15 .30, 56
33:4 .57, 260
39:1-4 46

Psalms

8:3-6 176
20:1 68
21:17 68
33:6, 9 45
36:9 260
51:5 56
71:6 30
82:3-4 . . . . .34, 130, 260
93:1 57
96:10 57
104:15 68
104:29-30 .57
106 129
127:3 47
128:113 47
139:13-16 . . .30, 33, 44, 46, 56, 130

Proverbs

6:16-17 . . . . .29, 260
9:2 68
23:29-35 68
24:11-14 . . . . .136, 167, 260
30:16 47
31:4 63
31:4-7 68

Canticles

4:2 48
6:6 48
8:2 68

Isaiah

1:17 216
8:3 45
13:8 47
13:18 36
14:4 134
26:17 47
28:7-8 68
38 216
39 216

44:2 130
44:24 . . . . .30, 130
44:24-45:5 57
45:9-11 .163
47:8 134
49:1 .57, 118
49:5 56
54:1 . . . . .47, 48
56:4 48
61:1-4 260

Jeremiah

1:5 . . . .30, 31, 44, 48, 57, 118, 130
4:31 47
5:26-29 .136
7:3-34 260
7:30 51
7:30-34 .129
15:7 48
20:14-18 .52
20:15 47
20:17 50
22 130
22:16 136
22:23 47
31:15 51

Ezekiel

5:17 48
16:1-5 51
16:6 45
37:5 57

Daniel

1 68
4:30 134
10:3 68

Hosea

4:11 68
9:11 48
9:14 48
13:16 36

Amos

1:13 . . . . .45, 46, 129
5:15,22-24 216

Jonah

4:3 52

Micah

6:7 . . . . .129, 260
6:8 260

Matthew

1:20 57
1:23 260
2:16-18 51
4:23 202
5:21-22 .202

5:43-48 . . . . .34, 260
6:24 133
7:1-2 260
8:28-33 .202
9:2,36 202
10:28 62
16:19 . . . . .64, 202
16:21-24 . . . . .131, 260
18:1-6 141
18:10 34
19:4-8 63
22:39 260
23 202
24:19 .30, 51
25:40 . . . . .134, 163
26:24 59
27:46 202

Mark

1:14-15 .202
10:13-16 . . . . .141, 202
10:45 140
11:15-17 202
14:21 59

Luke

1 . . . . .34, 37
1:7, 13 47
1:15 . . . . .57, 142
1:13-17 31
1:31 30
1:36 47
1:41 . . . . .46, 142
1:52-54 .260
2:52 179
4:16-19 .202
9:23 135
12:6 118
12:16-21 133
14:28-30 202
14:33 134
15 34
15:3-6 165
18:11-13,24 133
22:42 261

John

1:1 45
1:3,4 260
1:14 132
1:29 260
2:25 202
3:16 . . . . .34, 177
8 35
8:2-11 260
10:10 . . . . .120, 202, 260
10:11 165
11:25 . . . . .120, 261
13:34 . . . . .140, 260
14:6 202
15:13 169

17:1-5 133
17:3 260
18:22-23 260

Acts

15:20 119
17:11 260
17:25 260
17:28 260
17:30 63
20:35 260

Romans

1:25 134
3:5-6 260
3:23 260
4:17 57
5:6 . . . . .34, 131, 260
5:8 260
5:17 202
6:1,2 260
7:13-25 .260
8:1, 14 260
9:20-21 .163
12:2 . . . . .259, 261
12:20 260
14 64

I Corinthians

6:19-20 . . . . .34, 59, 135, 218
7 39
8-10 35
12:27 202
13 260
15:8 48

Galations

1:15 . . . . .30, 31, 34, 44, 57
5:13 260
5:20 50
6:1 260
6:2 260

Ephesians

2:2-9 260
2:3-6 . . . . .34, 131
3:10-11 .202
5 261
5:5 .35, 133
5:18 68
6 261
6:6 261

Philippians

2:1-11 260
3:12 131

Colossians

1:13-14 35
3:5 . . . . .35, 133

266

I Thessalonians
5:23 260

I Timothy
1:15 . . . . .34, 260
3:8 68
6:5-11 . . . . .35, 133

Titus
3:4-5 . . . . .131, 260

Hebrews
7:9-10 57

James
1:27 260

4:2 . . . . .35, 133
5:3-6:3 . . . . .35, 133

I Peter
1:18-19 .260
2:9 260
2:24 260

I John
2:2 . . . . .132, 260
3:2 260
3:16 . . . . .132, 169, 260
3:17,18 .260
3:18 138
4:8-11 260
4:10-11 .132

Revelation
9:21 50
12:11 260
18:23 50
21:8 . . . . .50, 260

Other:

Sirach
19:11 46

I Maccabees
1:61 46

INDEX OF PROPER NAMES

Abernathy, Virginia, 213

Acton, Dr., 73

Akron v. Akron Center for Reproductive
Health, 224

Alexander, Leo, 128

Alton, David, 143

Angello, Michael, 81

Apollo, 55

Asclepius, 55

Assyrian Law, 49

Athenagoras, 56

Atrahasis epic, 45

Aquinas, St. Thomas, 178

Augustine, St., 221

Bajema, Clifford E., 58

Barnabas, 56

Barry, Vincent, 126

Battle Creek, 71, 72

Beach, Walter R., 31

Beethoven, 135

Bellotti v. Baird, 223

Berlioz, Louis Hector, 98

Biggers, J., 62

Binding, Karl, 128

Blackmun, Justice, 223

Bracken, Michael, 200

Brennan, Justice, 223, 224

Bull, Malcolm, 209

Bunyan, John, 93

Burger, Chief Justice, 223

Cahill, Lisa, 213

Callahan, Daniel, 148

Callahan, Sidney, 213

Calvin, John, 92

Charles I, 92, 93

Clement of Alexandria, 56

Coke, Lord Edward, 222

Coles, Larkin B., 71

Cromwell, Oliver, 93

Darwinism, 214

David, Henry P., 226

De Medici, 92

Denes, Magda, 199, 200

Diamond, James, 61

Didache, 132

Doe v. Bolton, 125, 156, 222, 223

Douglas, Justice William O. 173, 176

Dred Scott, 127, 227

Duge, John, 32, 35

Dyck, Arthur, 217

Enuma Elish story, 45

Falwell, Jerry, 175

Fletcher, Joseph, 210

Fontenaille, 81

Fredericks, Richard, 28, 29, 30, 34

Geisler, Norman, 58

Grew, Henry, 98

H. L. v. Matheson, 223

Haring, Bernard, 149

Health, 55

Helms, Senator Jesse, 173

Heschel, Abraham Joshua, 199

Hill, Christopher, 92

Hill, Margaret, 176

Hippocratic Oath, 55, 128

Hitler, Adolf, 89, 128, 215

Hobbes, Thomas, 97

Hoche, Alfred, 128

Kant, Immanual, 81, 97, 98

Keeler v. Supreme Court, 222

Kellogg, John Harvey, 71ff

Koerbel, Pam, 137

Koop, C. Everett, 163
Kubo, Sakae, 28

Jerome, St. 221
Jesus Christ, see Index of Subjects
Jewett, Paul, 59
Josephus, 55, 58
Juan, Don, 97

Laud, Archbishop, 93
Leridon, Henri, 62
Leo X, 92
Locke, John, 98
Londis, James, 28, 29, 32
Luker, Kristin, 148
Luther, Martin, 92

MacDougall, Joseph, 164, 166
Maher v. Roe, 224
Marshall, Justice, 223
Marty, Martin, 94
Marxism, 206
Maxwell, Maureen, 31
McCarthy, Joseph, 97
Meehan, Mary, 65
Meiner, Felix, 128
Mill, John Stuart, 215
Milton, John 93, 98
Mohr, James, 72
Mosk, Justice, 222
Mozart, Wolfgang, 97, 98
Muggeridge, Malcolm, 164
Müller, Richard, 28, 29, 31, 32, 36, 37

Nazis, 59, 128
Newton, Sir Isaac, 81
Nuremberg trials, 128

Panacea, 55
Parvin, Professor T., 73
Paschal, 81
Paulson, Kevin, 31

Pearson, Michael, 208
Pelt, John, 221
Philo of Alexandria, 68
Pieper, Joseph, 102
Plato, 92, 95, 98, 114
Pol Pot, 89
Pomponazvi, Pietro, 92
Powell, Justice 223
Provonsha, Jack, 28
Pseudo-Phocylides, 55

Rawlsian, 213
Reagan, Ronald, 173
Rehnquist, Justice, 224
Rex v. Brain, 222
Robinson, John, 180
Roe v. Wade, 125, 127, 156, 176, 213, 222-224, 228
Rubinstein, Artur, 117
Ryder, Norman, 148

Schweitzer, Albert, 117-123
Seidman, Louis, 213
Shakespeare, 43, 53
Shettles, Landrum, 61
Sibylline Oracles, 55
Singer, Peter, 215
Stalin, 89
Storer, Horatio, 72
Storrs, George, 98
Sweem, Ardyce, 29, 38

Taney, Justice Roger B. 127
Teale, Edwin, 123
Tertullian, 56
Theobald, R., 149
Tillich, Paul, 115
Troeltsch, Ernst, 206
Tushnet, Mark, 213

Verdi, Giuseppe, 98

Waddell, Ralph, 32, 24, 239
Waltke, Bruce, 58
Watson, James, 162
Waugh, Evelyn, 97
Weber, Max, 206
Westoff, Charles, 148
White, Ellen, 55, 62, 67, 68, 102, 111-112,
   142, 151, 173-183, 227, 234
White, Justice, 224
Williams, Roger, 93, 94, 175, 180

Willimon, William, 139
Willke, John, 138
Wilson, Neal C., 187
Winslow, Gerald, 31, 32, 34-37, 197
Wittschiebe, Charles, 32
Wood, Miriam
Woodward, Clarice, 31

Youngberg, John and Millie, 28,36

Ziprick, Harold, 27, 28, 38

INDEX OF SUBJECTS

Abortion
  ancient traditions of, 55-56
  legal aspects of, 77-79, 82, 143-144, 221-232
  medical aspects of, 3, 4, 12-14, 19-24, 75, 76, 253, 254
  natural (spontaneous), 48-50, 62, 95, 114, 122, 182
  psychological aspects of, 14-16, 66, 69, 107-108, 136-140, 158, 211- 212, 226, 263
  repeat, 106, 200
  statistics, 62, 65, 66, 125, 137, 157, 207, 242-246
  therapeutic, 239, 240, 242, 243, 245, 254
  trimester, 1st, 9, 21-22, 233, 244, 254, 257; 2nd, 10, 22-24, 233, 244

AIDS, 52, 162-164

Anencephalic infants, 63, 115, 116, 247

Bible
  silence on abortion, 27, 28, 38, 55-56, 151
  as guide for principles, 27, 33-40, 63, 64, 100-104
  as source for rules and facts, 29ff
  misuse of, 29, 33, 35
  see Scriptural Index

Birth control, see Contraception

Catholic views, 77-78, 92-94, 136, 174, 185, 222, 226

Choice, freedom of, 34, 138, 248, 258, 259, 260

Childbirth, biblical aspects of, 46, 47

Compassion, 39, 40, 123, 135-140, 195-199, 258, 259, 260

Conception, 4-6, 43-45, 47, 52, 57, 159

Conscience, individual, 207, 248, 255, 258-260

Contraception, 7, 20-21, 51-52, 56, 74-75, 99, 178, 259

Creation, 31, 43, 44, 53, 101, 102, 105, 108, 110, 111, 119, 122, 167, 176, 177

Death, 61, 103, 114, 116, 126, 128

Economics in abortion, 35, 133-134, 136

Embodiment, 62, 94-98, 105-106, 114-116, 150-151, 255, see also Human nature and Life

Embryological development, 8-9, 59, see also Fetus, development of

Ethics, 65, 71, 87ff, 99, 109, 110, 117, 188, 209

Euthanasia, 126-127, see also Death

Family, 258, 259

Fathers, 73-74, 106, 212-213, 258

Fetus,
  abnormalities, (includes congenital and mental retardation), 3, 16-20, 19, 34, 63, 75, 76, 91, 95, 122, 134, 146, 240, 259, 262
  development of, 9, 10, 45, 45, 209-210
  value of, 37, 50, 76-78, 113, 130-132, 209-210, 255, 256, 258, 260
  viability of, 10, 16, 113-114, 255, 263

Forgiveness, see Grace

Gestation, see Fetus, development of

Grace (in abortion), 35, 83, 103-104, 108, 131, 132, 136, 188, 199, 200

Handicaps, see Fetus, abnormalities

Hospitals, Seventh-day Adventist, chapter 16, 256, 257, 262-264

Human nature, wholistic view of, 114-116, 179-180, 255, see also Life

Image of God, 34, 35, 117, 122, 177-178

Incest, 34, 52, 194, 196, 252, 259, 262, see also Rape

Infanticide, 50, 51, 130

Infertility, 4, 47-48

Informed Consent, 254

Jesus Christ, 59, 82, 84, 89, 102-105, 109, 110, 115, 118, 120, 130-135, 138, 159, 153, 179, 182, 183, 188, 192ff, 206

Justice, 34

Law, see Abortion, legal aspects of

Life,
    beginning of, 4, 28, 31, 43, 56-61, 77, 113, 221-222, 238-239
    definition of, 10-12, 114-115, 176-177
    personhood, 60-66, 90, 91, 116, 122, 126-127, 130, 176-180, 209-121, 239, 255-256, see also Embodiment
    sancitity of, 89-91, 100, 104-105, 111, 113-123, 127, 221, 247-248, 258-260
    symbolic, 65, 91, 115, 240, 256, 257
    value of, 30, 83, 84, 113, 126, 256, 260 see also Fetus, value of

Mental Retardation, see Fetus, abnormalities

Ministry to those facing abortion, 108-111

Miscarriage, see Abortion, natural

Mother
    teenage, 135, 139, 140, 184, 188-190, 198, 240, 257
    health and life of, threatened in abortion cases, 14, 17, 23, 24, 122, 164-166, 240, 254, 257, 259, 262, 264

Murder, 29, 58, 72-73, 77-80, 129, 132, 137, 159, 181-182, 190, 222

Natural law, 71, 74-76

Personhood, see Life, personhood

Political action, 81-82

Pregnancy, 17-19, 48-50, 107, 108, 115, 121, 165, 254, 257, 262-264

Pro-choice, 59, 65, 127-128, 144, 148, 157, 175, 177, 197, 210, 213

Procreation, biblical views, 43-45, 51, 67, 74, 102

Pro-life, 60, 65, 144, 148, 152, 167, 174, 197, 208, 210, 214

Protestant views, (related to abortion), 92-93

Rape, 34-35, 52, 65, 91, 108, 125, 135, 156-161, 194, 196, 240, 254, 259, 262

Religious liberty, 174-175, 207-208

Sabbath, 149, 184, 185

Second Coming, 182-183

Seventh-day Adventist,
    guidelines on abortion, 253-264
    sociological aspects, 147-152, 205-209

Sexuality
    activity and responsibility, 65, 72-75, 78-79, 81, 84, 102, 105-107, 108, Victorian views, 73-75

Slavery, 127-128

Sterilization, 106

Stillbirth, 50, 51

Soul, see Embodiment

Tays-Sachs disease, 63, 94, 95

Women
    specifics in abortion cases, 101, 105, 111, 188-194, 210-212
    sexuality of, 99-100